AF477896

Simona Milio is Associate Director of the Economic Social Cohesion Laboratory at the London School of Economics and Political Science (LSE). She holds a PhD in European Studies from the LSE, and is the recipient of the first prize for the best doctoral thesis in the Committee of the Regions 2009 Thesis Competition, awarded by the European Parliament.

FROM POLICY TO IMPLEMENTATION IN THE EUROPEAN UNION

The Challenge of a Multi-Level Governance System

SIMONA MILIO

TAURIS ACADEMIC STUDIES
an imprint of

I.B.Tauris Publishers
LONDON • NEW YORK

Published in 2010 by Tauris Academic Studies
An imprint of I.B.Tauris & Co Ltd
6 Salem Road, London W2 4BU
175 Fifth Avenue, New York NY 10010
www.ibtauris.com

Distributed in the United States and Canada
Exclusively by Palgrave Macmillan
175 Fifth Avenue, New York NY 10010

Library of European Studies 13

ISBN 978 1 84885 123 8

A full CIP record for this book is available from the British Library
A full CIP record for this book is available from the Library of Congress

Library of Congress catalog card: available

Printed and bound in the UK by CPI Antony Rowe, Chippenham, Wiltshire
Camera-ready copy edited and supplied by the author

To my brother

CONTENTS

LIST OF ILLUSTRATIONS

Figures

Tables

LIST OF ABBREVIATIONS

AN	*Alleanza Nazionale*
AP	*Alianza Popular* (Popular Alliance, Spain)
Agensud	*Agenzia per lo sviluppo del Mezzogiorno* (Agency for the promotion of development in the Mezzogiorno)
BNG	*Bloque Nacionalista Galego* (Nationalist bloc of Galicia)
CA	*Comunidades Autònomas* (Autonomous Communities)
Casmez	*Cassa per opere straordinarie di pubblico interesse nell'Italia meridionale* (Fund for the South)
CCD	*Centro Cristiano Democratico* (Christian Democratic Centre)
CEECs	Central and Eastern European Countries
CFP	Common Fisheries Policy
CICO	*Comitato Interdipartimentale di Coordinamento Organizzativo* (Interdepartmental Committee for Management Coordination)
CIS	*Comitato per l'Indipendenza della Sicilia* (Committee for the Independence of Sicily)
CODIPA	*Comitato di coordinamento dei dipartimenti* (Committee of Coordination of the Departments)
COR	Committee of Regions
COREPER	Committee of Permanent Representatives
CP	*Coalición Popular* (Popular Coalition, Spain)
CRPE	*Comitato Regionale per la Programmazione Economica* (Regional Committee for Economic Planning)
CSF	Community Support Framework
CTI	*Commissione Tecnica Interdipartimentale* (Interdepartmental Technical Commission)
D.lgs.	*Decreto Legislativo* (Legislative decree)
DC	*Democrazia Cristiana* (Christian Democratic Party)

DGFC	*Dirección General de Fondos Comunitarios y Financiacion Territorial* (Directorate General for Community Funds and Regional Finance)
DPS	*Dipartimento per le Politiche di Sviluppo e Coesione*
DS	*Democratici di Sinistra* (Left Democrats)
EAGGF	European Agricultural Guidance and Guarantee Fund
EC	European Commission
ERDF	European Regional Development Fund
ESF	European Social Fund
EU	European Union
EVIS	*Esercito Volontario per l'Indipendenza della Sicilia* (Voluntary Army for the Independence of Sicily)
FI	*Forza Italia*
FIFG	Financial Instrument for Fisheries Guidance
GDP	Gross Domestic Product
IDFM	Institutional Development Framework Method
IFA	*Instituto de Fomento Andaluz* (Institute for the Promotion of Andalusia)
IGRUE	*Ispettorato Generale per i Rapporti Finanziari con l'Unione Europea*
IMPs	Integrated Mediterranean Programmes
IOP	Integrated Operational Programme
IRDP	Integrated Regional Development Plan
ISTAT	*Istituto Nazionale di Statistica*
IU	*Izquierda Unida* (United Left Party – Spain)
L.cost.	*Legge Costituzionale* (Constitutional Amendment Law)
LOFAGE	Law 6/1997 on Organisation and Functioning of the General Administration of the State
L.R.	*Legge Regionale* (Regional Law)
LN	*Lega Nord*
MA	Managing Authority
MIS	*Movimento per l'Indipendenza della Sicilia* (Movement for the Independence of Sicily).
MLG	Multi-level Governance
NDP	National Development Plan
NPM	New Public Management
NUTs	Nomenclature of Territorial Statistical Units
PER	*Plan de Empleo Rural* (Rural Employment Plan)
PHARE	Poland and Hungary: Assistance for Restructuring their Economies

POP	Pluri-fund Operative Programme
PA	Public Administration
PA	*Partido Andalucista* (Party of Andalusia)
PC	Programme Complement
PCI	*Partito Comunista Italiano* (Italian Communist Party)
PLI	*Partito Liberale Italiano* (Italian Liberal Party)
PLN	Polish zloty (currency)
PP	*Partido Popular* (Spanish Popular party)
PPI	*Partito Popolare Italiano* (Italian Popular Party)
PRI	*Partito Repubblicano Italiano or Repubblicani* (Republicans)
PSdG-	*Partido Socialista de Galicia* (Socialist Party of Galicia)
PSDI	*Partito Social Democratico Italiano* (Italian Social Democratic Party)
PSI	*Partito Socialista Italiano* (Italian Socialist Party)
PSOE-A	*Partido Socialista Obrero Español de Andalucía* (Spanish Socialist Party of Andalusia)
QMV	Qualified Majority Voting
RDP	Regional Development Plan
ROP	Regional Operational Programmes
SEA	Single European Act
SFs	Structural Funds
SIMIC	IT system for SF management (Poland)
SMEs	Small and Medium Enterprises
SNAs	Sub-national Authorities
SOP	Sectoral Operational Programme
SOP ICE	Sectoral Operational Programme Increase of Competitiveness of Enterprises
SWOT	Strengths, Weaknesses, Opportunities, Threats – Analysis
UCD	*Unión de Centro Democrático* (Union of Democratic centre)
UDCC	*Unione dei Democratici Cristiani e Democratici di Centro*
UKIE	*Urządu Komitetu Integracji Europejskiej* (Office of the European Integration Committee
USCS	Unione Siciliana Cristiano Sociale

PREFACE

This book explores possible reasons for deficiencies in policy implementation across the European Union (EU) and asks why Member States have difficulties implementing EU policies. Public policy and planning, although important, are little more than statements of intent, whereas implementation is the crucial subsequent step of policy cycles, enabling a realisation of ideas and outcome.

It has become apparent that there is a clear gap between EU-level policy-making and Member State implementation. Previous literature has neglected full definition of the factors that encourage or prevent implementation processes, and has focused instead on upstream decision-making processes or downstream effects of policy. This book argues for a shift in focus to policy implementation, since this constitutes a crucial common pathway that determines whether a policy is effective or not (Chapter 1).

Deficiencies in implementation reflect some of the problems created by the multi-level governance (MLG) structure of European policy-making. Indeed, although MLG has been described by the White Paper on EU governance (EU Commission, 2001c) as the most appropriate governing framework for the EU, I believe the EU has a limited chance of succeeding in implementation unless it manages to persuade relevant policy actors at national and subnational levels to cooperate with its policy goals. However, cooperation is not possible unless all parties manage the complex policy requirements and implementation regimes necessary for European policy enforcement.

Cohesion policy is chosen as an output variable, which has in the last twenty years demonstrated a dramatically different pace of implementation among Member States (Chapter 2). The literature on cohesion policy implementation is relatively recent, and lacks a consistent conceptual framework for fully assessing the issue of absorption problems. First, its main analytical tools had to be borrowed from economic development literature dealing with bilateral and multilateral aid. Second, while there is a rich case study literature examining the Central and Eastern European Countries (CEECs), there is little systematic comparative research that has investigated members of the EU15. Italy appears to be a puzzling case study given its constant struggle to conform to EU directives and implement cohesion policy. Retrospective data reveal that, although at a national level there has been a lower than average ability to implement cohesion policy, in some southern Italian regions a higher than average ability has been demonstrated. Chapter 2 considers some of the factors which might account for this regional variation in implementation performance.

The aim of this research is to validate some preconditions – administrative and political – which are deemed necessary for MLG to work as an implementation model. I provide a definition of administrative capacity and a model of analysis which allows measurement of the concept and cross-country comparisons. Having established a measurement of regional administrative capacity, this book tests the concept that administrative capacity is influenced by three political factors – political interference, stability and accountability – which are thoroughly defined and investigated (Chapter 3).

Using my definition and suggested indicators, the administrative and political variables are empirically measured in two Italian regional case studies (chapters 4, 5 and 6). In order to enable an investigation of implementation difficulties in a broader range of Member States, these preconditions are further tested in Spain (Chapter 7) and Poland (Chapter 8). I am grateful to Dr Fabiola Mota and Dr Andrea Noferini for their work on Chapter 7, and to Dr Justyna Glusman for her work on Chapter 8, parts of which are adapted from her recent doctoral dissertation completed at the London School of Economics.

Chapter 9 summarises the main findings and their implications for judging the adequacy of MLG as a policy implementation framework.

This work has been made possible thanks to the support and advice of Professor Helen Wallace and Dr Robert Leonardi. Similarly, I thank all the members of the European Institute, especially Dr Bob Hancke and Dr Waltraud Schelkle. I owe personal thanks to the staff of the Economic and Social Cohesion Laboratory, particularly to Ms Aurora Cantone, who has supported me throughout the writing and polishing of the manuscript. This book could have not been written without the loving and constant support of my family and my husband.

PART I

THE STRUGGLE TO IMPLEMENT EUROPEAN UNION POLICIES

Political and Administrative Factors in the Member States

1

MULTI-LEVEL GOVERNANCE AND THE IMPLEMENTATION GAP

1.1 Implementation: A Growing Concern for the EU

This opening chapter focuses on what is known as the 'implementation gap' – the gap that exists between formulation of a European Union (EU) policy and its actual implementation. Section 1.2 reviews the literature and main theories related to this issue and identifies possible explanatory factors. Particular attention is given to the analysis of multi-level governance (MLG) as an implementation model (section 1.3) and the case of cohesion policy is examined as emblematic of the difficulties that the involvement of subnational authorities in policy-making and policy implementation gives way to.

Deficiencies in the implementation of EU policies have become a growing concern for the European Commission (EC) owing to the fact that non-compliance threatens the effectiveness and legitimacy of European policy-making, and consequently of the EU itself (Börzel, 2001). At first sight, the issue regarding the analysis of the implementation of EU law may appear inconsequential as Member States are legally bound by the EU treaties to transpose and implement Community law in a complete, correct and timely manner (EC Treaty, art. 249). However, national implementation practices differ widely, so that we can certainly talk about a disparity between implementation in theory and in reality. Therefore, in analysing in detail the gap between EU-level policy-making and Member State implementation, this book aims to achieve a shift in the focus of study of from the policy-making to the policy implementation. But to focus only on implementation would be too narrow, and a better starting point for analysis is to examine the more comprehensive issue of how governance systems deliver policy outcomes, and more specifically, how the institutional configuration of the EU impacts upon the implementation phase. In general terms, one could argue that the basic reason for the implementation gap is the 'structural imbalance in the institutional makeup of the EU', as defined by Jordan (1999: 86), which is due to the way the EU has come into being and the direction the integration process has taken, from the initial merely intergovernmental configuration to the more complex supranational, federal or MLG setup that has developed in recent years.

In the EU there is an explicit division of competences in relation to the implementation of policies between the EU institutions and the Member States, with the EU Commission responsible for monitoring the correct transposition and application of Community law while responsibility for the execution of policies lies with the Member States. Policy implementation is in general a delicate phase of the policy-making process, more so in the EU, where deviations in the implementation phase from the original policy objectives are recurrent. The EU also experiences significant difficulties in establishing the real impact of EU policies at a national level, due on the one hand to measurement and data problems and, on the other hand, to the sheer complexity of the multi-level interactions that inform the EU integration process.

In Knill's (2006) opinion the rather late politicisation of implementation deficits – i.e. until the mid 1980s implementation of EU policies was practically ignored by the political agenda – does not mean that such deficits were absent but rather that in this first stage of the process of EU integration there was a greater focus on the formulation of common policies than on their implementation. This corresponded to the Commission's interest in expanding its political authority without endangering the Member States' political support through interventions aimed at questioning the implementation and enforcement of policies; this position was also congruent with that of the Member States, not keen on Community actions aimed at investigating their eventual implementation failures. The completing of the integration of the common market was critical in changing this status quo (Jordan, 1999). In addition to this, the efforts of the European Court of Justice (ECJ) in establishing the principles of the supremacy and direct effect of community law at national level facilitated the politicisation of implementation problems. Therefore, following the development of these issues, implementation of EU policies became an increasingly discussed theme and a central issue on the European political agenda in the 1990s.

1.1.2 Two Stages of Implementation: Legal and Effective

Implementation in the EU system has acquired a particular meaning connected to the process of transposing and enforcing European norms at the domestic level (Sverdrup, 2007). Literature has mainly focused on the implementation of EU directives because other types of EU binding legislative instruments (such as regulations or decisions) are directly applicable in the national legal systems, whereas directives need to be transposed into national legislation before they are legally effective and can be put into practice by domestic administrative structures. Consequently, implementation of EU policies has been divided in two stages: legal implementation (incorporation of EU legislation into national law) and final or effective implementation (administrative operations for the actual application of EU law necessary to ensure compliance).

Transposition applies to the first stage of implementation, relative to the incorporation of the directives' provisions into national laws – it is the phase of the EU implementation process that has received most attention by scholars. Member States are granted a period of time ranging from some months to a few years to transpose directives. After directives have been transposed, implementation agencies within the domestic administrative structure need to become familiar with their monitoring and supervising tasks, the target groups of the policies must be informed about their rights and obligations, and compliance to the law needs to be monitored and, if necessary, sanctioned. But transposition predetermines the subsequent moves in implementation. Accordingly, the European Court of Justice (ECJ) considers timely transposition, that is, within the period prescribed by the directive, as a rigorous obligation (Haverland and Romeijn, 2007).

Therefore, non-compliance in regard to EU legislation may be grouped in two categories. The first category consists of failures to legally implement directives correctly and on time. The second category of violations consists of non-compliance in the application of EU rules: directives (and other EU rules, laws and regulations) that have been legally implemented must be correctly applied, and Member States must conform to the rules laid down by EU legislation. Measuring the degree of compliance to EU policies has been attempted only in relation to legal implementation, since the concrete application of EU rules is difficult to monitor and evaluate. Sverdrup, in this regard, talks of 'neglected outcome studies' (Sverdrup, 2007: 205), referring to the limited attention given to the study of the outcomes of EU policies. In fact, Falkner *et al.* (2005: 330) say, quite bluntly, that 'to establish if EU law is actually applied in practice is probably the most challenging task in research on European integration'. Establishing the level of 'effective implementation' is complicated, first, because results are difficult to measure – it can take decades to see evidence of them – and, second, it often happens that different policies may affect the same area, contributing to bring about the same result. Moreover, there is not a homogeneous measure of implementation: one Member State could judge a directive implemented when some specific results come out, while another could set completely different goals within the same implementation process – this situation is defined as lack of 'standards of evaluation' by Sverdrup (2007: 206).

1.1.3 Measuring the Gap

Monitoring the implementation of community law is a task assigned by the Treaty of Amsterdam to the EU Commission. To achieve this, the Commission can refer itself to notifications of a Member States' actions (Member States are required to inform the Commission on the implementation of EU directives). Another means of quantifying the implementation gap is examination of the infringement statistics based on the number of infringement procedures. This data is gathered and revised by the Commission and then published in Annual Reports on the Monitoring of the Application of Community Law. Both of these methods have been judged as rather unreliable: notification rates are biased because they are exclusively the expression of the Member State's opinion that directives have been transposed, while infringement figures neither say anything about the qualitative nature of the infringements nor do they comprise undetected cases of infringement (Bursens, 2002; Börzel, 2001). Indeed, Falkner *et al.* (2005) state that with infringement procedures what is ranked is not non-compliance but just the Commission's reaction to presumed non-compliance: therefore they don't reveal what the actual level of non-compliance is. In fact, non-compliance is not systematically addressed by the Commission, due to limited resources and also to political opportunity; for some directives, perceived as more important, enforcement may be pursued in a firmer way, while in other secondary cases the Commission might settle with a superficial compliance. In Börzel's opinion (2001: 804), if you control for time trends and the statistical artefacts that inflate numbers of infringement proceedings, the data available does not allow estimation of the absolute level of non-compliance but only variations across time, Member States and policy sectors. Therefore, there are different opinions on the actual size of the implementation gap. In this regard, Falkner *et al.* controversially observe that research on EU compliance has so far been conducted in an ambiguous way, implying that even though the dependent variable has always been compliance with EU rules, studies make use of different country samples, policy sectors, time sequences, policy instruments, stages, reasons and length of the infringement procedures: 'owing to this multitude of criteria – which are not always clearly marked off – it comes as no surprise that results are incongruous' (Falkner *et al.*, 2005: 203).

In any case, both notifications and infringement statistics are directed at assessing the transposition of directives and not the effective implementation of EU law and policies, which – as already stated – remains a largely unexplored field of research. After analysing some of the reasons that might explain the implementation gap, with particular attention for the problems posed by MLG as an implementation model, we will concentrate on cohesion policy as an output variable. Cohesion policy has been chosen principally because it is the policy field where MLG has flourished (Barca, 2009) but also because it allows us to focus on effective implementation as measured by expenditure rates (i.e. the spending of the resources allocated in the assigned time-spans), in contrast to the abundance of studies carried out on legal implementation.

There is not an extensive literature which addresses implementation as part of the public policy process. Most scholars – as already stated – have concentrated on the upper-level phase of the policy process, analysing the policy-making stage in detail while the implementation of policies has largely been disregarded. Implementation studies aim basically to investigate why, how and by whom policies are put into effect. This requires the policy analyst to investigate States' capacities and interests at different levels, and also to combine and ignore the distinction between politics and administration: even though implementation is also undeniably a political process, it has often been treated merely as a problem in efficiency (Stone, 1985). Implementation studies have, in fact, focused on identifying factors that might affect the implementation process within a framework that is perhaps excessively concerned with the top-down/bottom-up argument. At the European level, studies on implementation of policies have been conducted chiefly in relation to environmental policy and, to a lesser extent, cohesion policy. But there is a need to take implementation studies beyond the current models in order to reflect the new reality which is emerging, paying attention to the new structures in public service organisation and in particular to the implementation of the partnership principle, the importance of evaluation in the policy cycle, and the increasing fragmentation of the policy process itself (Schofield, 2001).

1.2 Reasons for the Implementation Gap

In analysing the reasons for the deficiencies in implementation across the EU, existing research has so far focused on the following variables as explanations for non-compliance: misfit between European policy and national institutions; domestic constrains; and EU-level constraints. In the following sections I give a brief overview of the main theories.

1.2.1 Europeanisation Studies

An important wave of research that started in the late 1990s is related to Europeanisation studies, which focused on investigating the domestic impact of European policies from a top-down perspective, in particular through the 'goodness of fit' hypothesis. These scholars (Duina, 1997; Börzel and Risse, 2000; Héritier, 2001) theorise that compliance and implementation performance depend on the degree of fit between European policy and national institutions. The thesis is that if EU policies do not match existing traditions (such as national administrative structures and regulatory traditions, domestic policy instruments and standards) implementation will be contested and delayed with risk of failure, whereas in the reverse case implementation should be unproblematic.

Europeanisation studies also relate to rational choice and sociological institutionalism research as two different mechanisms to understand institutional change resulting from Europeanisation processes. According to the rational institutionalist perspective (Downs *et al.*, 1996; Hurd, 1999; Jönsson and Tallberg, 1998; Martin, 1993), Europeanisation is conceived as a political opportunity structure which offers some actors additional resources to exert influence, leading therefore to change in the national structures through a diverse empowerment of actors that is the consequence of a redistribution of resources. Sociological institutionalism (DiMaggio and Powell, 1991; Knight, 1992; Olsen, 1996; March and Olsen, 1998; Checkel, 1999; Risse, 2002), instead, conceptualises Europeanisation as the emergence of new rules and practices to which Member States are exposed and which they have to incorporate in their domestic structures, understanding domestic change as a result of collective learning processes; Börzel and Risse (2000: 12) in fact define them as the 'two logics of domestic change'.

1.2.2 Domestic Constraints

Studies on implementation within specific countries or policy sectors ascribe delays to the States' implementation 'capacity' or 'willingness'. Different scholars (Börzel *et al.*, 2007; Falkner *et al.*, 2005) suggest distinguishing theories on non-compliance according to the source of non-compliant behaviour, analysing whether defection on part of a Member State is intentional or unintentional in order to understand the reasons for lack of implementation and thus devise courses of action aimed at ensuring compliance, in accordance with the enforcement and management approaches. The origin of voluntary non-compliance could be traced to both economic variables – i.e. the desire to avoid compliance costs – and political variables – i.e. pressures from interest groups – while involuntary defection is theorised as due to lack of capacity to comply.

Analysis of the EU policy-making process starts from two basic assumptions: (1) each Member State has its own administrative structure, and (2) each State tries to maximise its own utility, and minimise its costs. Nevertheless structural change can occur even in spite of high adaptational costs if such change is supported by a clear political will. This has led many authors to consider the influence of the political factor as a dependent variable of EU policy implementation, even though not all the authors highlight the same characteristics. Falkner *et al.* (2005), for instance, observe that there may be a political logic to domestic adaptation in addition to, and sometimes instead of, misfit logic. Thus, even far-reaching changes could be implemented if they coincide with a governing party's preferences, and, conversely, even minimal changes could be obstructed if they did not match with the governing party's values or priorities. Falkner *et al.* (2005: 277) talk of 'opposition through the backdoor', when national states, having failed to gain acknowledgement of their preferences during the EU decision-making process, decide to not implement a policy or to delay its implementation in order to protest against certain policies.

In addition, Lampinen and Uusikylä (1998) identify a Member State's prevailing political attitude towards the EU as an important variable in determining the cooperative conditions that facilitate implementation processes. Interest groups also play a role in implementation failure or success, both at the national and at the EU level: 'Interest groups and entrenched bureaucracies constitute the key mechanisms through which the requirement of behavioural change influences government compliance decisions' (Tallberg, 2002: 628). It is true that interest groups do not possess formal veto powers, but they are important players who exert influence in the political process and also in the implementation phase. Börzel (2003), in particular, argues that interest groups may be a 'pull' factor, exerting pressure on administrations to comply with EU law.

Another political variable to be considered is the existence of multiple veto points in a nation state's constitutional structure: the theory of veto players asserts that the capacity of a political system to reform itself decreases as the number of actors whose agreement is required to pass such a reform increases. Cowles *et al.* (2001) point out that the more power is dispersed among different actors, the more it is difficult to foster a willing coalition that will eventually allow for structural changes. Thus the existence of multiple veto points in a given policy-making process is likely to block or considerably hinder any pressure for European adaptation. In the same vein, Azfar *et al.* (1999: 11) remark that performance of services is likely to be influenced by fragmentation in government, therefore the greater political instability (national or subnational) the greater the difficulty in policy-making (the issue of the effect of political instability on implementation performance and administrative capacity is addressed in greater detail in Chapter 6).

Therefore, if Member State non-compliance to EU directives is motivated by a precise choice based on strategic cost-benefits calculations, the way to assure a higher level of compliance to EU policies is by making 'costs for non-compliance exceed the benefits of non-compliance' in accordance to a rationalist logic (Börzel and Panke, 2005: 19), changing the actors' pay-off matrices to bring them to comply through the threat of sanctions. Enforcement theories, in fact, stress a coercive strategy of monitoring and sanctions; sources and solutions to non-compliance stem from the incentive structure. States choose to defect when confronted with an incentive structure in which the benefits of shirking exceed the costs of detection. Compliance problems are therefore best remedied by increasing the likelihood and costs of detection through monitoring and the threat of sanctions.

On the other hand, if a Member State's failure to comply with EU directives arises from deficient capacities, then the appropriate course of action is to launch capacity-building processes that change actors' preferences through learning processes. Management theory in fact recommends a problem-solving approach based on capacity building (Tallberg, 2002). In regard, as I will examine in more detail when investigating the performance of Member States in the implementation of cohesion policy, several scholars (Leonardi, 2005; Mairate, 2006; Keating, 2008; John, 2000; Roberts, 2003) have pointed out that the main 'added value' of Structural Funds (SFs) – and perhaps their greatest impact – has been their role in fostering the capacity to enforce rules and transfer methods and good practices of policy planning, management and implementation, providing an arena for mutual learning and thus enabling 'practitioners in institutionally weak environments to learn by doing' (Begg, 2008: 306). In fact, a general conclusion of research focusing on the link between EU and national governance has been that it allows the researcher to conceive of the European level as an 'opportunity structure' which domestic actors may be able to exploit to further their own interests, depending on national interests and resources (Kohler-Koch and Rittberger, 2006: 38).

1.2.3 EU-level Constraints

In analysing the Member States' implementation failures, EU scholars have identified several EU-level constraints on transposition. The role of the Commission as transposition monitor and its limited resources and tools to ensure enforcement have already been analysed. Other institutional factors considered at the EU level are (1) the decision rule applied to the directive; (2) the length/nature of the directive; and (3) the amount of time allocated for transposition as reasons that could account for delay in implementation (Giuliani, 2003; Mastenbroek, 2005; Haverland and Romeijn, 2007; Bursens, 2002; Falkner *et al.*, 2005).

Lastly, complexity, ambiguity, inconsistency and poor quality of directives could be a further reason for implementation delays. In their study on transposition delays of social directives in five EU countries, Haverland and Romeijn (2007: 775) state that the empirical evidence gathered does not support these arguments. However, Falkner *et al.* (2005: 288), analysing 90 case studies relating to the transposition and implementation of six social directives across EU Member States, reach the opposite conclusion, that implementation could be improved by drafting clearer directives; but they are also conscious that 'ambiguous wording is often an inbuilt consequence of the negotiation dynamics prevailing at the European level' and an instrument to facilitate the reaching of agreements and common positions. Another variable that can affect transposition and implementation performance is the time available for transposition, as delay can be caused by too short time-frames assigned by the Commission for transposition of directives.

1.3 Multi-level Governance as an Implementation Model

1.3.1 Origin of the Concept

The review of the literature on implementation deficit shows a dominant focus on law implementation and compliance rather than policy implementation. We believe that this is because studying policy implementation requires a more detailed investigation of policy requirements and Member State's capacities and interests at different levels – i.e. national, regional and local. Indeed, the EU principle of subsidiarity calls for a direct involvement of levels of government closer to the citizen. Subsidiarity is the general principle according to which authorities should perform only those activities which cannot be carried out effectively at a more local level. The policy-making architecture which implements this arrangement is MLG, a system by which the responsibility for policy design and implementation is distributed between different levels of government and special-purpose local institutions (Barca, 2009:2)

The novelty of this implementation model resides in 'the difficulty of having to coordinate governmental and non-governmental actors at different territorial levels in ways that do not conform with the hierarchical relations or the mechanisms of consultation currently in place in the member states' (Piattoni, 2008: 71).

The MLG theory is consistent with a bottom-up policy perspective, where actors from the subnational level have an important role to play and wide space for manoeuvre. Bottom-up models are far more capable of dealing with complexity and are well suited to situations where policies are layered upon each other: the 'bottom-up' perspective takes account of the fact that implementation processes are hardly ever characterised by an unambiguous definition of competencies between the political and administrative actors involved at different levels:

> Implementation more often implies complex interactions between public and private actors and organisations at the national, regional or local level, with potentially diverging interests, beliefs and perceptions with regard to the underlying policy problem. From this perspective, implementation is seen less as being based on hierarchically defined and controlled requirements and is understood more as a bargaining process between a great number of organisations and administrative agencies participating in the implementation process (Knill, 2006: 362).

Analysing the EU policy implementation process in the light of the importance given to the subsidiarity principle, it is certainly consistent with a bottom-up bargaining approach, where interdependence prevails on hierarchical control.

Most of the literature in this field deals with MLG as a descriptive theory highlighting the vertical relations and boundaries between actors located at different territorial levels, and shifts in horizontal relations between state and society (Bache, 2008a). The concept thus indicates on the one hand the dispersal of modern governance across multiple centres of authority and territorial levels, and on the other hand the interconnection of multiple political arenas in the process of governing (Hooghe and Marks, 2003).

MLG therefore can be conceived as the 'outcome of the simultaneous process of European integration and regionalisation, both of which led to a diffusion of powers away from the national state' (Conzelmann, 2008: 31). The expansion of the EU's powers and activities and the consolidation of its structures, especially after the passing of the Single European Act (SEA) in 1986, have led to increasing dissatisfaction with traditional approaches to the nature of the European political system. European integration, in fact, – as stated by Hooghe and Marks (2003) – does not fit neatly into any class of political phenomena. It is common among scholars to refer to the EU as an institution *sui generis*. There is an emerging consensus that in conceptualising the EU, the confines between the domestic and international spheres, as well as between state and society, are ever more fluid and indistinct – and the concept of MLG has been remarkably successful in describing these changes:

> multi-level governance crosses the traditionally separate domains of domestic and international politics: it highlights the increasingly fading distinction between these domains in the context of European integration and supranational, national, regional, and local governments are interrelated in territorially overarching policy networks (Bekemans, 2008: 95).

In sum, multi-level governance is a concept that emerged in the context of EU integration studies basically as an 'alternative model' to the state-centric intergovernmentalist approach (Marks *et al.*, 1995). While adherents of a state-centred perspective consider national governments as the key actors in the EU system, the debate on MLG is chiefly concerned with decision-making competencies of actors on different levels. Thus, although MLG has been widely discussed and analysed by EU scholars as a descriptive model, instead we will concentrate on MLG as an implementation model – on which, to date, relatively little has been said.

Before analysing in depth the connection between MLG and implementation, it is necessary to introduce Hooghe and Mark's (2003) distinction between type I and II MLG to give a more detailed theoretical framework to our analysis, without which MLG might remain a vague concept of questionable utility.

Type I MLG describes jurisdictions (international, national, regional, local, and so on) at limited number of levels that are general-purpose and non-overlapping, with each level catering for a particular territory. The intellectual foundations for type I MLG are federalism and subsidiarity, and the unit of analysis is the individual government rather than the individual policy. Type II governance jurisdictions, conversely, are not aligned on only a few levels but operate on numerous territorial levels, with jurisdictions that are task-specific, over-lapping memberships and a flexible design, referring therefore to *ad hoc* governance bodies established for delivering specific services. The unit of analysis is the individual policy rather than the individual government. The advantage of many overlapping jurisdictions is that different authoritative functions can be tailored to meet the needs of different constituencies.

In analysing the EU, scholars disagree on how best to define it as a specific type of MLG. The Type I concept implies that the EU should be compared to a federal system; but, when applied to the EU, type I MLG clashes regarding characteristics of EU governance relating to the wide variety of regional and local structures across Europe and the absence of agreement relative to the role that these subnational structures should play in the member states (Conzelmann, 2008). Therefore a type II governance arrangement would seem in some respects to be a more adequate basis on which to build. In reality, in contemporary Europe general purpose and task-specific jurisdictions coexist, because they suit different objectives. Bache (2008b: 63), in fact, suggests that understanding MLG as a combination of type I and type II governance allows for the stability provided by formal institutions of government overlaid by more flexible arrangements that ensure greater effectiveness by bringing the appropriate local stakeholders into the policy process. Barca (2009: 41) sheds light on this, observing that the defining features of MLG are conditionalities and subsidiarity. The former allows the higher levels of government to establish and enforce the rules of the game, while the latter simultaneously allows the lower levels to design and implement interventions and advance towards the policy goals on the basis of their knowledge and preferences.

1.3.2 How Multi-level Governance Impacts on Implementation

Thus, if MLG as a theoretical descriptive model has been analysed in detail, less attention has been paid to MLG as an implementation model – which is precisely the focus of the present research. MLG is analysed as a framework for the implementation of EU policies, using cohesion policy as a case study. In fact, since the reforms of the SFs in 1988, the Funds have been commonly understood as a paradigm case of MLG structures in the EU and of adjustment of regional structures to the principles of cohesion policy. Cohesion policy, in fact, is based on a network system of actors (European, national, regional, local, civil society representatives) and interactions governed by a hierarchy of rules that give way to a multi-level and multi-actor governance structure (Leonardi, 2005). Barca (2009: 98) in this regard uses the term 'paradigm shift' to define this 'new method of running public investments' associated with a process of decentralisation, and, more generally, the development of new forms of governance including regional and local actors as well as non-governmental groups aimed at providing public goods and services tailor-made to specific contexts, as opposed to the traditional top-down approach to regional policy based on financial transfers to firms and on public works managed by the central administration.

The goal of this research is twofold: (1) to scrutinise the possible deficiencies in the implementation of EU policies that arise as a consequence of the crucial importance given to subnational actors in the implementation phase of the SFs; (2) to identify and test a set of preconditions necessary for implementation to succeed in the MLG framework. The starting point of observation is that, while the MLG model satisfactorily explains the complexity of the current EU policy-making system, as an implementation model it has led to mixed results: sometimes the active involvement of subnational actors has been judged as positive, while in other cases the multiplication of tiers and procedures has mostly created confusion among the actors. Most importantly, our analysis will highlight that effective involvement of subnational actors in the implementation process is subordinate to some preconditions: the presence of administrative capacity and political stability.

The question to be answered is this: is MLG an efficient way of governing or not? Is this governance approach, based on multi-level cooperation and characterised by 'soft ties', effectively, the best solution for facing development problems? And if so, under what conditions?

In analysing the connection between MLG and implementation, it is necessary to consider how the implementation gap is influenced by institutions and actors operating on a decentralised level.

Over the last twenty years, a process of decentralisation and regionalisation has occurred in all the Western countries but particularly in the EU; its consequence has been a proliferation of decisional centres and actors, with a progressively increased involvement of subnational authorities (SNAs) in the policy process. In the EU, in fact, SNAs interact with each other across national borders; they have their own channels of representation in Brussels, several lobbying offices and a role in various decision-making processes, among which their role in cohesion policies is dominant. According to the subsidiarity principle introduced by the Maastricht treaty, arranging a pliable system, in which SNAs deal directly with EU institutions in the decision-making process and then in the policy implementation phase, is the best way to have an accurate knowledge of the problems of each geographical area across the whole EU and, at a second stage, to respond to those problems in the most efficient way. In fact, the subsidiarity principle, entailing a change in the balance of responsibilities between EU institutions and Member States, and a shift downwards towards regional and local authorities, brings the decision-making and resource-allocation process closer to the people and the places that actually experience the problems. This should translate into an increased policy effectiveness which is the principal justification for the adoption of a decentralised system of implementation, providing an approach for regional planning which allows for flexibility and local initiative and responsiveness to changeable circumstances. As a matter of fact, in the theoretical debate between decentralisation and centralisation, the traditional question has been how to allocate responsibility for each type of public good and service between local and central levels, balancing the advantages of taking account of local preferences and greater accountability of government officials that derive from devolution against the advantages of scale economies and cross-border externalities which stem from centralisation (Barca, 2009).

The gist of the analysis presented here is that this approach works better and with greater effectiveness in countries with well-established institutional and administrative capacity and experience of promoting local and regional development. Before developing these arguments, however, a first theoretical consideration is the assumption that layers and levels contribute to deficits of implementation. In one of the first systematic studies of implementation, Pressman and Wildavsky (1973: xvi) define implementation, in the first place, as the process of interaction between the setting of goals and actions geared to achieving them; their insight is to theorise implementation as 'the movement from simplicity to complexity'. They argue that if action depends upon the number of links in the implementation chain, the longer the chain of causality, the more numerous the relationships among the links, the more complex implementation becomes; therefore there has to be a high degree of cooperation between actors if a situation is not to occur in which a number of small deficits add up to create a large underperformance. In some respects, Pressman and Wildavsky anticipate, focusing specifically on implementation, the 'joint decision trap' argument pointed out by Scharpf (1988) in relation to the general decision-making process: the participation of the regions as actors in the European policy-making arena produces new elements of interlacing and interlocking politics, increasing the complexity of policy-making through the involvement of so many actors that efficiency suffers. It can be assumed that with each additional territorial level and jurisdiction involved in the negotiation process, coordination costs increase, leading easily to situations of deadlock; this is especially true if negotiations take place in a non-hierarchical context.

These authors, indeed, seem to describe deficiencies in implementation as built-in consequences of any implementation process that involves multiple actors and institutional tiers. Since the links involved in the implementation process grow in number from the moment EU policies are defined in Brussels to the moment they have to be implemented on a regional level, one might expect the MLG model to be one of the reasons of failures in implementation. Hooghe and Marks (2003: 239) – the principal advocates of the MLG theory – are aware of this, stating that 'the chief benefit of multi-level governance lies in its scale flexibility. Its chief cost lies in the transaction costs of coordinating multiple jurisdictions.'

The idea is that, in conformity with the subsidiarity principle, dispersal of authority across multiple jurisdictions is more flexible than central state monopoly. Hooghe and Marks (2004: 16) claim that governance must operate at multiple levels in order to respond to variations in the territorial scope of policy externalities:

> because externalities arising from the provision of public goods vary immensely – from planet-wide in the case of global warming to local in the case of most city services – so should the scale of governance. To internalise externalities, governance must be multilevel.

To avoid the drawbacks of the joint decision trap, cooperation and coordination between actors and levels is fundamental as well as clarity in the definition of roles. Hanf and Scharpf (1978: 2) observe that

> the conventional response for this state of affairs has been to provide central governments with the capacity for formulating and putting into effect comprehensive and integrated policies, implemented through instruments of central control and designed to ensure that lower units will be more effectively guided by the policy objectives of more inclusive levels of government.

In short: re-centralisation of power in the hands of higher levels of government – exactly what happened in Poland, as we will see in Chapter 8. In reality, a centralised approach is simply not adequate in the long term. An MLG framework must be developed, and within it the performance of service delivery depends on the design of the institutional and decentralisation arrangements that govern its implementation. In this framework, a prerequisite for effectiveness is a clear delineation of roles and responsibilities. Benz and Eberlein (1988) in fact claim that differentiation of intergovernmental or intraregional decision making structures is the precondition for the successful management of a multi-level system; that is, problems are divided into partial tasks to be dealt with by separate arenas.

Moreover, a further complication can be ascribed to the fact that the need to coordinate implementation efforts among relatively autonomous actors causes implementation problems due not only to administrative difficulties but also to institutional tensions that might arise between supranational, national and subnational bodies. Boland (1999) develops the concept of 'contested multi level governance' to indicate that relations between the participants in MLG are frequently keenly disputed and that the problems centre on policy development, resource distribution, power and accountability. Contested governance occurs at many spatial scales because all players have their own goals and agendas, and it therefore happens in some countries that efforts on the part of regions or local governments to bypass the central state and build direct links with the European level create political turbulence. The sometimes conflicting positions of relatively autonomous subnational actors have to be taken into account and compromises have to be found. In the same vein, Marks *et al.* claim (1996a) that cohesion policy sometimes has contributed to the exacerbation of rivalry and conflict at the territorial level, between the regional and central authorities. Central governments control financial resources, and in countries with weak regional structures most of the EU funds are distributed in the framework of sectoral/national rather than regional programmes. It may thus be argued that the occurrence of power devolution is contingent on domestic factors, such as pre-existent administrative structures and culture. Likewise, Leonardi (2005) states that in cohesion policy the exact functions carried out by each level below that of the EC depend on the institutional structure of each member state. The role of regional and local actors is more pronounced in regional or federal systems: 'In other words, where functioning regional institutions were not operative, there was a lot less of multi level governance applied to the operationalization of cohesion policy' (Leonardi, 2005: 24).

Therefore, maybe the most important – if somewhat obvious – consideration in analysing MLG as an implementation model relates to the fact that if implementation of policies is to be entrusted to regional authorities, then the constitutional, institutional and administrative systems of the country and the regions involved become the fundamental factors in determining the policies' outcomes and the extent of the responsiveness of domestic actors to the EU principles and policy requirements. That is, on the one hand the degree of subnational involvement depends on the pre-existing constitutional arrangements and institutional structures of the individual member states; and on the other hand successful implementation depends very much upon the effectiveness and soundness of the regional political-administrative system.

The EU – and particularly EU cohesion policy – is commonly credited with exercising a strong influence on the evolution of regional-level structures and systems, as part of the design and implementation of regional development policies in the member states. Regional mobilisation in response to SFs has undeniably occurred across Europe, influenced by several factors: the pre-existing distribution of power and resource dependencies among central, regional and local governments in each country; the regions' democratic legitimacy deriving from popularly elected governments; the political skills and economic importance of different regions allowing them to lobby Brussels directly and more effectively; and the ability of central executives to structure the conditions under which regional governments interact with each other and with the Commission in the implementation of SFs (Pollack, 1995: 376). In fact, as observed by Rhodes (1995: 10): 'The less institutional autonomy a region has, the more disadvantages it accumulates. Regions without an elected tier of government are unable to wield the same influence in national and EU policies and to impose priorities.' This is confirmed by Barca (2009), who, analysing the data relative to the share of cohesion policy resources managed by regional authorities, concludes that only in those countries where regions enjoy considerable autonomy (i.e. Germany, Italy and Spain, among the ten countries benefiting most from support for lagging regions) are greater resources managed at the regional level than at the national one. A decentralised implementation is obviously easier if the member country has already a federal or regional system in place; for example, Mayntze (1999: 112) remarks that EU integration is particularly disruptive to unitary states, while in a federal system organised interests are used to being involved in the policy process and, similarly, the national government is used to sharing powers and to negotiating.

1.4 Preconditions for Multi-level Governance

The arguments presented above suggest a prerequisite for effective implementation of policies (and more specifically of cohesion policy) under the MLG framework is that a Member State already has in place a decentralised institutional structure: if subnational institutions and administrations are weak, EU intervention will not yield positive results. In this respect considerations relative to the new accession countries of Eastern Europe provide enlightening insights. The literature on the impact of the EU on the governance of accession countries is somewhat at odds regarding the varied policy outcomes produced: some scholars advocate the regionalising effects of EU accession and SFs, while others advance the hypothesis that it is instead the centre that has been reasserted. This is an interesting point from which to analyse the response of national/subnational actors and administrative structures to the challenge of SF's implementation (see Chapter 8 for a literature review on this issue).

This book aims to show the success of implementation depends not so much on recognised subnational institutions as it does on the administrative capacities and political features developed by the subnational tiers. Indeed, it seems that the MLG model's main point of strength coincides with its main point of weakness. MLG, in fact, creates high deregulation, opens doors to different and not homogeneous actors, and allows regions to implement their self-model of development. In short, MLG brings regions to the centre of the political arena. MLG, though, reaches its limit when a specific region is not able to manage this self-development model. As we will see in more detail in the following chapters, it may be necessary to recentralise the policy-making process when regions lack the economic, political and administrative capabilities to self-govern themselves (see Chapter 8 on Poland). MLG is not then a model generally suitable in every context but has to be calibrated. It has to be *governed*. In this respect, the central government's coordination and steering role is crucial. Anticipating some of the conclusions that will be drawn after analysis of the case studies, it can be said that even if recentralisation as a consequence of regional and lower tiers' incapacity may be a good short-term move to boost compliance, in the long term it is an unfeasible and anachronistic strategy: centralisation is not an adequate approach. Member States need to develop a multi-level framework and subnational authorities need to be helped in their institutional/capacity-building processes in order to be capable of implementing policies effectively and efficiently. This opinion is reflected in the Committee of the Regions' White Paper on Multilevel Governance (2009), where MLG is portrayed as a crucial means for enhancing the EU's capacity to perform its role and achieve its objectives:

> The legitimacy, efficiency and visibility of the way the Community operates depend on contributions from all the various players. They are guaranteed if local and regional authorities are genuine 'partners'

rather than mere 'intermediaries'. Partnership goes beyond participation and consultation, promoting a more dynamic approach and greater responsibility for the various players. Accordingly, the challenge of multilevel governance is to ensure that there is a complementary balance between institutional governance and partnership-based governance. The development of political and administrative culture in the EU must therefore be encouraged and stimulated (CoR, 2009: 5).

The originality of this research lies in its investigation of (1) the administrative and political preconditions which are necessary to implement EU cohesion policy in the MLG framework, and (2) whether regions met such preconditions. The interest of this enquiry is underlined by the following declaration of a Commission source: 'We never found a way to judge administrative capacity among the existing Member States. It was only in the case of the CEECs candidates knocking on our door that we erected the barrier of administrative capacity' (quoted in Dimitrova, 2002: 178). This book attempts to fill this research lacuna first by identifying the component elements and measures of administrative capacity, and then testing the existence of this capacity in selected case studies in Italy.

This approach is extended in the last two chapters of the book to Spain (Chapter 7) and Poland (Chapter 8) in order to outline a more comprehensive picture by considering first one of the most decentralised 'old' Member States followed by one of the new accession countries.

2

COHESION POLICY

A Case Study of Implementation Variation among Member States

2.1 The Reform of 1988 Challenges the Regional Governments
The four Structural Funds (SFs) were created in different periods and acted in an uncoordinated fashion until 1988:

1   The European Social Fund (ESF), established in 1960, is the main instrument of Community social policy. It provides financial assistance for vocational training, retraining and job-creation schemes.
2   The European Agricultural Guidance and Guarantee Fund (EAGGF) has financed the EU's common agricultural policy since 1962.
3   The European Regional Development Fund (ERDF), which is intended to help reduce imbalances between regions of the Community, was set up in 1975. In terms of financial resources, the ERDF is by far the largest of the EU's SFs and it is the main financial instrument of EU Regional Policy.
4   The Financial Instrument for Fisheries Guidance (FIFG), the last Fund to be created, in 1994, draws together the Community instruments for fisheries.

The major reform adopted in 1988[1] radically transformed the largely isolated way in which the SFs had previously operated into a global system of integration of their respective roles, within which they worked together towards the goal of economic and social cohesion under the same regulatory framework. The reform provided for SFs to become the instrument of EU cohesion policy and have as a main target Objective 1 regions, defined as those whose development is lagging behind – i.e. where the Gross Domestic Product (GDP) per capita is at or below 75 per cent of the Community average.[2] The Brussels European Council of February 1988 approved the principles under which the SFs would operate; namely concentration, programming, additionality and partnership. Concentration was intended to direct funding towards a limited number of objectives, focusing on spatially defined areas of greatest need, on the severest problems and on certain thematic areas. Programming was a process intended to lead first to the diagnosis of problems, then to the formulation of a strategy to address them, and, last, to a definition of the specific measures or projects necessary to implement the strategy. Additionality provides that the expenditure of SFs on a programme shall be additional to and not a replacement of what would otherwise have been spent by the relevant national public authorities on that area of activity. Partnership suggests that the broad plans for using the SFs are achieved through

> [c]lose consultations between the Commission, the Member States concerned and the competent authorities designated by the latter at national, regional, local or other level, with each party acting as a partner in pursuit of a common goal. The partnership shall cover the preparation, financing, monitoring and assessment of operations. (Council Regulation n. 2052/1988 Art 4)

At the broadest level, partnership is seen, at least by the Commission, as an application of the principle of subsidiarity in public policy, reflecting the value of decentralisation and the involvement, at all levels, of the relevant authorities in lower tiers of government, from the preparatory stage to the implementation of the measures (cf Section 1.3.2).

Partnership, both institutional – between different levels of government and within the same government level – and social, is deemed necessary at all stages (planning, implementing and monitoring) in order to allow the transfer of knowledge needed to produce a framework programme – defined as the Community Support Framework (CSF)[3] – that would subsequently be translated, at regional level, into multi-Fund Operational Programmes (OP).

Since 1988, three cycles of SFs have been completed – 1989–1993, 1994–1999 and 2000–2006 – and a fourth one is currently under way – 2007–2013. Each planning period has been characterised by changes in the rules and regulations of the practical operation of SFs.

The landmark reform introduced key principles such as focusing on the poorest and most backward regions, multi-annual programming, strategic orientation of investments and the involvement of regional and local partners. The second reform of 1993 strengthened the rules on partnership, evaluation and publicity of SFs expenditure. The third reform in 1999 was much stronger and was intended to tighten the rules on financial control and discipline. For the first time a form of sanction was introduced for those not spending SFs according to the timeline set by the Commission – i.e. the 'n + 2' rule. According to this rule, failure to provide proof of payment within two years means that the allocation is lost. In addition, stronger involvement of Member States and regions in programme monitoring and assessment was imposed by a system of ex ante, mid-term and ex post evaluations.

All this innovations opened the way for a completely new approach to regional development policies within the EC, based on multi-year integrated programmes that were no longer centred on the exclusive role of one institutional level (i.e. the national). Instead, the new regulations required the participation of several levels – i.e. the Community, national, and regional/local levels (Leonardi, 2005).

The institutionalisation of cohesion policy with the reform of the SFs in 1988 changed the state-centred regulatory model of the European institutions. Indeed, cohesion policy prompted the gradual evolution of an MLG form of decision-making and implementation, which became increasingly focused on the programmatic approach and partnership model. The reform did away with the old didactic intergovernmentalist bargaining model in regional policy by admitting subnational actors into a tripartite decision-making and implementation process. In addition, the new approach required the active participation of both public and private actors at various levels of policy-making.

But how were Member States coping with these changes? Were they keeping up and implementing SFs according to the rules and regulations or were they struggling, widening the implementation gap? Retrospective data on the rate of SF expenditure across the Member States show strong variation, with Spain and Italy being respectively the best and worst performing. Interestingly, though, closer examination of individual regions' performance within Spain and Italy reveals strong variations. Section 2.2 considers how we might explain these differences in regional performance. Section 2.3 reviews the existing literature on SFs implementation, focusing on the introduction of a new approach to regional development policies based on the increasing role of subnational governments; this had consequences in terms of both the institutional and administrative changes required within Member States to enable them to implement SFs. It became clear that not all regions were able to become active partners with the national government and the European Commission, because of differences in their administrative roles, decision-making autonomy, and policy-making and implementation capacities.

2.2 Cohesion Policy Variation across the EU

From the beginning, there have been significant differences between regions in the way they have implemented their allocation of funds. The EC defines implementation as '[t]he operational process needed to produce expected outputs' (CEC, 1999c: 55).

Implementation, therefore, is that part of the cycle by which inputs are converted into outputs. The outputs produced can be of two kinds: (1) quantitative implementation, i.e. spending the allocated resources in the given time span; or (2) qualitative implementation, i.e. investing the resources in 'good' projects in order to generate economic growth and job creation.

Why do some regions spend more funds than others? This question is relevant for two main reasons. First, unspent resources are lost and this has a negative impact on, among others, a country's general public, which sees the loss as a failure of the government. Second, the future allocation of SFs is determined, among other factors, on the basis of a region's spending capacity. A Member State which does not spend its allocation therefore risks losing future funding and opportunities to foster regional development. This aspect is currently of particular importance since the EU redefined its budgetary allocations for cohesion policy for the present policy cycle, 2007–2013, after the 2004 enlargement brought into the EU nine Member States whose national GDP per capita is below the 75 per cent threshold.[4] Although the newly joined countries have already begun to receive SFs, it remains to be seen whether all will be able to utilise these resources as prescribed by the rules and regulations.

The qualitative aspect of implementation is equally relevant but needs to be tackled separately, since rather than the relative objectivity of resource expenditure it requires a different methodology and the identification of indicators for assessing the quality of a project, a somewhat contentious process.

Empirical evidence on the expenditure rate of SFs in EU Objective 1 regions shows that the overall performance of Italian regions has consistently lagged behind that of other countries whereas Spain has always been among the best performing countries (Table 2.1)

However, analysis of regional performance within both Member States reveals the existence of strong intraregional variation. Indeed, analysis of the

Table 2.1 Percentage of SFs expenditure[a] – EU Objective 1 regions

	1989–1993 (%)	1994–1999 (%)	2000–2006 (%)[b]
Ireland	95	87	82
Portugal	91	89	75
Spain	87	82	75
Denmark	n/a	81	n/a
Germany	n/a	n/a	77
Austria	n/a	77	74
Finland	n/a	n/a	72
Sweden	n/a	n/a	79
Greece	84	73	53
Belgium	n/a	72	66
France	84	67	64
United Kingdom	83	67	66
Netherlands	n/a	67	72
Italy	73	67	60

Source: European Commission – Respective Annual Report on SFs

Notes
a   % of expenditure is calculated as expenditure/total allocation
b   Expenditure is calculated until December 2006

Italian Objective 1 regions, all located in the southern part of the country – best known as the *Mezzogiorno* – shows that not all followed the same general trend. Retrospective data suggests that SFs implementation over the past three planning periods has varied markedly between these regions (Table 2.2).

Although all regions began to implement SFs with no prior experience, some regions, such as Basilicata, have consistently performed well. Conversely, other regions, such as Sicily, have shown constant delays in the pace of expenditure over the three periods. So, although on the national level there has been a lower than average ability to implement allocated funds, some southern Italian regions have demonstrated, in contrast, a higher than average ability to spend the resources.

The same puzzling evidence applies to Spanish regions, with Galicia's rate of absorption being higher than Andalusia's for all the considered periods (Table 2.3)

Why is this the case, and what has been happening in some Objective 1 regions *vis-à-vis* others? How can we explain these differences in regional performance? This research explores these differences and aims to identify potential variables that may have influenced the evident variations in implementation.

Table 2.2 Percentage of SFs expenditure – Italian Objective 1 regions

	1989–1993 (%)	1994–1999 (%)	2000–2006 (%)[b]
Basilicata	92	100	64
Abruzzo[a]	80	100	n/a
Molise[c]	77	99	73
Sardinia	77	92	63
Calabria	80	84	64
Campania	62	80	51
Puglia	64	77	55
Sicily	57	75	46

Source: Author's elaboration on Italian Ministry of the Treasury data.

Notes
a   Abruzzo is in 'Phasing-out' stage – i.e. it exits obj. 1 status at the end of 1996
b   The data for this period are updated at December 2006
c   Molise is in 'Phasing-out' – i.e. it exits ob. 1 status at the end of 2003

Table 2.3 Percentage of SFs expenditure – Spanish Objective 1 Regions

Autonomous Communities	1989–1993 (%)	1994–1999 (%)	2000–2006 (%)
Andalusia	94.0	82.69	77.68
Asturias	106.5	71.77	90.01
Canary Island	102.6	87.26	76.45
Cantabria[a]	—	78.95	112.01
Castile-La Mancha	101.7	89.16	93.62
Castile and Leon	110.3	92.18	102.67
Extremadura	100.0	61.54	87.70
Galicia	107.2	91.84	82.20
Murcia	110.4	83.03	77.81
Valencian Community	102.9	85.69	74.98

Source: Spanish Ministry of Economy and Finance

Notes
a   Objective 2 in 1989–1993; phasing out in 2000–2006

2.3 The Existing Debate on Cohesion Policy

Throughout the literature there has been little attention paid to the implementation of resources. Indeed, all the studies and analyses that have been developed in the past can be classified into two main areas.

The first area focuses on the design of the decision-making process and is dominated by the opposing ideas of intergovernmentalism theory

(Moravcsik, 1993, 1995) and multi-level governance (Hooghe, 1996; Jeffery, 1996). Intergovernmentalists argue that national governments perform the role of 'gatekeepers' between supranational institutions and their domestic system. Multi-level governance theory suggests that a new form of policy-making is developing in the EU. According to this perspective, as illustrated in the previous chapter, central governments remain vitally important but do not hold a monopoly on decision-making powers. Instead, policy-making responsibility is now shared among a number of actors at European, national and subnational levels.

The second area of studies investigates the economic impact of SFs. It is divided between the supporters of negative results (Rodríguez-Pose, 1998) – i.e. the view that SFs do not succeed in backing economic growth – and the advocates of positive results – those who corroborate that a process of regional convergence has been taking place since the SF reform of 1988 (Leonardi, 1993, 1995, 2005). Indeed, the discussion of whether the different growth of the regions is related to SFs implementation has been the object of a large-scale debate (Beutel, 2002; Keating, 1995a; Basile *et al.*, 2001).

Therefore, I suggest that there is a significant need to change the focus of the analysis. Indeed, previous authors confirm that mismanagement or lack of implementation of Funds has no economic impact (Ederveen *et al.*, 2002). They argue that, putting implementation problems to one side, the EU's Structural Policy has beneficial effects with regard to economic and social cohesion.

In the light of the above considerations, it is clear that the significance of the contribution made by SFs to economic development is still controversial. Furthermore, so much has already been said that I do not wish to contribute to this debate. Instead, I want to tackle the implementation phase, which, positioned as it is in the less visible back-end of the process, is completely neglected. Indeed, since implementation constitutes the last major and the most important component of a policy – that is, it determines whether a policy is effective or not – it is important to understand the factors that encourage or prevent its occurrence. If resources are not spent, then they will definitely have no impact.

Clearly, the creation of the SFs and the strengthening of an EU regional development policy through the adoption of the CSF approach has significantly changed the nature of relations between institutions and has led to the emergence for the first time of regional institutions as significant policy actors. This is true with regard to participation in the formulation and implementation of SFs. Policies are no longer structured in an exclusively top-down approach. Instead, they now combine both top-down and bottom-up characteristics.

The implementation of the new decision-making mechanisms associated with MLG proved to be far more complex and difficult to carry out than was initially expected. Adaptation to the new EU rules and regulations was not automatic. The new approach required both political and administrative changes at both the national and subnational level. In order to create modern efficient forms of governmental activities, the institutions involved needed to develop (1) differentiated vertical and horizontal distribution of powers and responsibilities, and (2) considerable planning, programming and coordination capacities (Tömmel, 1987).

In each Member State, national government and subnational actors have different degrees of participation in decision-making. This reflects factors such as the distribution of competencies between national, regional and local levels, political interests and linkages, the amount and scope of co-funding available, the number and scope of programmes to be dealt with at each level, and administrative experience of managing economic development. It follows that practical arrangements for programming also vary, including the approaches to programme development, project generation, selection, monitoring and evaluation, and the extent to which these tasks are subsumed within the existing administrative structure or whether parts of the implementation are carried out by dedicated administrative structures and how these are organised (Taylor *et al.*, 1999).

It is clear that, with the 1988 reform of SFs, the regions gained a key role in the design and implementation of EU regional policy. However, several authors (Bailey and De Propris, 2002; Keating, 1995b) argue that differences in the forms and structures of local governance throughout Europe have weakened the aim of structural policies to achieve economic and social cohesion. As Bailey and De Propris (2002: 9) put it, '[s]ome regions had never before been involved in European policies and thus had never started or developed a dialogue with European institutions, in other cases regions did not even exist as geographical, administrative and political entities'.[5]

To be clear about how MLG can work efficiently, therefore, it is necessary to understand what preconditions are necessary at regional level for favouring implementation.

3

ADMINISTRATIVE AND POLITICAL PRECONDITIONS FOR EFFECTIVE MULTI-LEVEL GOVERNANCE

3.1 Introduction

The administrative capacity and efficiency of the Member State is a decisive variable in determining its implementation performance, for both domestic and EU policies. Many scholars have linked administrative efficiency with implementation performance; Milio (2007), analysing Structural Fund implementation, provides evidence that successful implementation definitely does depend on the level of administrative capacity of the bureaucracy. The combination of a lack of horizontal coordination between departments, vertical fragmentation and responsibilities divided between a vast number of internal units and offices, and deficiencies in staff, technical expertise and infrastructure, leads inescapably to administrative inefficiencies that delay and hinder effective compliance and implementation. In this context, some scholars have argued that there is a 'Southern problem' related to the notorious lack of administrative efficiency that characterises countries like Italy or Greece. The difficulties experienced by southern European countries in complying with EU law, their poor implementation record, and their reputation of being 'laggards' in the implementation of EU policies have also been defined as the 'Mediterranean syndrome' (La Spina and Sciortino, 1993).

The first part of my central hypothesis is that positive administrative factors are a necessary precondition for successful implementation, but this alone is not sufficient. If it is indeed true that the variation in implementation of resources among regions can be explained by a different regional administrative capacity, what is it that determines the degree of this capacity at regional level? The second part of my central hypothesis is that the features acquired by the key components constituting administrative capacity are influenced by political factors: namely political interference, government stability and political accountability. Political stability is particularly important aspect since it 'allows for continuity and coherence in administrative actions' (Milio, 2008: 915) and is thus conducive to improved administrative performance. Moreover, coalitional crises and frequent changes of government may hinder the passing of laws required to transpose EU directives.

The two parts of the central hypothesis – i.e. administrative and political factors are preconditions for implementation success in the MLG framework – are developed in sections 3.2 and 3.3, while section 3.4 outlines the methodology and the case studies – i.e. Sicily and Basilicata in Italy, and Galicia and Andalucía in Spain – which address the central hypothesis.

3.2 Defining Administrative Capacity

3.2.1 Approaches to Administrative Capacity

An exploration and review of the concept and substance of administrative capacity must overcome one main problem, which must be declared from the outset. It is, quite simply, that what the literature offers is too general and too broad. This obstructs attempts to develop an assessment of administrative capacity that aim to establish a common understanding across countries of what capacity actually is and what capacities might be required for various forms of implementation activities. Therefore, my characterisation of administrative capacity aims to be more specific in order to be operationalisable and applicable across countries. Naturally, some of the specification will be related to resource implementation, but it will be easily applied to any financial resource and not merely to SFs.

My review begins by analysing a recently developed line of thought which focuses on building administrative capacity in order to improve SFs implementation in the CEECs (Shoylekova, 2004; Kun-Buczko, 2004). Studies on the EU-15 are rare, which seems unfair given that administrative capacity is an issue for all EU countries.

It was during the negotiations with the CEECs for EU accession that interest in administrative capacity first emerged (Bollen, 2001). It became clear that '[s]tates with weak administrative capacity at the regional and local levels were more likely to have serious problems with the mismanagement of funds, or even with accessing them' (Hughes *et al.*, 2004a: 532–3).

The EC recognised that the allocation of SFs to new Member States had to be underpinned by a capacity building programme, in order for these countries to develop adequate administrative and management skills (CEC, 1999b). Chapter 21 of the *acquis communautaire* states that '[t]he candidate countries have to define clear tasks and responsibilities of all the bodies and institutions involved in SFs preparation and implementation, and have to ensure appropriate administrative capacity' (CEC, 2004a: 68).

As enlargement progressed, administrative capacity requirements grew in importance and complexity – from 'administrative capacity' to 'institution building' (Dimitrova, 2002; Hughes *et al.*, 2004b: 85–118). To help achieve these goals the CEECs were supported by the PHARE programme whose first priority, 'institution building', was defined as the process of helping candidate countries to develop the structures, strategies, human resources and management skills needed to strengthen economic, social, regulatory and administrative capacity (Papantoniadou, 2004). However, neither a clear definition of administrative capacity nor a strong and coherent assessment model can be found in the existing literature (Dimitrova, 2002; Hughes *et al.*, 2004a: 534).

Current thinking on capacity is significantly broader than the definitions applied ten years ago. Capacity is closely linked with performance. Improvement and development of capacities is in turn linked with strategic management to ensure that performance directly reflects the objectives of the organisation and the system (Milen, 2001: 4). In recent years, many authors have focused on the weakness of the institutions in responding either to the goals set by policies or to the demand of the society.

In general, capacity has been defined as 'the ability to perform appropriate tasks effectively, efficiently and sustainably' (Hilderbrand and Grindle, 1994: 15), or as 'the ability to perform functions, solve problems and set and achieve objectives' (Fukuda-Parr *et al.*, 2002: 3).

What makes a country able to perform a function, solve a problem or achieve an objective? This is very country-specific, since a country's approach to a particular problem will be embedded in its complex history, institutional setting and social fabric. The approach that Fukuda-Parr suggests is that a country should determine the actions that it is willing to take, and then assess what capacity such actions require. Indeed, research suggests that most instances of non-compliance with international agreements are not intentional but are caused by lack of state capacity (Brown Weiss and Jacobson, 1998; and cf. section 1.3.2 of this book). If the gap between *existing* capacity and the capacity that is *required* is too large for a particular policy option, it could become virtually impossible for a country to abide by what it has committed to do, either domestically or internationally. In this framework, the level of existing capacities in a country is likely to define the next step it can take. However, it is also hoped that capacity will grow with each step and allow for a progressive strengthening of actions over time.

Other authors (Mentz, 1997; North, 1992) argue that administrative capacity is related to personal capacity, since any administration is staffed with civil servants, and it is therefore their capacity that ultimately determines service delivery. Similarly, Cohen's (1993) definition of capacity in the public sector is linked to the strengthening of human resources (managerial, professional and technical), particularly institutions, and to providing '[t]hose institutions with the means whereby these resources can be marshalled and sustained effectively to perform planning, policy formulation, and implementation tasks throughout government on any priority topic' (Cohen, 1993: 10).

Cohen's approach to capacity appears to be narrower, more operational and more oriented towards problem solving. Still, it does not tell us what capacity is required, nor how we are to assess administrative capacity. The question here is what capacity is needed for the region to improve its performance. How capacity is defined determines what kind of strategies and actions should be taken in order to improve its output.

Further insights can be found in the literature on institutional capacity, which encompasses the whole organisation rather than just the administrative sphere. Although this latter is a broader concept than administrative capacity, it is worth considering existing definitions of institutional capacity for support in formulating my definition of administrative capacity.

3.2.2 *Towards a Definition of Administrative Capacity*

The international development community is increasingly focusing on institutional capacity as one of the missing elements in any successful development strategy. This was inevitable in light of accumulating evidence that development programmes failed because of institutional and managerial weaknesses. Broadly, the literature views institutional capacity as a means to achieve higher-level programme results (USAID, 2000).

The concept of institutional capacity is constantly changing. Institutions are not just discrete organisations (e.g. government agencies) but also, more generally, are sets of rules, procedures or practices that prescribe behavioural roles for actors, constrain activity and shape expectations (Keohane, 1988). Institutions are durable: they are sources of authority (formal or informal) that structure repeated interactions of individuals, companies, civil societal groups, governments and other entities. Thus, institutional capacity represents a broader 'enabling environment' which forms the basis upon which individuals and organisations interact. In this context, training individuals and strengthening organisations can only succeed in the long term if it is consistent with existing institutions, or if it helps transform these institutions, so that actions are based on rules, processes and practices that can be sustained over time (Willems and Baumert, 2003).

The existing approaches to defining and studying institutional capacity can be classified under three main headings: the systemic, the functional and the constituent approach. I will be using a combination of these three approaches to define my operationalisation of administrative capacity (cf. section 3.2.3).

The *systemic approach* is based on the notion that institutional capacity has developed over time:

> the concept of institutional capacity is a moving target since the field has evolved over the years from an initial focus on building and strengthening individual organizations and providing technical and management training to support integrated planning and decision-making processes between institutions. [...] Today, institutional capacity often implies a broader focus of empowerment, social capital, and an enabling environment, as well as the culture, values and power relations that influence us. (Segnestam *et al.*, 2002: 10)

This approach is characterised by the assumption of the inherently systemic nature of institutional capacity and conduct within a broader definition that distinguishes between three levels of institutional capacity (Forss and Venson, 2002, cited in Willems and Baumert, 2003: 11): a micro level, i.e. the individual; a meso level, i.e. the organisation; and a macro level, i.e. the broad institutional context.

Willems and Baumert (2003: 15) warn that such a broad definition of institutional capacity, which includes social norms, values and practices, could be viewed as 'blurring any distinction between *ability* and *willingness* to implement a particular policy or international commitment', and provide a clear example of how this could happen:

> a Party could argue that it has *in a narrow sense* the ability of taking on a particular commitment, because it has sufficient human and financial resources to do so, but that its own civil society is not ready to accept this particular policy, because of its own values or way of life. Is this national government not *willing,* or not *able,* to implement a particular policy or commitment? (Willems and Baumert, 2003: 17)

My research focuses on assessing the capacity an institution needs in order to implement a policy, and what factors cause variations in that capacity. My definition of administrative capacity therefore excludes social norms, values and practices in order to avoid any of the 'blurring' suggested by Willems and Baumert.

A second approach to institutional capacity, the *functional*, analyses the functions that need to be performed in order to achieve a policy objective. Any policy process must include different functions in order to be successful. These functions can be grouped into three distinct phases of the policy process: (1) national assessment, strategies and goals; (2) policy design and implementation; and (3) monitoring, reporting, review and enforcement. These phases may overlap in time, but essentially follow a logical order. The challenge for any policy process is to be able to perform all such functions in an efficient manner, given that they are interdependent. Thus, there needs to be capacity for each of these functions if the policy process is to be sustained over time (Willems and Baumert, 2003).

Willems and Baumert argue that in most countries there is often an imbalance in the capacities devoted to each of these clusters of functions. In some cases, most capacity development is devoted to the actual implementation of policies, with little capacity left for strategic assessment. This may result in the lack of a long-term view and in badly designed policies. A lack of capacity in the monitoring and reporting area may lead to difficulties in sustaining policy efforts, given that information that might improve policies over time would be lacking. In other cases, it may be that a sophisticated strategy has been formulated, but there are no means to implement it.

The *constituent approach* defines the concept of institutional capacity through a list of constituent elements. It can be found in, among others, Loubser (1993) and the United States Agency for International Development (USAID, 2000). Loubser lists the following elements of capacity:

> specified objectives, including vision, values, policies, strategies and interests; efforts, including will (motivation, drive) energy, concentration, work ethic and efficiency; capabilities, including intelligence, skills, knowledge and mental sets; resources, including human (for collective participants), natural, technological (infrastructure), cultural and financial; and work organization, including planning, designing, sequencing and mobilizing. (Loubser, 1993: 23)

USAID defines an institution as an organisation, or a system of related components that work together to achieve an agreed mission. It therefore identifies a list of organisational components (Table 3.1), which is neither all-inclusive nor universally applicable to all organisations. Rather, the components are representative of those of most organisations involved in development work and will vary according to the type of organisation and the context in which it functions. Consequently, the institutional capacity of the chosen organisation is given by the combination and performance in the areas which are fundamental for the organisation to succeed in its task.

Finally, some authors have suggested that institutional capacity might be the result of the combination of two or more areas/dimensions. White argues that '[g]overnment institutional capacity has two dimensions: whether the instruments of government per se are adequate to a task, and whether a specific government has the necessary powers and resources' (White, 2003: 6).

Defining institutional capacity as the product of instruments/tasks and power creates a circularity that does not leave space for intervening variables. Indeed, if both the political power and the administrative tasks are

Table 3.1 List of components

Areas	*Key components*
Administrative and support functions	• Administrative procedures and management systems • Financial management (budgeting, accounting, sustainability) • Human resource management (staff recruitment, placement, support) • Management of other resources
Resources	• Human • Financial • Other
Technical/programme functions	• Service delivery system • Programme planning • Programme monitoring and evaluation • Use and management of technical knowledge and skills
Structure and culture (political organisation)	• Organisational identity • Vision and purpose • Leadership capacity and style • Organisational values • Governance approach • External relations

Source: USAID Center for Development Information and Evaluation (2000).

incorporated in the definition as being equally important, there will be nothing left to hypothesise about regarding what influences the functioning of the government instruments. This is the main reason why my investigation is divided into two parts, intended to disentangle the administrative sphere from the political.

3.2.3 A New Definition

As shown in the previous section, the definitions of administrative capacity found in the literature are too general and tell us little about which activities should be performed. However, investigating the broader concept of institutional capacity provides useful benchmarks and inspirations to help formulate a new definition of administrative capacity, which will allow us to measure the concept empirically.

In the context of SFs policy, as in any other policy area, reaching a definition of administrative capacity requires an understanding of what we are trying to achieve. This should allow us to achieve a definition that is narrower, more operational and more oriented towards problem-solving than the existing ones. Indeed, as Honadle (1981: 575–6) points out,

> [d]efinitions of capacity vary to the extent to which they specify the activities that should be performed versus the results that are sought. It is unlikely that a consensus definition of 'capacity' will ever be reached. Nevertheless, a reasonably integrated framework for pursuing this Holy Grail would help capacity builders map a sensible course.

In pursuing such a goal, I suggest that administrative capacity is related to the ability of institutions to manage SFs policy according to their own rules and procedures. I therefore propose that administrative capacity should be defined as being characterised by four key components:

1   management
2   programming
3   monitoring
4   evaluation.

This choice is based on a combination of the three approaches emerging from the literature review, a thorough scrutiny of the principles and structures of SFs,[1] and an analysis carried out by Boijmans (2003). The four actions are defined in the following section.

3.2.4 The Four Key Components of Administrative Capacity

I believe that high performance in the administrative area is determined by the functioning of the four key components identified above. Therefore, the intraregional variation we observe in both Italy and Spain could be explained through the analysis of each key determinant within the regional government.

I outline below definitions of these key components and their associated expectations in terms of improving SFs implementation. I also introduce the indicators proposed to measure the performance of each action, which are discussed in detail in section 3.4.1

Management

Management covers overseeing the correct implementation of the overall programme. In the case of the SFs development programme, the responsibility for each Operational Programme (OP) is allocated to the Managing Authority (MA), which is appointed by the Member States (Council Regulation n. 1260/99, Art. 9). The responsibilities and powers of MAs have increased over time. Their tasks cover the implementation, correct management and effectiveness of the programmes (collection of statistical and financial data, preparation and transmission to the Commission of annual reports, organisation of the mid-term evaluation, and so on). The establishment at regional level of a MA in charge of overall fund management is necessary given that there are many actors and departments involved. Since, in fact, the funds cover various areas of intervention – natural resources, human resources, cultural resources, local development, agriculture, transport, environment, and so on – it is necessary that the most appropriate departments are in a position to manage them. This could lead to a department acting in an isolated fashion and dealing only with its own part of the funds, without an overall vision of the whole programme. It is necessary that the funds are implemented following an integrated logic among the various departments. This is possible if the regional MA provides an efficient horizontal coordination.

An additional consideration that emerges from examination of primary and secondary sources[2] is the unclear division of responsibilities in day-to-day activities. This uncertainty leads most of the time to a duplication of workload and confusion. Indeed, a survey carried out in 2003 by ÖIR-Managementdienste GmbH provided evidence to suggest the following:

When management structures are clearly defined, with roles and coordination processes well implemented, the system works well.

In the case studies that have been completed for this survey, this is the situation in Alentejo, Burgenland, Ireland, Saxony, Spain, Valencia, Portugal POE, Italy, France, Lorraine, East Midlands, Bavaria, Veneto. This is not to say that there are no problems in these regions, but there exists a solid basis on which to resolve the practical problems as they emerge. Where management structures are not clearly defined, as for example in cases where newly devolved structures are just being implemented, there are problems. This is clear from the case studies of Wales, Greece Transport, Finland, Central Macedonia. (ÖIR, 2003: 129)

Taking into account the above observation, I propose two indicators to measure the functioning of the MA, namely:

a   coordination between each level involved;
b   clarity of the roles carried out by personnel.

Through the measurement of these indicators, we can understand the degree and quality of management present in each region.

Programming

Programming is conducted on a multi-annual basis and involves the determination of objectives to be achieved against the background of an analysis of the socio-economic context, SWOT analysis (Strengths, Weaknesses, Opportunities and Threats), and the identification of priorities and measures capable of converting these objectives into projects in which to invest the available funds. If the identification of priorities is incorrect, it will be difficult to spend the resources. Programming is not just at the heart of the SFs implementation system but is a key factor in any public policy. Although the principles and main concepts of programming have not changed over the three periods considered, demands on the quality of programme documents have increased significantly. One primary factor that influences the implementation of resources is the preparation of the multi-annual development plans,[3] based on national and regional priorities, which include two fundamental requirements: programme design and programme decisions. In the first case it is necessary to have a precise description of the socio-economic context of the region (disparities, lags, potential development) based on a SWOT analysis; a determination of the most appropriate strategy for achieving the previously identified objectives; and indications as to the use and form of the contribution from the Funds. Second, it is important that the time lapse between the approval of the national document and the regional document is as short as possible to avoid wasting time; this is because the national development plan is set for a period of five years (or more), and so the regional plan needs to respect that timeframe in terms of start and end dates.

In light of the above remarks, I suggest the following two indicators to measure the functioning of programming activities:

a   programme design;
b   programme approval.

Monitoring

Monitoring aims to ensure that projects are implemented according to agreed strategic priorities. It involves an exhaustive and regular examination of the resources, outputs and results of public interventions, based on a system of pre-established indicators. It verifies the sound management of the interventions and produces a regular analysis of the progress of programme outputs (Council Regulation n. 1260/99, art. 36).

The logic behind monitoring is twofold. First, it gives the MA updated information on the pace of expenditure, so that it can intervene and adjust the implementation in progress in case of problems or delays. The need for a monitoring system has always been stated in the regulations, but in the first two planning periods its role was not clearly defined. It was in the latest planning period, 2000–2006, that it became a crucial element in the implementation of the funds. Detailed monitoring of a multitude of indicators measuring the output, results and impact of each measure has resulted in a significant data management challenge for programme implementation. Where monitoring activities have been carried out properly this has favoured the implementation of the programme and expenditure of resources.

I suggest the following indicators to assess the functioning of the monitoring system:

a   introduction of a system of indicators and of monitoring procedures responding to nationally agreed standards.
b   guaranteeing the availability of financial, physical and procedural data.[4]

Evaluation

Evaluation judges programme implementation on the basis of the outputs, results and impact on society: 'The purpose of evaluation is to check the *raison d'être* of a public intervention, to confirm both reproducible success stories and failures not to be repeated' (CEC, 1999c: 55). The capacity to evaluate the results of the implemented resources is relevant at three different stages: *ex-ante*, *in itinere*, and *ex-post* (Council Regulation n. 1260/99, art. 40). *Ex-ante* evaluation serves to clarify the needs of the territory and to verify the existence and nature of the problems within the territory; it helps to ensure that the final programme is as relevant and coherent as possible. The mid-term evaluation (*in itinere*) is performed halfway through implementation of the interventions, and serves to highlight and adjust eventual deficiencies. An *ex-post* evaluation serves to examine whether the needs or problems still exist and whether the programme has achieved the expected results. *Ex-post* evaluation provides exceptional support and guidance to the administration in programming future financial interventions and organising the implementation of actions so that subsequent programming cycles are successful. Therefore, where such a task has been carried out internally, the regional government is in a much better position to learn from past mistakes increase the rate of implementation in future programming efforts.

From my perspective, it is fundamental that the regional MAs have the capacity to evaluate – collect and analyse data – on a continuous basis. At present, evaluations are contracted out to private independent companies according to the dictates of the EU regulations. Thus there is a large reliance on the outside professional community for evaluation skills and competencies in providing independent analysis and aiding the regions in the process of institutional learning.

In light of the above remarks, two benchmarks appear to be adequate to gauge the functioning of the evaluation system:

a   production of evaluation reports accordingly to the three stages in time;
b   integration of the evaluation method and culture in the implementation system.

It can be argued that other components of the administrative arena should be taken into account, but I will demonstrate that the ones included here are not only the most relevant in accounting for variation in the implementation of resources, but are also the tools the institution needs to deal with *any* public policy.

The administrative capacity loop

My definition of administrative capacity encompasses both the activities that the regional government should be performing and the results it should be achieving. Taken as a whole these actions create a framework which

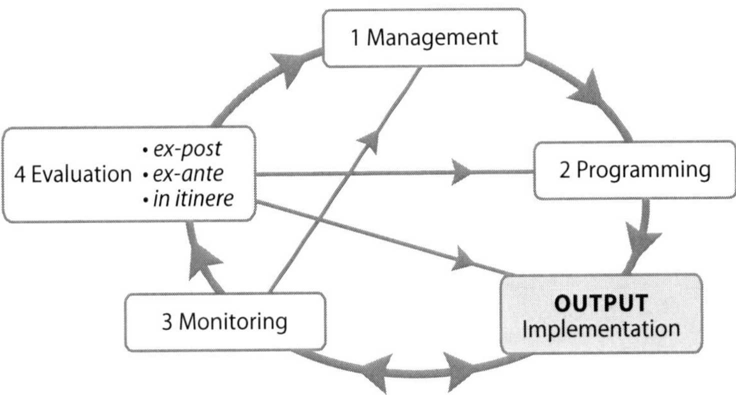

Figure 3.1 Administrative capacity loop

Note: implementation represents the output of the four actions, which constitute administrative capacity.

operates as a system – i.e. the key components are related to each other so that the outcome of each one is closely related to the other. This creates a loop where if every action is performed correctly, a high level of SFs implementation occurs (Figure 3.1). In sum, a conceptual framework for administrative capacity should include all of these components. Individually, none can provide a sufficient definition of capacity.

3.3 What Determines the Degree of Administrative Capacity?

Once I have tested whether the variation in SFs implementation is determined by regional administrative capacity (cf. Chapter 5) – i.e. the first part of the central hypothesis and the first set of preconditions for MLG to work – my subsequent aim is to establish which factors determine the degree of administrative capacity of a region, i.e. why administrative capacity varies across regions (cf. Chapter 6). This will provide a full picture of the preconditions necessary for implementation success within the MLG framework.

3.3.1 The Role of Political Factors

The second part of my central hypothesis concerns the role of internal political factors in contributing to variation of administrative capacity. In this context, my work finds strong support in two publications by Putnam, Leonardi and Nanetti, namely *La Pianta e le radici* (Putnam *et al.*,1985), and *Il Caso Basilicata* (Leonardi *et al.*, 1987).

The starting question of their research asked why some institutions (regions) succeed while others fail. What they meant by 'succeed' was the capacity of the institution to fulfil its goals in an efficient way in order to satisfy the various interests (Putnam *et al.*, 1985). The two studies answer this question by examining, respectively, contextual factors and endogenous factors.[5] They do not only examine the socio-cultural aspects but highlight the influence of the political factor on regional performance:

> Responsible for the weakness of the regional administrative performance was the political class, which in recruiting the staff was driven by clientelism and party affiliation criteria rather than expertise and qualification criteria (Putnam *et al.*, 1985: 347)

> The higher performance of Basilicata over the period 1970/1984 is due to the extraordinary role played by a small group of regional *dirigenti*, who have collaborated with unusual solidarity (Leonardi *et al.*, 1987: 32; author's translation).

Hence, we must examine the behaviour of the relevant individuals within the institutions to understand how they may influence the degree of administrative capacity. Much of the literature on public institutions is concerned with how politics and political interests with competing agendas constrain institutions' technical capacity: 'It is rare to encounter a significant instance where political leaders make serious and concerted attempts to structure an institution for the explicit purpose of increasing its capacity to design and implement policy in a particular domain' (Desveaux, 1995: 7).

The above was the case for southern Italian regional government. Piattoni (1997, 1998a, 1998b; Piattoni and Smyrl 2002), among others, has extensively studied its political aspects and reached the conclusion that

> the explanation of the differentiation in policy efficiency among various regional governments does not lie in their formal institutional layout, which is identical, nor in their informal institutional capacities, be they embodied in civicness or strong regional identity. Rather, it lies in the different capacity and willingness of the regional political class to promote the adequate requirements for implementing the funds … Politics, far from being irrelevant or altogether deleterious for southern development, has played a fundamental role in the development of the most successful southern regions. (Piattoni, 1998b: 50)

Similarly, Allum and Cilento (2001) successfully tested the hypothesis that the charisma, personality and commitment of politicians can have a genuine effect on the improvement of regional performance. In their article 'Parties and Personalities', which recounts the case of Antonio Bassolino, former Mayor of Naples, they show how the charismatic leader carried out the so-called 'Bassolino revolution' to change the city fundamentally. He introduced a new form of leadership, a new style of governing and a new style of policy-making, which demonstrated the innovative forms of development that were possible in Naples.

On the specific issue of regional policy implementation, Smyrl (1997) has identified two factors that seem to improve the effectiveness of regional empowerment in the implementation process: political engagement within and on behalf of the region, and the institutional capacity to build and sustain a Regional Policy. According to Smyrl, the empowerment of the regions depends heavily on whether, and how, opportunities are perceived at the regional level, and on the constructive (or unconstructive) way in which regional political leaders and regional state officials respond to those opportunities.

Following the line suggested in this literature, my hypothesis on the relevance of political factors suggests that the political component exercises an impact on the administrative machinery and consequently on the policy output and outcome. The aim of my study is therefore to characterise a model of political behaviour that influences the key actions of administrative capacity and eventually determines its variation across regions. The political aspects I will consider – i.e. political interference, government stability, and political accountability – are defined as follows.

Political interference refers to the restrictive or disruptive and invasive action by the political class towards the administrative sphere. It is benchmarked by the formal and informal separation of powers and responsibilities between the two spheres of activities. In order to be capable of saying what a public organisation will do (and how it will do those things) we must first have some conception of *who* will perform its tasks and for *what* purposes. There should be a clear distinction between administrative responsibilities and the political arena of power. In Chapter 4 I discuss the 1990 reform of public employment in Italy. Recognising that a major source of delays and inefficiency was the working methods and general attitude both of the political class and the civil service, in 1993 Italy embarked on a series of reforms, which it has pursued more strongly since 1998, whose aims were threefold: (1) to de-politicise the civil service; (2) to separate the political sphere from administrative tasks; and (3) to instil new management practices across the

Public Administration (PA) system. The outcome of these reforms was a formalisation of the separation of power, under which the political leader cannot, in any circumstances, revoke, reform, reserve for himself, remove to a higher level, or otherwise adopt provisions or actions which are the responsibilities of an administrator. These reforms were first implemented at the national level and then put into practice at the regional level, although not all of the regions adopted it at the same time.

Government stability[6] through the entire period of tenure – i.e. five years – ensures continuity and coherence in the programming process. I define a government as stable when it has an average of one or two cabinets for each five-year legislature. Conversely, a government is unstable if it has witnessed more than three cabinets in each five-year legislature, or if the *assessori* are turned over mid-way through the government's tenure. Political stability firstly acts as the basis for the credibility of the administrative context within which the efficiency of the implementation system is determined, and secondly creates the 'glue' that unites civil servants in their pursuance of a common goal.

Recurrent changes of government can negatively affect the programming of a long-term development plan in administrative systems that depend on political appointments to key policy-making positions. This is even more relevant in the case of the SFs, whose use is based on a multi-annual programme. Regional governments that change constantly have more difficulty in maintaining a strong commitment to multi-annual programmes. Additionally, unstable governments are more likely to witness change, not only in the political class, but also in the civil servants responsible for sustaining development programmes. This is likely to cause a significant amount of discontinuity and delay in the overall administrative system. A multi-annual programme takes years to deliver results, while a cabinet that lasts less than a year can only deal with short-term matters. Furthermore, such a government would not invest in monitoring or evaluation activities, since a one-year lifespan does not allow for any adequate review of implementation performance or any opportunity to learn about how to improve the programme for the future.

Political accountability, in its simplest form, means

> the requirement of a public organization (or perhaps an individual) to render an account to some other organization and to explain its actions. Further, the accounting may be financial or administrative, or about the policy decisions that were made. Accountability, therefore,

depends upon some external organizations to assess what it has been done and to evaluate it (Peters, 2001: 301).

In politics, and particularly in representative democracies, accountability is an important factor in securing good governance. Accountability constrains the extent to which elected representatives and other office-holders can wilfully deviate from their theoretical responsibilities. The goal of accountability is at times at odds with the goal of leadership. A constituency may have short-term desires that are at odds with long-term interests, and in such a context policy makers are likely to pursue their own political agenda and be interested in enriching themselves. This is particularly true in relation to SF implementation, which not only is based on long-term planning but also can be used by the political class to finance projects. Such projects do not always represent a priority for regional development but are useful in building consensus for other goals. Therefore, a political class that is not accountable will try to manipulate every form of information and publicity seen by the public about the use of the funds. The purpose of monitoring and evaluation systems is to feed this information to the MA, the national government, the EU and ultimately the public. The presence of efficient monitoring and evaluation procedures for policies adopted and implemented leaves policy-makers less able to divert resources to other goals or to use them for self-interested purposes.

I believe that political accountability influences monitoring and evaluation practices – i.e. the less accountable a political class is, the more it will try to obstruct forms of monitoring or evaluation activities, even though the less there is information available on the policy implemented, the lower will be the flow of resources.

3.3.2 Model of Analysis: Testing the Relevance of Administrative and Political Preconditions

My model of analysis to test the relevance of administrative and political preconditions suggests that each of the three political aspects influences each of the key components of administrative activity. Through the analysis of the case study, I will test the following corollary relationships (Figure 3.2):

1   Strong political interference increases deficiency in management on the part of the MA.
2   High governmental instability might account for poor programming and follow-through on implementation.
3   Political accountability affects monitoring and evaluation practices.

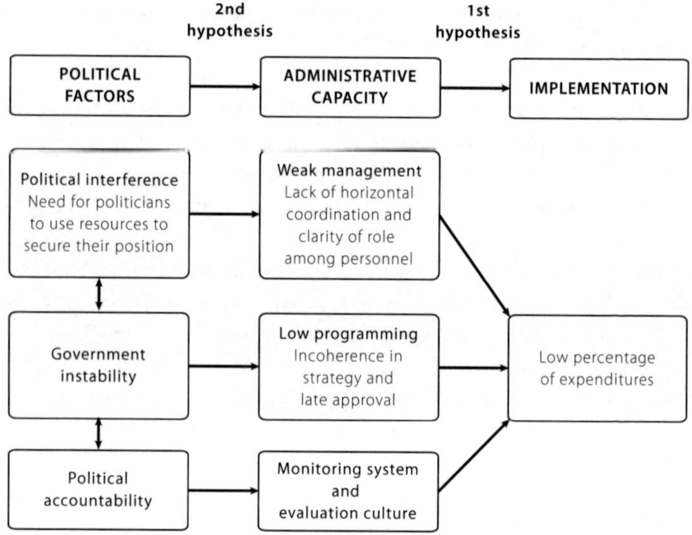

Figure 3.2 Model of analysis: interaction between political factors and key administrative components.

Furthermore, as anticipated, I believe that the three political factors are strongly interconnected. Indeed, I expect to find that in a region where the government is unstable, the political class will act in an interfering manner in order to pursue its own short-term interests during its tenure, and will be not be accountable for its action. Vice versa, I presume that where the government is stable, the political class will be less inclined to interfere and will act to pursue the long-term interest of the region and its own political status.

3.4 Method of Analysis

3.4.1 *Measurable Indicators of Administrative Capacity*

My analysis will follow two main steps. First I will assess the degree of administrative capacity in the selected regions in order to establish the first set of preconditions and to test the first part of my central hypothesis that there is a positive correlation between capacity and SFs expenditure rates. Second, I will explain why capacity varies across regions and establish the second set of preconditions – i.e. the second part of the central hypothesis.

In order to perform the first part of the analysis, I need to have adequate indicators to assess the degree of capacity within a region with regard to SFs implementation. Table 3.2 (overleaf) shows the indicators for the administrative arena, which have been deduced according to the definition of the objective that each key determinant aims to reach. The indicators have been selected in order to guarantee comparability across organisations and over time. The method chosen to measure the performance of each key component, following progressive stages, is an adaptation of the Institutional Development Framework Method[7] (IDFM) used by the Centre for Development and Evaluation of USAID (2000). There are four identified stages of administrative capacity along a capacity development continuum: Absent, Starting, Developing, and Consolidated. The criteria for each progressive stage have been adjusted to the expectation for each phase.

Each indicator will be rated on a scale from 0 to 3, as follows: 0 = Absent; 1 = Starting; 2 = Developing; 3 = Consolidated. Consequently, all components will be averaged together to provide a summary score for the administrative area (Table 3.3).

The rating scale will be calculated for each key component and then for the overall activity. This will provide a comprehensive indication of where the institution is in its stage of development for that particular key determinant and for its overall approach to administration. The four final stages are defined below (Table 3.4).

Table 3.3 Range of scores for each area

Score	0–0.5	0.6–1.5	1.6–2.5	2.6–3.0
Stage	Absent	Starting	Developing	Consolidated

Table 3.4 Progressive stages of administrative capacity

	Administrative capacity
Absent	Most of the components measured are non-existent. The output produced is very low.
Starting	Administrative capacity is in the early stages of development. All of the components measured are in rudimentary form. The output produced is low.
Developing	Administrative capacity is developing. Structures for management, programming, monitoring and evaluation practices are in place and functioning. The output produced is medium/high.
Consolidated	Administrative capacity is fully functioning and sustainable. The output produced is high.

Table 3.2 Indicators and progressive stages in benchmarking administrative capacity

Key components	Indicators	Absent	Starting	Developing	Consolidated
1 Management	a) Clarity in the definition of role	Staff roles and responsibilities unclear and changeable	Staff roles and responsibilities vaguely defined	Staff roles and responsibilities defined	Roles of personnel well defined; Staff increasingly able to shape the way in which they participate in management
	b) Coordination and cooperation between departments	Poor inter-staff and inter-department communications; Lack of formal and informal channels.	Modest amount of inter-staff and inter-department communication; Emergence of formal channels for dialogue and decision-making	Communications are open and inter-hierarchical; Formal and informal channels established and utilised	Organisation periodically reviews communication flow to ensure free flow of information through both formal and informal channels
2 Programming	a) Programme design: SWOT Analysis	Absence of a SWOT analysis	Introduction of a SWOT analysis; important territorial problems still overlooked.	SWOT analysis is supportive of the programme, although interventions selected still not fully targeted.	SWOT analysis is thorough. It allows full correspondence between the budget and targeted territorial needs
	b) Programme approval: time lapse between the beginning of the CSF and approval of the ROP	Approval of the ROP significantly delayed (by over two years)	Approval of the ROP delayed by up to two years.	Delay in the ROP approval contained to 1 year	ROP starts within six months

Key components	Indicators	Absent	Starting	Developing	Consolidated
3 Monitoring	a) Introduction of a system of indicators and monitoring procedures responding to national/European agreed standards	No monitoring system	System has been introduced but indicators and procedure are not functioning properly	Indicators and procedure are coherent with national/European guidelines but still not fully operational	Indicators and procedure are coherent with the national/European guidelines and fully operational
	b) Guaranteeing the availability of financial, physical and procedural data	No data available	Only partial data available	Data available without much delay	Data available and used in support of the policy process
4 Evaluation	a) Production of evaluation reports	No reports produced	Ex-ante report produced, but no initinere or ex-post report	One report still not produced	All three reports produced
	b) Integration of evaluation method and culture into the system	The evaluation method considered time consuming and not useful	Although considered important, it is too difficult to perform	Evaluation performed as thoroughly as possible	Evaluation considered a fundamental tool to improve policy implementation

3.4.2 Case Study

The core of the methodology presented here is an in-depth case study. The purpose of the case study is to provide a thorough insight into the specific administrative features that prevail in the selected regions and to provide a basis for comparative analysis based on empirical facts in order to generate evidence to validate my hypothesis for the conclusions to be reached. One of the major benefits of the case study approach is that it facilitates the presentation of processes and complexities that are impossible to see in any other way. This is most useful in testing a theoretical hypothesis against a detailed insight into the reality of daily actions in the field (ÖIR, 2003: 33). An in-depth case study provides a clear view of the way in which the administrative machinery operates and how it affects institutional performance.

Case study research excels at bringing us to an understanding of a complex issue or object and can extend understanding or add strength to what is already known through previous research. For the purpose of the hypothesis I aimed to test, which had not been previously investigated, the case study and associated fieldwork were essential in providing original information that may validate my hypotheses.

In order to use the case study method optimally and successfully, I followed four fundamental steps in organising and conducting the research:

1   selecting the case study that is of most use in answering the questions;
2   determining data gathering and analysis techniques;
3   collecting data in the field;
4   evaluating and analysing the data.

The two case studies were chosen to ensure the representation of two contrasting performances: Sicily and Andalucia are examples of low implementation of the funds; Basilicata and Galicia has the highest implementation rate.

3.4.3 Data Collection

The data collection is based on three methods to ensure reliability of findings: (1) document analysis; (2) interview data – questionnaires, focus groups, semi-structured interviews; and (3) direct observation (Johnson, 2005: 185–304). For the Spanish regions, only document analysis was carried out.

The analysis covers the third (2000–2006) planning period of SFs, referring, where possible, to the first (1989–1993) and second (1994–1999) period.

The data collection for the Italian case originates from a questionnaire designed (1) to assess regional administrative capacity in terms of the selected indicators; and (2) to investigate the eventual relationship between the administrative key actions and the correlated political factors. The questionnaire was divided into three sections, one for management, the second for programming and the third for monitoring and evaluation. Each section was divided into two parts: the first assessed the administrative components; the second asked relevant questions about the political factors. The respondents to the questionnaire were the politicians and civil servants involved in the implementation of SFs. Based on the questionnaire, I also designed an interview guide to support semi-structured interviews with key actors within the regional government, including both administrative staff and political leaders (cf. Table 3.5).

Like other analytical approaches (ÖIR, 2003) the case studies were conducted over three stages, as follows.

Stage 1

Deskwork involving a detailed review of all primary source documentation associated with the region concerned – i.e. the CSF 1989–1993; CSF 1994–1999; CSF 2000–2006; CSF *ex-post* evaluation 1994–1999; CSF Intermediate Evaluation 2000–2006; Pluri-fund Operational Programme (POP) 1989–1993; POP 1994–1999; Regional Operative Programme (ROP) 2000–2006; each POP and POR *ex-ante, ex-post* and intermediate evaluations for each period;[8] the annual reports on SFs implementation produced each year by each regional administration; and all of the available documentation produced by each regional and national Monitoring Committee on the status of SFs implementation; the corresponding European, national and regional legislation covering this policy area.

Stage 2

Fieldwork in the selected region involving consultation with members of the MA, general managers, civil servants, and relevant political assessors (*assessori*) involved in SFs implementation. In detail, in Sicily, I interviewed three assessors and seven general managers, who also completed the questionnaire. In addition, the questionnaire was completed by one assessor, eight general mangers and 10 civil servants, reaching a total of 29 opinions. In Basilicata, I interviewed two assessors, 17 general managers and managers, and seven civil servants. The written part of the questionnaires was returned by 10 managers and five civil servants, making a total of 41 completed questionnaires. In both Sicily and in Basilicata the consultation covered all of the

Table 3.5 Synoptic structure of questionnaire and interview guide

Analytical dimensions	Aims	Main questions
Basic information		Name of the interviewee; Position in the organisation; Date of interview; Duration of interview
Section I Assessment of the management activities	Assessing management with a focus on the coordination activities and the clarity of roles among personnel; the questions are also retrospective, in order to capture any improvement or variation over the three different periods of analysis – i.e. 1989–1993; 1994–1999; 2000–2006. Some of the questions require self-evaluation of past administrative behaviour.	1 Which have been the major changes in the Managing Authority (MA) over the three planning periods? 2 Which have been the major difficulties faced by the MA and how have they been solved? 3 Describe the coordination activity carried out by the MA. Is there clarity of role between the different departments and within the departments as far as SFs are concerned? Is there clarity of role among personnel?
Investigation of the relationship between the political and administrative classes	Understanding whether there is a separation of power in the region and how the relationship between these two spheres influences SFs management.	1 Define the interaction/relation between the MA and the political class. 2 Has the separation of powers between the political and the administrative sphere had any impact on the SFs management? 3 Define the influence of political power on SFs management before the Regional Law that formally separated it (12/1996 in Basilicata and 10/2000 in Sicily). 4 Which level is more suited to managing the SFs? 5 Despite the formalised separation of powers, is there still political interference in the management of SFs?

Analytical dimensions	Aims	Main questions
Section II Analysis of the programming activities	Investigating how the regional government has reacted to the novelty of the multi-annual planning approach introduced by the SFs. Particular attention is given to: (i) the use of a SWOT analysis to link the interventions planned with the real needs of the territory; (ii) the time taken to approve the designed programme, in order to ascertain the reasons for eventual delays.	1 Was the programme supported by a SWOT analysis? Were there previous experiences that guided the regional administration in adapting to the multi-annual planning approach introduced by SFs? 2 How has the programming capacity evolved over the three different periods 1989–1993, 1994–1999, and 2000–2006? 3 What is the main cause of the delay in the approval of the Regional Operative Programme (ROP)
Description of the regional government stability	Capturing the eventual repercussions for the continuity of the SFs programme.	1 Does government stability affect SFs programming? What kind of effect does it have? 2 Which are the major problems in terms of SFs programming related to eventual changes of government? Is the programme implementation strictly related to the government stability and continuity?

Continued overleaf

Table 3.5 continued

Analytical dimensions	Aims	Main questions
Section III		
Scrutiny of the monitoring and evaluation system	Assessing how the monitoring system works and whether it is positively correlated with improvements in the implementation of SFs. The two dimensions investigated are the setting up of a monitoring system and the availability of data. Similarly, the questions regarding evaluation activities aim to capture the perception of evaluation in the region and assess the spread of an evaluation culture.	1 Which were the major difficulties encountered in the establishment of a monitoring system? How has the monitoring system evolved during the three planning periods? 2 Has an adequate system of monitoring indicators and procedures been introduced? If yes, which one? 3 Does the monitoring system guarantee availability of up-to-date financial, physical and procedural data? 4 Each planning period should be supported by an ex-ante, intermediate and ex-post evaluation. Have these reports been produced accordingly? 5 Is the culture of evaluation spreading within the regional government?
Self-evaluation of the accountability of the political class	These questions ask the personal opinion of the interviewees on political accountability and eventually on the influence that the political class might exercise in impeding or propelling the diffusion of monitoring and evaluation systems.	1 Is the political class accountable? Are there any procedures in place to ensure accountability? 2 Which are the main reasons for poor accountability? 3 Is the improvement of monitoring and evaluation activities supported by political leaders? 4 Does the political class openly support the practice of monitoring and evaluation? 5 Has the political class propelled or impeded the diffusion of an evaluation culture? 6 How would you define the perception by the political class of the practice of monitoring and evaluation?

assessors involved with SFs, all of the general managers, 75 per cent of the managers, and 75 per cent of the civil servants concerned with the policy.

The principal purpose of the fieldwork was to conduct interviews, to ensure the correctness and completeness of the desk-based research on the basis of the documentation available, to collect supplementary or additional documentation, and to determine the management, programming, monitoring and evaluation structure in place. The fieldwork represents the core of the research. Indeed, a preliminary analysis of the documentation revealed the lack of adequate information on the variable I was investigating and so the main source of information became the interaction and interviews with the key actors involved in SFs implementation.

Stage 3

Relevant players in the regions were consulted via email, telephone and fax with a view to completing the analysis of the region and verifying the correctness of the analysis.

Further information, data and primary source evidence was gathered from two other projects in which I was involved. The first project, 'The ex-post evaluation of the Pluri-fund Operative Programme (POP) in Sicily 1994/99', lasted one year and focused on analysing nine projects financed by the SFs in Sicily between 1994 and 1999. The second project, 'The intermediate evaluation of the Community Support Framework Objective 1, Italy 2000/2006', lasted three years and it aimed to scrutinise the performance of the seven southern Italian regions in implementing SFs, by focusing on specific sectors of intervention – transport, rural development, research, tourism, professional training and territorial integrated projects.

PART II

MULTI-LEVEL GOVERNANCE AND IMPLEMENTATION PERFORMANCE

Lessons from Italy

4

FROM THE *INTERVENTO STRAORDINARIO* TO MULTI-LEVEL GOVERNANCE

Policy Shifts in Italian Regional Policy, 1992–2004

4.1 Overview of the Analysis

The second part of this book analyses the implementation of EU cohesion policy in Italy. Italy provides an interesting and somewhat puzzling case study, given the country's constant struggle to conform to EU directives, regulations and policies, and the ambiguous results it has achieved in implementation. Empirical data reveal that, although implementation has been below average at the national level, within Italy's regions there are consistent performance differences, some regions having demonstrated a higher than average ability than others to implement SF programmes. Why this is the case, and the factors accountable for variation in implementation performance, will be addressed in the following chapters.

This introductory chapter outlines the Italian regional administrative and political system, with attention to the institutions connected to cohesion policy, and presents the data on national and regional performance. This retrospective analysis is intended to provide an interpretative framework for the case studies. Chapters 5 and 6 assess the existence and characteristics of the two sets of preconditions which are the focus of my hypothesis.

Italian regional policy can be divided into two main phases, 1950–1992 and 1992–2004. The first phase was characterized by the introduction of regional policy in Italy under a special agency, the *Casmez*,[1] and its evolution over the period 1950–1992 was based on a top-down, centralised approach. The Italian experience with top-down regional policy approaches was not much different from what took place in other countries that experimented with regional policy, such as France, Great Britain, Spain and Greece. It is not only the nature of this top-down approach but also, more specifically, the Italian variety of that approach that undermined any possibility of sub-national institutions developing planning and implementation capacities with regard to regional development. Indeed, there was no attention paid to the modernisation of the regional administration in terms of supporting the building of administrative and political capacities so that the regional government might carry out its own development policies; there was no provision for long-term planning; there were no monitoring or evaluation procedures; and there was a generalised distribution of expenditures over all regions rather than on targeted areas.

The policy's endogenous approach and lack of a specific territorial component doomed the policy to failure. The choices made by the political class and the use of regional policy for the purpose of building political patronage also did not help the overall success of the policy. Indeed, the ruling class at the time constantly intervened in administrative activities according to personal agendas rather than economic motives; the extreme instability of the government created a political class more focused on short-term rewards than long-term planning; and, moreover, any accountability of actions was non-existent. Gualini's (2004) interpretation of this period is that the national government aimed not to build any autonomous capacity into the regional government, but to gain support from the local political class and keeping the regions strongly dependent upon the centre.

Thus the adoption of a centralised approach to regional planning cannot explain in any way the differences in the implementation performance of individual southern regions observed after the abolition of top-down policies. Indeed, national regional policy was an external constraint that applied equally to all regions.

In the 1990s profound changes to the planning of policies for the development of the *Mezzogiorno* took place. These changes followed three concurrent events: the closure of the *Casmez*; the beginning of radical reform of the Public Administration (PA); and the sudden drop in public expenditure which directed attention towards the SFs as the only available funding for development purposes. All these events took place between 1992 and 1993, which is why many authors refer to 1992 as the 'turning point' in Italian regional policy (Bodo and Viesti, 1997; Barca, 2001b).

At this point a new, bottom-up method, based on the central role of the region, emerged: these transitional years introduced a phase of reorganisation for the central management of development policies and structural actions. Institutional, administrative and organisational adjustments were made in order to manage the conversion from a centralised management approach to a multi-level, decentralised one. Regional governments were formally recognised as equal actors in this new system and were called upon to contribute to the planning and eventual management of the EC resources. The operationalisation of these changes proved to be far more difficult than expected, which confirmed that the *Casmez* had acted as a substitute for the lack of territorial institutional capacities, and led ultimately to the consolidation of a policy environment that could be defined 'as if the whole of the activities related to local development could be conceived and realised outside of the regional administrative structure' (Barca, 1998, as cited in Gualini, 2004).

In order to analyse the impact of these changes in relation to my case studies and SF implementation, this chapter is divided into three sections. Section 4.2 looks at the massive and revolutionary regulatory reforms implemented from 1992 onwards with the aim of modernising the PA and improving the devolution of powers and the separation of responsibilities between the political and administrative classes. I will disentangle and study the reform under two headings; administrative changes and political changes. Section 4.3 focuses on the impact of the reforms on regional policy. It considers the end of the *Intervento Straordinario* and its consequences for the national and regional governments, focusing particularly on the sudden relevance given to the SFs and the EU cohesion policy, and the consequent adoption of the multi-level governance model. Section 4.4 scrutinises the first three periods of SFs (1989–1993, 1994–1999 and 2000–2006) and the events that raised public awareness of the necessity of promoting administrative capacity at the regional level.

This retrospective account, apart from providing background information, is structured to enable analysis of past events from the perspective of the two parts of my central hypothesis and its correlated variables – i.e. the relevance of administrative capacity for the implementation of policies, and the political factors that intervene to determine the degree of administrative capacity. The investigation of the different political and administrative reforms that have taken place in Italy will also provide an interpretative framework for the case studies analysed in the following chapters.

4.2 The Reform of the 1990s:
A Revolutionary Shift in the Italian Tradition

At the beginning of the 1990s,[2] when the entire Italian political system was going through a period of severe crisis, the most important reform of the Italian State since 1860 began, including a major review of the constitutional framework. Not one central, peripheral or local organisational structure and decision-making process or procedure managed to escape this wave of change, which swept over the formal rules and the procedures of public sector management (Rebora, 1999; Capano, 2000).

Italian local government is based on a precise hierarchy: at the bottom the municipalities, then the provinces and then the regions. The Constitution of 1946 provided that the regions be endowed with extensive law-making powers, conceiving them as independent centres of decision-making. In reality, Italian governments have always kept a tight grip on the regions, delaying for countless years the passing of legislation necessary to fulfil the constitutional provisions related to the autonomy of the regions. Thus, for more than 20 years there was no clear framework defining the powers of the regions and their relationship with the central state. As a matter of fact, the Italian Constitution distinguishes between 'ordinary' and 'special' statute regions; the five special statute regions, created at the same time as the Constitution, were established as such for geographic, ethnic and linguistic reasons, and granted wider autonomy and powers than the ordinary regions in order to better safeguard their peculiarities. The institutional reforms necessary for the establishment of the ordinary statute regions were carried out only in the 1970s; in fact, the first elections for the regional councils of the 15 ordinary regions were held in 1970 and most of the administrative functions were transferred from the central state to the regions in 1977. Even if the range of competencies attributed to the regions was at this point more or less defined, regions were seen by the state basically as implementers of central government policies, appointed to spend resources transferred from – and controlled by – the national level. The situation of uncertainty and disarray in the distribution of competencies, in the organisational structure of local powers and in the centre–periphery relationship, lasted till the 1990s.

The poor results of centralised intervention, along with the fiscal and economic problems of the early 1990s associated with the huge public debt, and the move during the beginning of the 1990s to eradicate government corruption, sowed the seeds for change (Ceccanti and Vassallo, 2004).

The 1990s have in fact been commonly defined as a watershed in the country's institutional and political system. Until the 1990s a proportional electoral system was in place both at the national and local level. Combined with an excessively fragmented party system, this led to a political paralysis, with governments and councils that rarely lasted their full tenure. In 1993 reforms were passed introducing a majoritarian electoral system and also providing for the direct popular election of mayors. The passage of the reformed parliamentary electoral law in 1993, and the uncovering of the corruption scandals that led to the disappearance of the old political parties and most of their representatives, were hailed as marking the beginning of the 'Second Republic'. In parallel, the federal question entered the political agenda in the 1990s with the electoral success of the Lega Nord, and in the following years a process of decentralisation of functions and competencies was undertaken, reaching its peak with the reform of the Constitution in 2001. Before 2001, the institutional framework was based on the hierarchic supremacy of the centre over the regions. The reform formalised a federal framework, extending considerably the legislative powers of the regions and giving more space for regional participation at the EU level.

The changes that occurred in the 1990s in the political system were mirrored by the changes that took place in the same period in the administrative system. The end of the First Republic, marked by the mismanagement of public resources and frequent episodes of corrupt behaviour among party politicians and civil servants, triggered demands for greater efficiency, effectiveness and transparency in the Italian Public Administration, which had traditionally distinguished itself for a bureaucratic culture characterised by the extended politicisation of the top administrative ranks, enduring patronage and clientelism patterns in recruitment to the public sector, uneven distribution of human resources, and excessive formalism and legalism (Anessi-Pessina and Steccolini, 2005).

European policies – the single market programme, competition law and policy, the use of EU funds, and monetary and fiscal rectitude that was the price of entering the euro area, and the Maastricht criteria[3] – greatly influenced the Italian regulatory and administrative environment.

The Italian reforms of the 1990s were part of an international trend characterised by a new approach to administrative problems. This solution has been labelled the New Public Management (NPM), a definition that combines a variety of different, often contradictory, public management techniques, based on two previously existing general principles: the managerial approach of the American school and classical organisational theory (Gow and Dufour, 2000).

In the Italian case and in relation to the general use of SFs we also have to attribute the change in management approach to the impact of Europeanisation[4] – that is, the need to align the national and regional approach to cohesion policy according to the regulations and principles enunciated in the 1988 and subsequent reforms of the ERDF, ESF, and EAGGF (Leonardi, 2005: 48–56).

4.2.1 *The Administrative Reorganisation*

The PA reforms covered four important issues, summarized as follows:

1   The balance between the centre and subnational governments through the devolution of political-administrative power to the regions and to local authorities began (Law n. 421/1992; Law n. 59/1997).[5]

2   The reform of the central administration, the first of its kind since Cavour's days in the nineteenth century (when the Kingdom of Italy was founded), which involved '[m]erging bodies with similar missions; eliminating duplication and segmentation'; a 'more flexible internal organization', with 'freedom to choose between organizational models'; the presence 'of just one ministry for each mission: 22 ministries in 1990, 12 in the year 2001'; the creation of numerous agencies, that is, of 'company-like technical-operative structures' (Bassanini, 2000a: 11).

3   The civil service reform through the privatisation of the working relationship and separation of responsibilities of the political and administrative class in order to overcome the inefficiencies and bottlenecks created by a 'passive' civil service (D.lgs. n. 29/1993; Law n. 59/1997; Law n. 191/1998; Law n. 145/2002).

4   The simplification of the PA, procedures and controls.

The introduction of these sets of reforms was designed to transform the Italian PA from a form of administration in which only rules and procedures mattered to a performance-oriented administration. The reformers seemed to be strongly convinced that they had effected a break with the past, starting with the replacement of the 'old' legal paradigm with a 'new' managerial model (Bassanini, 2000b).

As a result, in less than a decade Italy took important steps away from being a highly interventionist state, in which law was devalued and the regional dimension was underestimated and disregarded, towards becoming a modern regulatory state based on transparent rules and MLG.

4.2.2 *The Political Implications*

As mentioned in the above paragraph, running parallel to the changes in the administrative arena were similar relevant reforms in the political sphere. These can be summarised under three headings: (1) increased devolution and decentralisation; (2) changes in party system; and (3) introduction of the spoils system.

First, the process of decentralisation and devolution initiated in the 1990s was formalised by Law n. 59/1997 and dramatically reinforced over the last years. Decentralisation was marked by the restructuring of the state apparatus (D.lgs. n. 300/1999) and the establishment of new relations between political forces, and the integration of new economic and social actors. Devolution – i.e. the transfer of powers to the regional level of government – was finalised with D.lgs. n.12/1998, which recorded the shift of political and administrative decision-making power in favour of the regions. This process reaches its peak in 2001 with the reform of title V of the Constitution (cf. Section 4.3.2).[6]

Second, the changes that took place in the Italian party system from 1990 onwards were not mirrored in the post-war history of any other western democracy. In the space of a few years, the parties that had dominated the parliament since 1945 either dissolved or re-branded themselves and transformed profoundly. New elites entered the political arena, causing serious consequences for politics and institutions (Newell, 2000). In fact, until 1994 there was never an alternating government and opposition: the Democrazia Cristiana (Christian Democratic – DC) party was always the leading party of government. Nevertheless this did deliver political stability for the country. Between 1945 and 1994, Italy had more than 50 governments, constituting one of the highest rates of government instability in western Europe. The high turnover of governments was accompanied by a remarkable persistence of the political elites.[7] This process was triggered by, among other factors,[8] the Referendum movement, which believed that the Italian system of proportional representation favoured clientelistic practices and party fragmentation, prevented the formation of long-lasting majorities, and therefore limited the duration and the stability of governments. A system of plurality, the movement believed, would instead reinforce accountability and trust, and deliver stronger and more stable governments. Between 1994 and 1996 the new rules stimulated the polarisation of the Italian party system, which has actually delivered a more stable government, although there remains much to do with regard to building trust and accountability (Diamanti, 2001). The end of the First Republic was marked by the passage of the reformed parliamentary electoral law and the uncovering of corruption scandals which led to the disappearance of the old political parties and most of their representatives. This raised hopes that changes in both the rules of the game and the people holding the most important institutional positions would lead to a more stable and transparent system of government 'based on electoral choice rather than inter- and intraparty negotiations' (Katz and Ignazi, 1996: 19). Some stability, as well as increased responsibility and accountability, was reached at regional level after L. cost. n. 1/1999 and L. cost. n. 2/2001 introduced direct election of the Presidents of the ordinary and the special status regions (the same electoral system based on direct elections had already been introduced in 1993 for the majority of municipalities).

Finally, the third change in the political scene was strictly linked to the administrative area, and in particular to the privatisation of public employment. Indeed, as previously discussed, this introduced the spoils system in Italy.[9] This practice, which reached its peak with Law n. 145/2002,[10] has been the subject of opposing debates. The greater concern was related to the choice of the highest bureaucrats by the politicians: the risk is that the administration becomes a mere executive instrument of politics (Cerbo, 2002).

This examination of administrative and political reforms, although brief and mainly descriptive, is relevant in putting into context the national and regional apparatus. As we have seen, these reforms were deemed necessary to improve Italian performance both nationally and internationally. In the meantime, regional policy was also subject to major reforms, due to the abolition of the centralised approach. A new bottom-up method, based on the central role of the region, emerged, as described in the next section. In sum, Italy was trying to get into line with EU dictates in order to be able to gain credibility and play a more active role in EU regional policy as well as in other areas of interventions. Have these reforms had an impact on the regional performance?

4.3 The Impact of the Reform on Regional Policy: A Bottom-up Approach

4.3.1 *From the* Intervento Straordinario *to Multi-level Governance*
The revolutionary administrative and political changes that took place in the 1990s marked the end of the *Intervento Straordinario*. Indeed, the logic behind the *Intervento* – i.e. centralised intervention, little autonomy for the regions, strong political interference, and poor attention to administrative performance – was incompatible with the needs of the Maastricht criteria for reducing government spending and with the EU regulation for SFs allocation.

The consequences of this event were twofold. First, there was a return to ordinary administrative procedures, that is, responsibilities were redistributed amongst the central administration bodies of the State according to their statutory competencies. Second, regional governments were formally recognised as key actors in this pluralist and decentralised system of responsibilities. This underlined the importance of their strategic as well as operational programming abilities, in terms of mobilisation, distribution and timing of resources – shifting the focus on the issue related to the regional administrative capacity.

The end of the centralised approach meant first of all a drop in public investments in the *Mezzogiorno*, from a peak level of 21 billion euros in 1992 to a lower level of 15 billion euros in 1996. European funding thus became the most important enabler of public investment for the southern regions. To implement SFs successfully, the country needed a radical change in its approach to regional policy. This meant an abandonment of the top-down centralised approach in favour of the bottom-up, multi-level approach; a focus on investments in an integrated, territorialised programmatic fashion rather than sectoral interventions; multi-annual rather than short-term plans as the basis for the investments; the adoption of an expenditure monitoring system; and the incorporation of an evaluation culture that had so far been missing.

These requirements proved very difficult to implement at both the national and regional level, due to their absolute novelty. An awareness of their fundamental importance, however, highlighted the need to provide positive support for administrative and political innovation at the regional level.. The closure of the *Casmez* in 1986, completed in 1993 with the demise of the *Intervento Straordinario*, was endorsed by a general reconsideration of the strategies for promoting regional development. The reframing of relationships between discourses on regional policy reform and on local development had been fostered by a shift towards negotiated and concerted models of inter-governmental and public–private relationships. The first step in this direction was the strengthening of the 'concertation model' of programming, based on tools aimed at promoting a negotiated coordination of public–public as well as public–private relationships, introduced into Italian political administrative practice in the early 1990s. This model was labeled *programmazione negoziata* (negotiated programming; Gualini, 2004: 195). The legislation on *programmazione negoziata* was based on the merging of previous local practices featuring experimental, bottom-up initiatives that had been adopted in the regions with the more advanced forms of regional economic planning, e.g. in Emilia-Romagna and Tuscany (Leonardi and Nanetti, 1991, 1998). Many initiatives developed, on the one hand, as a result of the SFs logic and, on the other, in order to put the SFs into operation.[11]

The main change arrived with the Bassanini reform, i.e. Law n. 59/1997, which introduced a general reframing of the competencies of regional and local governments in key areas of public action and regulation, moving towards a subsidiary pattern of inter-governmental relationships, which constituted a crucial premise for a 'territorialisation' of development policies outside what was already possible through the regional operational programmes. Law n. 59/1997, along with the reforms in the electoral system (direct election of majors since 1993, of regional presidents since 2000, and new executive powers) and fiscal system(regionalisation of fiscal revenues and budgeting since 2000), constitutes a major factor of change in State–local relationships towards a model of 'administrative federalism'.

Among the most important policy areas in which regulatory and/or managing responsibilities were devolved to the regions as of 1999 (D.lgs. 143/1997, D.lgs. 469/1997, and D.lgs. 112/1998) were active labour policies, local development promotion and incentives to SMEs, social services, tourism, waste management, transportation, environmental protection, and city and regional planning.[12] In all matters pertaining to territorial development, the central administration retained only those responsibilities pertaining to definition of the national preferences and managing special legislation (e.g. regional State aids) that required a national programming and coordination framework.

The reform assumed a particular importance in redefining the institutional context of local development policies. What made *programmazione negoziata* a crucial step in the renewal of the Italian states' approach to regional policies was that it embedded local development in a multi-level framework of horizontal, i.e. public–private and inter-organisational, as well as vertical, i.e. intergovernmental, forms of collaboration. Regions and local governments were identified as the primary actors in a much broader array of policies related to the promotion of territorial development relying on coordination among a plurality of actors rather than on direct public intervention.

4.3.2 *The Growing Role of the Regions in the Italian Institutional Setting*

Moving to Brussels

As explained in chapters 1 and 2, SFs explicitly promote a multi-tiered, compound system where national, subnational and European institutions co-operate with each other to produce public decisions. In the Italian case this multi-level governance approach clashed with the pre-existing diplomatic and centralist orientation towards European affairs, according to which only the Ministry of Foreign Affairs had the competence to represent the national interest at European level, and subnational authorities were prevented from establishing direct links with European institutions. SFs, thanks to the partnership principle and to the important role assigned to regional administrations in programming and managing European resources, clearly highlighted the inconsistency of such a framework and contributed to the modification of national legislation. Law n. 52/1996[13] finally allowed the Italian regions to establish offices in Brussels and to participate (with four representatives) in the national delegation within the European Council. This provision proved to be a crucial turning point in the management of SFs. Indeed, it allowed the regions to bypass the national state and to establish a direct link with the EC.

Thanks to this law, the Italian regions became increasingly legitimate actors in European decision-making, with a new role that was also acknowledged by the later constitutional reform of 2001. Despite this opportunity, not all regional governments fully exploited the chance to promote themselves as interlocutors at the European level; rather, their 'activation' in Brussels appears to have been strongly differentiated in terms of timing, numbers of channels, types of participation and strategies of representation, as demonstrated in a study carried out by Fargion *et al.* (2005). From this study it emerged that Italian regions can be divided into three groups: a leading group of 'proactive' regions, which became active before the removal of the national legislative constraint (that is, before Law n. 52/1996); an intermediate group of 'reactive' regions, that became active once the national law allowed them a presence in Brussels and elsewhere in Europe (that is, between 1996 and 1999); and a last group of 'inactive' regions, that became active only recently (between 2000 and 2002). The leading proactive group is composed of some Central and Northern regions, with the sole exception of one southern region, Basilicata. Conversely, the inert regions are led by a group of southern regions, including Sicily. These findings suggest that while Basilicata was developing an active role in the EU scenario Sicily was still in the shadows.

A Change in the Constitution

The success of the regional governments in emerging and acting according to the new form of multi-level governance that had entered Europe was marked by the changes in title V of the Italian Constitution, made in 2001 (L. cost. 3/2001) by the Amato government. Indeed, under L. cost. n. 3/2001, the republic was defined as a unit composed of municipalities, provinces, regions and the state. The legislative powers of the regions were considerably extended,[14] while government restrictions on regional legislation were curtailed. A new legal framework for governance was thereby created, and new criteria were established for the distribution of administrative duties among the state, regions, municipalities, provinces and metropolitan cities, while external controls were lifted. New provisions governing the financial autonomy of regional and local authorities were laid down. Finally, regional powers with regard to relations within the EU and at international level were redefined, and gave more space for regional participation.

All these changes irrevocably established a strong and autonomous role for the regional dimension within national boundaries. Although this book argues that for MLG to work it is not enough to establish and recognise tiers of government, it is necessary for each tier to possess a set of preconditions, both political and administrative.

4.4 Regional and Cohesion Policy in Italy: From Top-down to Multi-level Governance

4.4.1 *The Integrated Mediterranean Programme 1986–1992*

The Integrated Mediterranean Programmes (IMP), introduced in 1985, provided the first opportunity for the Italian administrative system to learn from contact with a decentralised rationale and medium-term programming:

> the new programmes exerted, in fact, an enormous impact on Italian administrative practices, dominated by non-integrated, fragmented competencies where sectoral ministries managed the single funds in a centralist manner, without significant procedures of participation and co-decision by other central or peripheral administrations (Gualini 2004: 137–8).

Along with the programming difficulties, problems also arose in the implementation phase leading to a very low level of expenditure. Indeed, by 1991 Italy had spent only 17 per cent of its allocation whereas France and Greece respectively had spent 58 per cent and 68 per cent of their allocation (Table 4.1 and 4.2).

A good performance was achieved in the northern regions, and relatively good one in small Mezzogiorno regions, whereas in large Mezzogiorno regions (Puglia, Sicilia, Calabria, Campania) an almost complete implementation deadlock occurred (Table 4.2).

Difficulties in implementing the IMPs were related to inconsistencies and duplication in the central administrative apparatus, as well as to the difficulties regions encountered in gaining full acknowledgement of their role

Table 4.1 IMPs allocations 1986–1992 (Mecu) and percentage of expenditure at the end of 1991

Member States	Total allocation (Mecu)	Payments (Mecu)	Percentage of expenditure
France	843.52	487.88	58
Greece	2,000.00	1,361.62	68
Italy	1,256.48	219.31	17
Total	4,100.00	2,068.81	50

Source: Corte dei conti, 1991
Note: Mecu = millions of Ecu. The European Currency Unit (Ecu) was a basket of the currencies of the European Community Member States, used as the unit of account of the European Community before being replaced by the euro on 1 January 1999, at the value €1 = 1 Ecu.

Table 4.2 Italy: regional IMPs allocations 1986–1992 and percentage of expenditure at the end of 1991

Region	Total allocation (Mecu)	Payments (Mecu)	Percentages of expenditures
Marche	88.97	17.17	19.2
Umbria	83.98	18.75	22.3
Lazio	58.15	14.55	25.1
Emilia Romagna	80.27	24.12	30.2
Liguria	52.12	11.59	22.3
Toscana	114.22	38.66	33.6
Laguna Adriatica	42.98	2.97	7.2
Total Northern Italy	520.69	117.81	22.6
Molise	58.57	15.43	26.3
Abruzzo	79.4	18.22	23.2
Puglia	99.97	20.82	20.8
Basilicata	93.49	16.78	17.9
Calabria	119.96	13.52	11.3
Sardinia	96.32	10.13	10.5
Campania	75.75	3.9	5.2
Sicily	112.33	3.7	3.3
Total Southern Italy	735.79	101.50	13.2
Total Italy	1,256.48	219.31	16.7

Source: Corte dei Conti, 1991

from the central government (Sapienza, 1993). Fanfani (2001) and Gualini (2004) have argued that the low level of expenditure was due, on the one hand, to the lack of technical expertise and administrative capacity of the regional governments when it came to designing and implementing integrated development programmes, and, on the other, to the new approach introduced by the Community, i.e. the need to coordinate a multi-level system of governance in relation to the policy.

However, neither Gualini nor Fanfani specify which administrative capacity was missing, whereas Buti (1995: 228) identifies some specific political and administrative factors that impeded the success of the IMPs, namely: extreme instability of the government; short-term strategies of regional development; fragmentation of responsibilities; and the absence of a culture of monitoring. The limitation of Buti's suggestion is that these factors were not in any way tested in the various regions.

The data shown above suggests that the centralised approach used in the south but not in the north may have influenced the lack of administrative capacity, in terms of the ability to manage, programme and implement the policy. Furthermore, the data corroborate the hypothesis that, in the south, irrespectively of the overall centralised approach, some regions were developing differentiated capacities to deal with issues related to economic development. Looking at the selected case studies, there is already a clear gap between Sicily[15] and Basilicata. Therefore, the overall centralisation of the policy cannot be considered an explanatory variable to account for differences among the regions.

4.4.2 The First Period of SFs, 1989–1993

In 1989, three years after the introduction of the IMPs, the first SF programming period began. Its framework clearly followed from the experience gained from the IMPs and was regulated by the 1988 reform that launched an innovative approach to regional policy, based on multi-level governance with regional governments taking part in the different stages of the policy cycle – i.e. decision-making, programming, implementing, monitoring and evaluation. Since then we have seen some dramatic changes in the internal structure of nation states. Where regions did not exist, they were created as a tier of governance to activate the partnership triangle of the European Commission, national government and regional government. Where they already existed, regions moulded their institutional setting to fit the European regulations. In both cases a process of institutional adjustment was set in motion, with institutional frameworks converging toward a two- or multi-tier system of governance according to the willingness of national governments to involve just regional governments or also to include local private, public and social partners in policy-making.

These institutional changes represented an important step forward in policy-making. Nevertheless, some authors (Bailey and De Propris, 2002; Hooghe, 1998) identify only an entitlement of the regions to European funding in the above process. Such studies claim that the 1988 reform over-estimated the capacity of the regions to activate such entitlement through effective participation.

On a more positive note, Nanetti (1996) looked at the participation of national, supranational and subnational actors in the implementation of the CSF after the 1988 reform in five of the seven Member States with Objective 1 regions: Italy and Spain, which had regional systems; Greece and Portugal, which had recently created regional administrative planning systems; and Ireland, where the whole territory was the basis for a regional plan. Nanetti (1996: 86–7) concluded that

> [d]espite national governments retaining almost exclusive powers of negotiation with the Commission over policy formation, the early years of implementation of the first CSFs proved the slow but steady emergence of the regional level as the new institutional partner of the Commission in the operationalization and monitoring of broad-based development policies.[16]

In such a framework, major problems arose at all stages. Again, the Italian implementation rate was very poor compared to that of the other Member States (cf. Table 2.1), and the variation between the southern Italian regions was accentuated cf. Table 2.2).

One consequence of this meagre implementation rate was the crea-tion of the system of national and regional steering cabins (the Cabina di Regia Nazionale and Cabine di Regia Regionali) in the attempt to achieve greater coordination and institutionalisation in the implementation of SFs. Although the literature on SF implementation in Italy over the period 1989–1993 is very limited, the failure to spend the funds allocation fully during the first planning cycle can be attributed to two main factors, which are consistent with my hypothesis: (1) blurring of responsibilities, both between national and regional government, and within the regional govern-ments, 'which gave rise to significant inter-institutional conflicts and led to inefficient policy-making and high coordination cost' (Grote, 1996: 260); and (2) the lack of alignment between Italian regional policy and the EU approach.

Concerning the first factor, most regional governments seemed to have accepted this unequal and unclear situation because the expected payoff seemed to be quite high (Hine, 1993). Indeed, in this confused and centralised situation, responsibilities for failure or for inefficient use of resources could always be shifted on to the centre. Ultimately, the lack of accountability of the regional political class left room for discretion in the expenditure of resources, not necessarily according to economic criteria but most of the time according to personal agendas. Following this hypothesis, Bianchi (1993) hints that poor administrative capacity at the regional level was attributable to the constant interference of regional politicians. This practice deprived the regional civil servants of discretionary powers, and forced them to become mere executors of administrative acts. Regional programming, in circumstances such as these, is destined to fail because planning becomes almost impossible. In Italy during this period there was no provision for the separation of powers and responsibilities between the political and administrative spheres, and so the political class acted in an intrusive fashion according to its personal interests, and was far from following a technocratic approach.

As regards the second factor, Trigilia (1992) points out that the Italian approach to regional policy did not contain many of the features that had been built into the EU's cohesion policy approach. This is the classical 'lack of fit' argument, which is used in other contexts to explain the difficulties countries have encountered in incorporating European level legislation into their individual policy structures (Cowles *et al.*, 2001). Indeed, at the national level and consequently at the regional level there was no management structure in charge of coordinating a long-term development plan; programming was based on short-term goals and most of the time these goals were not tied to real territorial needs; and monitoring or evaluation procedures were deficient. Therefore, the capacity to manage the new cohesion policy adequately was missing at both the national and regional level because of the policy's innovative structure and direction.

Additionally, I suggest two further elements may have impeded successful policy implementation. The first is the high level of government instability in Italy, which had 48 different governments between 1950 and 1992, an average of 0.9 governments per year. In this scenario, it is predictable that the regions, all subject to national intervention, would have felt the impact of government instability in undermining the predictability of government programmes. The fact that some regions, such as Basilicata, managed to perform well despite this is worthy of attention.

A second reason for the poor performance both during the IMPs and the first SF planning period could be attributed to the confusion and overlapping responsibilities created by the still existing *Intervento straordinario*. The centralised approach ended with Law n. 488/1992, which closed the *Agensud*. Then, in 1993, in *Decreto Legislativo* (D.lgs.) (Legislative Decree) n. 96, the term 'Mezzogiorno', used to refer to southern Italy, was replaced with the European Commission's phrase 'depressed areas or Objective 1 areas', and the content and principles of the interventions became those of the EU regional policy.

This D.lgs. marked the beginning of the second phase of regional policy in Italy, which was characterised by a bottom-up approach capable of considering the regional governments and supporting administrative capacity development.

4.4.3 The Second Period of SFs, 1994–1999

By the time the administrative and political reforms were in place and the top-down approach was eradicated the second CSF period, 1994–1999, was coming to an end and the level of expenditure of EU funding was repeating the poor trend of the previous period (cf. tables 2.1 and 2.2).

The failure to implement the IMPs and two rounds of SFs corroborate the thesis that the *Intervento Straordinario* did not have the effect of building at the regional level an autonomous capacity to participate actively in regional policy. Instead, the national regional policy had a perverse effect of delegitimising and transforming the regions into mere observers of a policy process that remained the responsibility of the centre (Gualini, 2004).

Once the institutional settings were in place, with the different tiers of governments empowered to take part in the multi-level form of governance, it was necessary to assess the quality of each level's performance in programming and implementing development policies. This meant addressing the requirements of administrative efficiency in a manner that was unprecedented within Italian experience.

The first step in aligning Italian regional policy with EU procedures was the creation at central level of a department responsible for general coordination of regional policy and, in particular, of cohesion policy. The new department, Dipartimento delle Politiche di Sviluppo e Coesione (DPS or Department for Development and Cohesion policies), was established in 1998 within the reformed Ministry of the Treasury. The DPS was conceived as an administrative body strategically placed with regard to interests, procedures, and patterns of relations involved in implementing EU regional and cohesion policy.

The DPS played a significant role in re-orienting the Italian attitude towards European matters, seeing the procedures ruling SFs more as an opportunity to promote and foster administrative modernisation rather than merely as binding constraints. The top-down, centralised approach that had steered Italian regional policy until 1992 had left the southern regions with a burdensome legacy, and by the end of the second planning period it was clear that administrative bottlenecks had to be addressed at both the national and regional level.

4.4.4 The Third Period of SFs, 2000–2006

In 1999, in preparation for the third CSF, the DPS invested a lot of its energy and resources into a campaign to promote the modernisation of Italian public administrative structures and behaviour (Ministero del Tesoro, 2002, 2003, 2004, 2005). Appropriate incentive systems had to be created so as to persuade regions to implement administrative reforms and pursue high levels of outputs. The same approach was also applied to the central administration.

The first step in this direction was taken by the EU, with its initiative to increase the effective use of SFs, Council Regulation n. 1260/1999, which provided for the creation of a performance reserve (art. 44). This performance reserve was considered an opportunity to hasten the upgrading of the MA and reach higher quality standards in the implementation of the programmes. Its level was set at 4 per cent of the commitment appropriations.[17] The logic behind the reserve was that within three years from the beginning of the programming cycle (2003), Member States that had reached a specific set of implementation, management and financial targets would bean extra sum of SFs as a prize.

The Italian government considered the performance reserve a key incentive for improving the implementation of SFs for the period 2000–2006 in Objective 1 areas. On this basis, it decided to strengthen the Commission's proposal by adding to the 4 per cent reserve an extra 6 per cent national performance reserve to be attributed by the end of the second year of SFs cycle (2002).[18] The latter was conceived as a tool to incentivise regional government to implement some of the administrative and political reforms previously discussed – e.g. delegation of managerial responsibilities to officials (D.lgs. n. 29/1993); increasing the rate of expenditure and the quality of public spending; and developing the capacity of the public administration to interpret and study the socio-economic conditions of each regional territory where investments were to be directed. Overall, the reserve mechanism aimed at modernisation of the public administrative structure, which was deemed essential to reaching the expected results.

The design of the 6 per cent reserve was divided into three blocks of indicators, namely institutional enhancement, integration and concentration.

The first block included 10 indicators for regions. For institutional 'enhancement', among the different features of the administrative reform, the performance reserve mechanism rewarded the transition from the former normative-hierarchical approach to administration towards a performance-oriented one where officials were delegated higher responsibilities and had defined targets, and where such elements are part of a contract that is monitored (indicator A.1.1). The reward for implementing an internal management control system is formulated along the same lines (indicator A.1.2). As previously highlighted, the success of the CSF depended mostly on the capacity of regional governments, to whom implementation of the majority of funds was delegated, to screen and select the interventions that were most relevant for their territory, and to monitor and evaluate their impact in terms of their contribution to improving supply externalities and intermediate objectives. A proxy for this is the indicator that measures if regional and central administrations have set up and implemented monitoring and evaluation mechanisms and equipped the responsible units with sufficiently qualified human resources to perform those functions (indicator A.1.5).

As for integration and concentration, both criteria were based on the underlying assumption that when resources are limited, as they always are, only a restricted number of objectives can be achieved and that, for each objective to be reached, all pertinent interventions have to be implemented following both a logical and temporal integration path.

Clearly the main purpose of the performance reserve and the correlated criteria was to reinforce at regional level the implementation of administrative reform that was taking place at the national level. The indicators suggested by the DPS only partially catch the aspect of administrative capacity defined in this book. Indeed, my definition and correlated indicators for measuring administrative capacity are more focused on the actions of the regional administration relevant to improving public spending. The concept used by the DPS, however, was broader, and covered various aspect of the whole institution (that is why the DPS phrased its performance objectives in terms of 'institutional enhancement' rather than administrative capacity building) (UVAL, 2002a).

Table 4.3 shows that by the end of 2002, after three full years of implementation, Basilicata was the region that fully satisfied the DPS institutional indicators and reached the highest level of performance in the three groups of indicators. Sicily, although not among the lowest performers, was still far behind Basilicata, given its inability to satisfy the indicator on the programming of resources in an integrated manner. As far as the institutional

Table 4.3 National Reserve. Percentage of satisfaction for set of indicators (December 2002)

Regions	A.1 Institutional enhancement (%)	A.2 Integration (%)	A.3 Concentration (%)	Total (%)
Basilicata	100	53	98	88
Calabria	30	0	59	27
Campania	60	100	58	70
Puglia	80	0	98	63
Sardinia	10	53	59	29
Sicily	80	0	59	57

Source: UVAL, 2002

indicators were concerned, Sicily managed to fulfil 80 per cent of the required objectives.

The Director of the DPS commented on these results as follows:

> The incentive device has definitely had a positive impact in terms of pushing the regions to implement the appropriate reforms. This experiment has proven that the central government should have a role in overall guidance and should not be invasive as in the past. There is evidence to support the idea that the regions, if correctly supported, can increase their (institutional) capacity and performance. (Recorded interview)

In summary, the 2000/2006 Objective 1 planning process gave the Italian government a chance to finalise the shift towards a more appropriate policy approach with the intention of increasing the capacity of the regional governments to manage, programme, monitor and evaluate the use of the available resources. The Italian government understood that for the MLG to function at his best, it was necessary to recognise the subnational level but most importantly it was fundamental that the regional level had the capacity to perform efficiently within the system.

5

THE FIRST SET OF PRECONDITIONS FOR MULTI-LEVEL GOVERNANCE

5.1 Assessment of Administrative Capacity in Sicily and Basilicata
This chapter, which marks the beginning of the empirical analysis in which I aim to explain the observed different rates of expenditure of SFs among Italian Objective 1 regions, tests the existence of administrative capacity – one of the two major preconditions which I believe is necessary for implementation to succeed under the MLG framework. Each of the chapter's four sections scrutinises a key action, in order to assess the degree of administrative capacity in Sicily and Basilicata according to the indicators established in Chapter 3. The analysis covers the third planning period of SFs (2000–2006), referring, where possible, to the first (1989–1993) and second period (1994–1999).

Besides using the available primary and secondary sources for each period, the analysis draws on my own observations and on interviews based on questionnaires completed by the four categories of relevant actors – (cf. section 3.4.3). All the quotations used in the text were obtained from personal interviews, which I have translated into English.

5.2 The Degree of Management
The introduction of the cohesion policy brought with it a new approach to the management and expenditure of resources. Indeed, the principles underpinning the expenditure of the SFs introduced a method of managing, programming, monitoring and evaluating resources that was previously unknown in Italy or in other Member States. Given that the SFs were awarded to a country or region on the basis of a signed contract – i.e. the Community Support Framework[1] (CSF) and the Operational Programmes (OPs) – the

task of coordinating the implementation and accounting for expenditures became a vital necessity. It was crucial therefore to identify explicitly at both national and regional level the person responsible for implementing the programme and for reporting expenditures to the Commission.

During the first CSF cycle, 1989–1993, this administrative exigency was not clearly spelled out and the administrative solutions varied from country to country. In contrast, in the 2000–2006 SFs cycle the creation of an explicit Managing Authority (MA)[2] was made the basis for finalising negotiations regarding the OPs, and thus in 2000 it was necessary to set up a MA within each level of government responsible for the expenditure of SFs. In Italy a national MA was created to oversee the entire CSF programme, while each national and regional OP had its own dedicated MA, to which was assigned the task of putting together the strategy, actions, priorities and funds allocated by the CSF. The CSF was broken down into seven Regional Operational Programmes (ROPs), which were managed individually by each of the seven Objective 1 regions.[3]

The ROP is a document comprised of a consistent set of priorities divided into sub-programmes and measures,[4] which derive from the CSF but are more specific and tied to regional needs. The implementation of the assistance strategy and priorities is detailed in a technical document, the Programme Complement (PC). Each regional MA had the responsibility of drawing up both the ROP and the PC. The regional MA was generally located within the Programming Department (Dipartimento della Programmazione), and a general manager was appointed to take responsibility for its activities.

In sum, the underlying framework of the SFs suggests that the regional authorities were ultimately responsible for the outputs of the programme and making sure that the Funds were spent on the objectives and projects outlined in the OP.

The key role of the MA is to be responsible for the efficiency of the overall programme in order to deliver the expected results by performing two main activities:

1   to clarify the role of personnel in the administrative structure of the MA (i.e. who does what, when and how); and

2   to coordinate the activities of the *assessorati* involved in the implementation of sectoral sub-programmes and measures (i.e. horizontal coordination).[5]

In accordance with the methodology I proposed in Chapter 3 (cf. section 3.4), I use the MA's key activities as indicators of the degree of management in the two case studies between 1989 and 2004. I will present the results of the analysis of the component parts for each region in sequence.

5.2.1 Clarity of Roles among Personnel

Sicily

The drafting and management of the Pluri-fund Operative Programme[6] (POP) for 1989–1993 was the responsibility of the regional government, which was divided into 12 *assessorates*. Within each *assessorato*, in addition to the political figurehead, the *assessore*, there is an administrative position of general manager (*dirigente generale*), responsible for the management of the programme. Along with the implementation of the POP, the regional authority was in charge of the IMPs, which started in 1986. The POP was organised in twelve thematic sub-programmes,[7] with implementation assigned to the appropriate *assessorato*. Following these criteria, the interventions financed by the ERDF came under the authority of the Programming Department of the regional Presidency: the EAGGF interventions were assigned to the Assessorato of Agriculture; and the ESF sub-programme was the responsibility of the Assessorato for Labour. The other *assessorati* were involved according to their area of responsibility.

From 1989 to 1993, a Joint Committee of the three different *assessorati* in charge of coordinating the activities of each Fund was created in order to guarantee coherence in SFs intervention (Arthur Andersen, 1995). However, the coordinating activities were only a formality.

An accurate review of the only available evaluation report (Arthur Andersen, 1997)[8] supported by my personal interviews, leads to two main conclusions. First, there was a lack of clarity in the roles assigned to the administrative personnel within the planning *assessorato* as well as in the other *assessorati* involved in the implementation of the sub-programmes and measures (Arthur Andersen, 1997: 90). Second, each *assessorato* acted independently, with no coordination within or between the departments comprising the regional administrative structure.

This state of affairs was caused mainly by the absence of a well developed coordination framework and the lack of preparatory measures taken to facilitate the introduction of a new and more complex method of implementing regional programmes as required by the SFs. No changes were made at the time to the administrative structure, and personnel were randomly overloaded with extra work. This created a situation of overall confusion and duplication of efforts among the personnel. In the absence of a coordination body to refer back to, everyone was left to act on their own. As revealed in the interviews, the main constraint on introducing an adequate framework within which to carry out the new tasks was the political class, which relied on such confusion to manage funds according to its personal agenda.

Similar problems characterised the period 1994–1999. It was only during the third planning period, 2000–2006, that the regional administration began a process of organisational restructuring on the heels of the explicit requirements introduced by the 1999 EU regulations. A new regional law (LR 10/2000) clearly distinguished political functions and responsibilities from the administrative duties relative to the management of the OPs. With Decision 332 (18 September 2001) the regional *giunta* approved the specification of the person responsible for the implementation of each intervention, and also established the conditions governing the coordination role of the MA. Setting these boundaries between the political and administrative classes contributed significantly to clarifying the roles of specific individuals and reducing the blurring of responsibilities.

Basilicata

The regional government of Basilicata, which is divided into six *assessorati*, behaved similarly to that of Sicily in the way it assumed the responsibility of implementing the 1989–1993 OP. The interventions financed by the ERDF fell under the authority of the Presidency, Programming Department, and the EAGGF and ESF interventions were allocated to the Assessorato of Agriculture. The remaining four *assessorati* intervened in their respective areas of competence.

The main difference between the OP management in Basilicata and in Sicily was that the former created an ad hoc structure – the 'Cabin of Direction' (Cabina di Regia) – to undertake technical and administrative coordination of the POP, under the guidance of the Programming Department. The benefits of such a structure relate not only to the administrative aspects of coordination but also to the major clarity it brings to the definitions of roles and responsibilities.

Some start-up problems were experienced at the beginning of the 1989–1993 programme because of the novelty of the SFs mechanisms. Those initial difficulties were definitively overcome by the beginning of the second planning period, 1994–1999. This was made possible by a series of formal and informal meetings between the staff working on the implementation of SFs, aimed at sharing information and experience (Ecosfera *et al.*, 1999), thus disseminating a better understanding of the mechanisms involved in the operationalisation of the SFs.

The experience accumulated during the previous two planning periods allowed the Basilicata region to set up its MA without difficulty in 2000, establishing a clear working framework that facilitated clarity of responsibility and the division of roles between personnel. Furthermore, the division of duties among personnel was coherent with each area of responsibility (Ecosfera, 2000: 29).

Moreover, what emerged from the interviews was an overall tendency among the staff at every level to collaborate, in contrast to the picture that emerged in Sicily. This attitude appears in both cases to have been stimulated by the political class. As I discuss in more detail in Chapter 6, in Basilicata 'a non-opportunistic, pro-active behaviour exemplified by the political class has favoured the spreading among the administrative class of a similar type of behaviour' (Mancinelli, 2001: 312).

5.2.2 Coordination of Activities among Different Assessorati

Sicily

In Sicily, there was another crucial factor accounting for the deficiency in management, along with the lack of clarity about the roles of personnel: poor coordination between the different *assessorati*. As we saw in the previous section, this was caused by the absence of a proactive structure/body dedicated specifically to the implementation of SFs intervention. Indeed, as both primary and secondary sources (documents and interviews) clearly reveal, the Joint Committee did not perform its role of coordination and was fundamentally a very weak body, as it was not recognised nor supported by the political class.

The coordination problems were increased also by a vertical and compartmentalised administrative hierarchy, rooted in the principle that each *assessore* was responsible for its *assessorato* in front of the Cabinet. Consequently, each *assessorato* acted totally autonomously, with no communication between the different branches.

Each *assessorato* was divided into two levels, departments (*dipartimenti*) and areas (*aree*), for a total of 12 *assessorates* and 22 departments. Each area was responsible for some activities, and again there was a lack of communication/coordination even within individual *assessorati*. This compartmentalised vision of the administration was an obstacle to the overall performance of the region as an implementer of policy.

The main result of such uncoordinated administrative behaviour was the poor performance during the period 1989–1993, when Sicily spent only 39 per cent of its total allocation, registering the lowest level of expenditure of all the eight southern Italian regions (cf. Table 2.2). In the light of these results, the regional government established that the Programming Department, in addition to being responsible for the ERDF, should coordinate all the different *assessorati* in activities related to the planning and implementation of the overall programme.

The new POP of 1994–1999 clearly spelled out the role of each *assessorato* and the regional officer within it responsible for managing the single sub-programmes and measures (Regione Sicilia, 1996: 6 Part V). However, despite the innovation of having the whole Programming Department in charge of overall coordination, operational incompetence still affected the regional administration. The technical personnel in charge of management, limited by the constant level of political interference, did not have freedom to manoeuvre – as Chapter 6 will reveal.

Finally, at the beginning of the 2000–2006 period, the regional administration set up an MA whose general manager was hired from the national administration.[9] There was a general agreement, corroborated by primary, secondary and interview sources, that with the creation of a centralised administrative structure headed by an individual from outside of the regional administration, the situation in terms of clarity of role and responsibilities and coordination improved significantly (Ernst & Young, 2003a). Furthermore, in 2001, Law n. 20 created a Committee of Coordination of the Departments (CODIPA – Comitato di Coordinamento dei Dipartimenti) within the Presidency of the region, whose tasks were to ensure full correspondence between managerial activities and political directives and to increase coordination between the operating structures of the administration, in order to achieve effectiveness of administrative actions.

Basilicata

Basilicata had a vertical structure similar to that of Sicily. The main difference, though, was the existence of coordination bodies at various levels. Three coordination bodies existed: the Interdepartmental Committee for Management Coordination (CICO – Comitato Interdipartimentale di Coordinamento Organizzativo) for general horizontal coordination; the Comitato di Direzione, operating within the single departments; and the Conferenza di Organizzazione, a more inclusive body comprising other third parties, such as the trade unions.

Clearly, this mechanism, ensuring coordination of activities at each level in Basilicata, was key in enabling the region to manage the EU Funds well and efficiently. What made the difference for the management of SFs in Basilicata was the creation of the Cabin of Direction, which was in charge of the coordination of the activities related to the POP of 1989–1993 and of 1994–1999. The Cabin of Direction was organised on two main levels: a political level where the decisions were taken by the regional Cabinet and the Mixed Committee (Comitato Misto); and a technical level where the decisions were taken by the Interdepartmental Technical Commission (CTI – Commissione Tecnica Interdipartimentale) and by the Staff Office for Community Policy and Programme (Struttura di Staff Politiche e Programmi Comunitari).

This management structure set up for the SFs was capable of guaranteeing an optimal implementation performance between 1994 and 1999. Indeed, the degree of expenditure reached 58 per cent in 1999 and after the two-year extension it rose to 100 per cent. This achievement speaks for itself.

Both the evaluation report completed by the independent evaluator and all 26 of the people interviewed in Basilicata agreed on the vital role played by the three coordinating bodies, valuing the existence of such technical bodies as the determining element of the successful implementation of the 1994–1999 Funds (Ecosfera *et al.*, 1999: 79). Such an optimal result was possible due to the room for manoeuvre left by the political class, which, instead of interfering, enabled civil servants to grow and develop their own technical capacities in administrating the Funds.

The next section will assess the second key component, namely programming. We can already anticipate that, since these activities are part of a loop, a weak management will definitely influence the level of programming performance.

5.3 Programming Performance

Programming is the second key determinant that needs to be addressed. Ideally, once the MA has been set up and roles have been clarified among personnel and various departments, the next step is to design and approve a development plan. The long-term nature of SFs interventions makes this factor a very valuable means of ensuring legal and financial certainty for planners, policy implementers, project promoters and managers over a prolonged period of time.

In this context, a programme is defined as an

> organised set of financial, organisational and human interventions mobilised to achieve an objective or set of objectives in a given period. A programme is delimited in terms of a timescale and budget. Programme objectives are defined beforehand; an effort is then made systematically to strive for coherence among these objectives (Tavistock Institute, 2003: Glossary).

Based on this definition, as previously discussed, two indicators have been considered in order to assess the degree of programming at the regional level: programme design and programme approval (cf. section 3.4.1). In terms of programme design, there are two essential elements to address: the correctness of the SWOT analysis, and the consequent development of a coherent strategy. These two steps are closely interrelated, so any imprecision in the SWOT analysis will compromise the success of the strategy. A SWOT analysis, in fact, assesses socio-economic strengths and weaknesses in addition to opportunities and threats, providing vital information that will assist the organisation in accomplishing its objectives or overcoming possible obstacles to achieve the desired results (Ferrell and Hartline, 1998).

The second factor necessary for successful programming is 'timing'. Indeed, the programme to implement SFs is spread over a length of time that usually spans between five and seven years and coincides with the beginning and end of the EU budgetary cycle. The logic behind multi-annual programming is that there is a certain amount of allocated resources that needs to be spent within the set period of time, or else it is lost. Therefore, any delays in approving the beginning of the programme reduce the time available to spend the resources.

In many Objective 1 regions, timing has been a major issue of concern, not only in terms of approval but also in terms of programme preparation. The preparation of operational programmes has been seen as a time-consuming exercise, which can be speeded up by an efficient MA (ÖIR, 2003: 82). In the next section, I investigate the characteristics of both programme designs and programme approval practices in Sicily and in Basilicata.

5.3.1 *Programme Design and Strategy Coherence*

Sicily

Programme design, in terms of appropriate strategy and coherence with real territorial needs, was not a familiar practice in Sicily: indeed, the drafting of the IMP programme and of the first POP 1989–1993 was the first real programming exercise undertaken by the region during its long history (Regione Sicilia, 1990).

In reality, the two POPs (1989–1993 and 1994–1999) were deficient in many respects. First, they did not contain an exhaustive SWOT analysis of the territory:

> the programme was written sitting around a table – i.e. it was written by a few people in charge who had conducted no territorial analysis and assumed, based on their own personal knowledge, that they knew what interventions were necessary for the region. The same people developed a strategy which was very shallow and in no way successful. (Recorded interview).

The strategy addressed regional disparities and individual problems, but without adopting an integrated model of development that considered the region as a whole (Regione Sicilia, 1990). This approach, based on the separate needs identified by each individual department, and without any recognition of possible links with other interventions, was in large part the result of sectoral programming and the lack of coordination among the different *assessorati*, thus creating the opportunity for individually self-justified initiatives. Consequently many development problems were left unsolved and very little was done (CENSIS and Vision and Value, 2001; 2002).

On the other hand, a scrutiny of the 2000–2006 ROP indicates the adoption of a more horizontal cooperative model, to replace the existing vertical one, and an improvement of the use of the SWOT analysis (Regione Sicilia, 2000a). This time, however, in attempting to be more inclusive the analysis became insufficiently selective, so that the programme developed was far too ambitious, addressed too many issues, and was extremely fragmented (Ernst & Young, 2003a). The result of this approach to programme design was that the strategy was spread between 77 intervention measures, far too many to manage in an integrated fashion (Regione Sicilia, 2000b).

Basilicata

The information on programming activities during the period 1989–1993 was collected mainly through interviews. Various key actors have pointed out two elements that set apart the programming activities in Basilicata. First was the experimental experience of the IMP, which was taken very seriously and used as an opportunity to learn about how to engage in integrated planning (Regione Basilicata, 1996c). This was not the case in Sicily, which continued to rely on the Funds of the Casmez; these were more easily accessible and were not accompanied by restrictive rules on their use. The second element was the efforts that the regional organisation made towards closing the gap between the ordinary administration of funding for development and the SFs procedures. Indeed, Basilicata immediately understood that the SFs principles could be more effective than the logic behind the Casmez interventions, and tried to apply these principles in its overall management and programming activities (Regione Basilicata, 1996c; 1997).

An investigation of the two benchmarks for programming activities reveals a positive situation in Basilicata. Here, the definition of the strategy for implementation of the funds began with what was considered an accurate SWOT analysis of the region's socio-economic structure (Regione Basilicata, 1989, 1995b, 2000a). The programming document for each period – i.e. POP 1989–1993, POP 1994–1999 and ROP 2000–2006 – was characterised by a strategy of continuity with the previous period. Furthermore, the interventions appeared to be strongly coordinated (Regione Basilicata, 1989, 1995b, 2000). This was possible because of the existence of the Cabin of Direction and the CTI (cf. section 5.2), which created an arena for discussion between all the departmental general managers and managers with a view to sharing strategy.

Naturally, the documents show a clear improvement in the use of the SWOT analysis over the course of the three planning periods. However, two common elements were always present: (1) a clear definition of priorities and an operationalisation of the interventions designed to provide solutions to the problems identified; and (2) a broad agreement between departments on the selection of priorities (Regione Basilicata, 1989, 1995b, 2000a).

I have scrutinised the latest ROP (2000–2006), and the elements which emerge in opposition to the contents of the Sicilian development programme are (1) a clear focus on four main development issues which the region aims to tackle; and (2) a limited number of measures – 45 – into which the programme was divided (Regione Basilicata, 2000a: 39–41). All the people questioned agreed that, as one interviewee put it, 'the number of measures is adequate to answer the territorial needs, and the programme is well coordinated and this makes it possible to eventually adjust the interventions to any changes in the scenario' (recorded interview).

Furthermore, in Sicily the weakness of the programme design was increased by constant revisions of the programme over the years. As an example, in the last planning period (2000–2006), the Sicilian programme underwent 17 revisions, against only 7 in Basilicata. On one hand these amendments are necessary in order to adapt the programme to inevitable changes in the economic scenario over time, but, on the other, the situation in Sicily was extreme and ultimately led to a decline in the coherence of the final programme.

5.3.2 *Programme Approval*

Along with poor programme design, another main problem that compromises programming performance is the pace of programme approval – the second selected indicator.

In Sicily, there was evidence of considerable delays in the approval of the programming documents which resulted in a late start and further delays in putting implementation structures into place.[10] As far as the first POP (1989–1993) was concerned, the sequence of events was similar in both Sicily and Basilicata: the programmes that were supposed to start in 1989 were approved after significant delays in 1990,[11] almost two years after the CSF began, and received an extension until 1997 for Sicily and 1996 for Basilicata, in order to increase the possibility of expenditure. Analysis of the documents from that period seems to show that the delay arose from the many innovative features of the programme, all of which required due time for consideration.[12] However, if we look at the end of the period, i.e. the end of 1993, the rate of implementation in Sicily was among the lowest, at only at 39 per cent of available Funds, whereas Basilicata had already spent

56 per cent of its total allocation. In comparison to the remaining Objective 1 regions in Italy, Basilicata's performance was the best. The factor that enabled Basilicata to accelerate its rate of expenditure was repeated by most of the interviewees:

> The regional administration has been able to spend the resources and reach an admirable level due to the strong coherence between the programme objectives and the regional needs. Having identified what was *really* needed, it was easy to spend resources to tackle those necessities. (Recorded interview)

The same type of delay that characterised the first cohesion policy cycle was repeated in the second. The 1994–1999 Sicilian OP was approved on 28 September 1995, again almost two years after the beginning of the CSF. The situation appears to have been very different in Basilicata, where the delay was contained to less than a year.[13] The reduction of the delay in Basilicata exemplifies the capacity of the region to adapt and improve its own performance, while Sicily remained wedded to its usual procedures and delays. Furthermore, the delay in approval on this occasion was due to the inadequacy of the POP presented by Sicily to the EC, which required Sicily to make changes and improvements to the document before it could be approved (recorded interview).

If we look at the other regions, we can identify a strong correspondence between the time of approval and delays in expenditure. Indeed, Molise, Sardinia and Calabria, which had their respective POPs approved by the end of 1994 with less than a year's delay, had by 2001 spent respectively 99 per cent, 84 per cent and 92 per cent of their total allocation. The remaining regions, on the other hand, suffered a delay of two years in the approval of their programmes and this had an impact on the expenditure (cf. Table 2.2).

The delays in Sicily were much less notable in the third planning period, 2000–2006. Even so, there was nearly a year of delay in the approval of Sicily's PC (Programme Complement), whereas Basilicata's PC was approved straight after the ROP (November 2000). The quarterly data on SFs expenditure available for the latter period show clearly how a delay in approval compromises the rate of expenditure. Indeed, by the end of the first year (31 December 2000) Sicily had not spent anything because its PC had not been approved, while Basilicata had managed to spend 1 per cent of its allocation. A delay in the start-up of the programme created a gap between the regions in terms of expenditure. At the end of 2001, Sicily had spent a meagre 0.74 per cent of its total allocation and Basilicata had spent almost 5 per cent.

5.4 Creation of a Regional Monitoring System

Monitoring was introduced during the first programming period (1989–1993). The provisions for monitoring requirements were laid out in Council Regulation 2052/88, Article 6:

> Community operations shall be constantly monitored to ensure that the commitments entered into as part of the objectives set out in Articles 130a and 130c of the Treaty are effectively honoured. Such monitoring shall, where necessary, make it possible to adjust operations in line with requirements arising during implementation.

However, monitoring activities were not carried out systematically in Italy or in other countries during the first period of planning of the SFs. The requirement was revisited during the second programming period (1994–1999) and it only really took off as a strict legal requirement and an integral part of the administration of SFs during the third period (2000–2006). Article 34 of Council Regulation 1260/1999 states that:

> [t]he Managing Authority, as defined in Article 9, shall be responsible for the efficiency and correctness of management and implementation, and in particular … for setting up a system to gather reliable financial and statistical information on implementation for the monitoring indicators referred to in Article 36.[14]

The basic criteria for the creation of a monitoring system for the period 2000–2006 were set in accordance with the following principles: (1) optimisation of the best monitoring experiences adopted during the 1994–1999 programming period; (2) adoption of the programme indicators system (financial, processing and physical indicators of the state of implementation); (3) standardisation of monitoring models in 2000–2006 CSF programmes (data tables, synthesis indicators, benchmarking, data processing) most suitable for the evaluation system and surveillance activity. Undoubtedly, the requirements concerning indicators and monitoring posed serious challenges to all MA.

Evidence from other EU Objective 1 regions suggests that, when performed correctly, both monitoring and evaluation contribute to the improvement of the implementation of Funds (ÖIR, 2003). On the one hand, the creation of a viable monitoring system contributes to increasing the professionalism of the PA by encouraging the creation of databases of relevant information on programme implementation. On the other hand, the systematic collection of data on specified indicators and the presentation of periodic evaluations provide the management with an ongoing update on the progress of the programme. In this respect, it supports the MA in spotting possible problems that might arise during the implementation, so that the MA can intervene during the process and initiate adjustments. However, it has to be said that not all of the regions came to terms with monitoring and evaluation procedures from the outset. According to Taylor *et al.* (2001), it took time for the requirements of the monitoring procedures to permeate the administrative machinery and to function fully.

In the next section I assess the degree of monitoring evident in my selected case studies, according to the indicators introduced in Chapter 3. The benchmarks for monitoring are: (1) the introduction of a system of indicators and of monitoring procedures responding to nationally agreed standards; and (2) a guarantee of the availability of financial, physical and procedural data to the MA.

5.4.1 *Constraints in Monitoring Procedures in Sicily*

An investigation into the features of monitoring in Sicily revealed that no monitoring system was in place over the period 1989–1993 (Arthur Andersen, 1997: 72). The costs in time and money of setting up a monitoring system were perceived as being too large relative to the value that they produced.

It was not until 1995 that the regional administration set up a system of data monitoring, with the support of the Technical Assistance service.[15] However, there is evidence to suggest that the monitoring system in Sicily did not fully comply with national and European standards over the whole period (Arthur Andersen, 1995; 1997; Ernst & Young, 2003a), failing to satisfy the need for accountability, and in particular the need for the Commission to report on the proper use of public funds. Apart from the lack of inter-departmental coordination in the operationalisation of the monitoring system, there was also the complexity associated with the exigencies of different fund-specific monitoring systems, which were time-consuming and costly. Furthermore, the monitoring functions were not integrated into the institutional framework of the PA systems, which resulted in the proliferation of information that was of little use in developing a full understanding of programme implementation. In response to a question about the efficiency of the system, the manager of monitoring activities in the 1994–1999 and 2000–2006 periods said: 'During the first two planning periods, 1989–1993 and 1994–1999, the monitoring system was not a "system": it was a random mass of information' (recorded interview).

Some improvements were made during the period 2000–2006. Sicily created a web-based, decentralised system in line with European and national standards. During the first two years, the system experienced many start-up problems due to the novelty of the web-based method, and even some years later there are still some departments that find it difficult to input their data into the system according to schedule. Nevertheless, the regional administration has made a lot of improvements in monitoring (Ernst & Young, 2003: 32).

Despite this progress, there still seems to be a dichotomy between the gathering of data for monitoring purposes and the management of programmes. Monitoring systems are primarily intended to satisfy the accountability needs of the system (in particular the need for the Commission to report on the proper use of public funds). However, they should also feed back into the management process, so that their information can be used to improve the implementation process. Instead, according to my analysis, it appears that the monitoring systems were developed solely to meet the requirements of SFs implementation rather than as the result of a perceived need at the regional level to improve the implementation process per se. This lack of connection between data gathering and management processes suggests that monitoring activities still need improvement and are not yet fully integrated into the functioning of the administrative system.

5.4.2 *The Monitoring System in Basilicata: A Model of Best Practice*

Basilicata first experience of setting up monitoring activities was with the initial IMP programme, and with the ERDF programmes in 1979 (Regione Basilicata, 1996b). The first monitoring methods were very basic: information was written on a file card, and later copied onto an electronic file.

System demands increased during the period 1994–1999. The Commission asked for a web-based monitoring system able to capture not only the physical data but also the financial information on programme outputs. Supported by the Technical Assistance service the region succeeded in implementing its first full monitoring system by the end of 1999 (Ecosfera *et al.*, 2002). The existence of this system was one of the reasons that the region was able to spend its entire SFs allocation. By guaranteeing the availability of both financial and physical data, the system has enabled the regional administration to keep the progress of expenditure under constant review and to take preventive action when potentially critical bottlenecks appear likely (Ecosfera *et al.*, 2002: 144).

Scrutiny of the documents which describe the monitoring system during the period 1994–1999 reveals that it was based on a complete and exhaustive set of indicators (Ecosfera SPA, 1999; 2000; 2001; 2002). Such a high level of performance, according to the two managers in charge of monitoring activities, was because both the administrative personnel and the political leadership believed that monitoring was vital: 'the reason behind such commitment to improving the monitoring system is that the regional government fully shared and understood the importance of such a system and its utility in improving public spending overall' (recorded interview).

During the period 2000–2006, the regional administration focused on two aspects. First, it tried to improve the degree of coordination among the different departments in collecting the necessary information to feed into the monitoring system. Second, it carried out further analysis to adjust the new set of indicators to the eventual changes in policy objectives and to keep it coherent with the EU and national guidelines. The result was a series of indicators that appears to be 'adequate and exhaustive' (Ernst & Young, 2003b: 54). In conclusion, the independent evaluator of the ROP in Basilicata in the period 2000–2006 affirmed that: 'the monitoring model set up in Basilicata represented an example of best practice for the other regions' (Ernst & Young, 2003b: 65).

5.5 Diffusion of the Evaluation Culture

Tied to the monitoring system is the issue of evaluation activity and culture, which relies both on the monitoring of results and on the collection of supplementary information. Initially, in the period 1989–1993, evaluation, although required by EU norms, was not strictly regulated. In the second SFS cycle (1994–1999) the subject received greater attention from EU policy-makers: a third type of evaluation, mid-term evaluation, was introduced in addition to the *ex-ante* and *ex-post* assessments. In the third period, 2000–2006, the required depth of analysis for all three types of evaluation increased significantly (ÖIR, 2003: 22).

At present, the *ex-ante* evaluation is carried out by the regional administration, whereas the intermediate and *ex-post* evaluations are usually contracted out to private independent companies. Thus there is a large reliance on the outside professional community for evaluation skills and competencies. An external assessor is arguably in a better position to ensure an objective analysis of performance, and it can also be expected that the need to interact with independent evaluators would encourage the PA to rationalise and render more efficient its activities.

The impact of evaluation on implementation is twofold:

First, the systematic identification of the best alternatives, as well as the careful consideration of the ability of ongoing or past programmes to reach their objectives in an efficient way. This can become a powerful tool for modernisation in the public sector for cost reduction and for greater responsiveness to citizens. Second, the opening up of the administrative 'black box' to the scrutiny of external stakeholders, as well as taking the interests of stakeholders and citizens into account when designing evaluation questions, is in itself an embodiment of the principles of democratic governance. (Tavistock Institute, 2003: 85)

Evaluation has become a standard, widely used tool to support the implementation process and is generally acknowledged to be an instrument that enhances transparency. Processes and outputs of the evaluation system are usually documented and used as a basis for future planning and management (ÖIR, 2003: 101).

Moreover, both monitoring and evaluation aim to ensure, on an ongoing basis, proper management of resources in accordance with standards of accountability.[16] I address accountability in Chapter 6, and will close this chapter by assessing the degree of evaluation used in the case studies according to the indicators introduced in Chapter 3: (1) production of the evaluation reports according to EU standards; and (2) integration of the evaluation method and culture in the implementation system.

5.5.1 'Inspection' rather than 'Evaluation' in Sicily

As with monitoring activities, evaluation activities in Sicily were very poor in the first planning period. The 1989–1993 POP was not supported by an *ex-ante* evaluation and the *ex-post* evaluation was carried out four years after the end of the programme, in 1997 (Arthur Andersen, 1997: 82). The administration was not prepared to manage this function, and appeared to regard the evaluation as more of an external control or obligation than as a support for improving the nature of the implementation. In addition, the Monitoring Committees[17] very rarely dedicated sufficient time to debating the results of the evaluation or created a task force to accompany the evaluator. This approach derived from the tradition of the administration, which was never receptive to formal controls or to the verification of results and accountability. This attitude was the main constraint on the introduction of evaluation to the decision mechanisms. In addition, the regional administration often misinterpreted the role and function of the independent evaluator, who was seen as 'an inspector' rather than a supportive figure.

The situation seemed to improve in the second period (1994–1999), when both an *ex- ante* and an *ex-post* evaluation was carried out (CENSIS *et al.* 2001; 2002), but, as the interviews revealed, 'there was no real interest in evaluation activities; neither were they considered of any importance in the implementation of the funds; the only reason to perform them was to conform to EU standards' (recorded interview).

It was only in the most recent planning period (2000–2006) that the evaluation culture spread throughout the administration. Until then the evaluation process was considered merely as an extra workload whose beneficial effect was not understood.

The region's *ex-ante* evaluation report for 2000–2006 appears to be more thorough and to show progress in the region's appreciation of the importance of such a task (Regione Sicilia, 2000d). The intermediate evaluation was commissioned to Ernst & Young in due course (Ernst & Young, 2003a). An interview with the independent evaluator revealed that:

The regional administration has definitely understood the utility of the evaluation activities, compared to the last planning periods; the results of the intermediate evaluation are actually taken into account by the administration. Furthermore, every member of staff has collaborated in providing information and material essential for the evaluation to be performed. (recorded interview)

5.5.2 Evaluation Culture in Basilicata: Developing Internal Expertise

In Basilicata, the Monitoring Committee itself carried out the evaluation activities during the first planning period (1989–1993). This responded to a practical need to spread the evaluation culture throughout the departments and to make everyone understand the importance of such an instrument. It seemed appropriate that the Monitoring Committee, due to its inclusive nature, should share this new activity within the regional organisation rather than assign it to an external firm. The logic behind this was that the regional organisation needed to develop its skills from the inside rather than relying on external consultants (recorded interview). This would have helped to spread the evaluation culture and awareness of its importance within the organisation. The Monitoring Committee produced both an *ex-ante* (Regione Basilicata, 1989) and an *ex-post* evaluation report (Regione Basilicata, 1995a).

In the period 1994–1999 the *ex-ante* evaluation of the programme was carried out by the Programming Department. The intermediate and *ex-post* evaluations were contracted out to an external evaluator whose appointment was delayed until the end of 1998. A similar delay was experienced in the other Regions, but in the case of Basilicata it was not due to a lack of recognition of the advantages of evaluation activities (Ecosfera SPA *et al.*, 1999: 73). It was because the regional administration wanted to develop an understanding of what to ask an evaluator and how to use the evaluation to improve the expenditure of Funds – so that the administration were familiar with the evaluation mechanism before appointing an external actor (Ecosfera SPA *et al.*, 1999: 73).

In 2000–2006 the *ex-ante* evaluation was again carried out by the Programming Department. A thorough analysis of the *ex-ante* evaluation reveals a great knowledge of regional territorial needs, a clear set of goals to be achieved and a coherent strategy of how to improve regional conditions (Regione Basilicata, 1999).

In contrast with the delays registered in the previous period, the independent evaluator, Ernst & Young, was this time appointed on schedule, within the deadline set by the EU.

One of the members of the evaluation group affirmed that 'the region of Basilicata is already familiar with the practice of evaluation. Here the evaluation culture has spread within the region, both in administrative and political spheres, which pay great attention to the results emerging from the assessment' (recorded interview). The leader of the evaluation group supported this statement by adding that: 'the regional administration considers both monitoring and evaluation two significant activities to improve resources implementation' (recorded interview).

5.6 Administrative Capacity: Scores and Cross-regional Comparisons

This chapter addresses empirically the first question of my central hypothesis – i.e. what accounts for the observed regional variation in the implementation of SFs? I suggested redefining administrative capacity as an independent variable that better explains the ability of the regions to implement SFs – i.e. where there is a higher degree of administrative capacity there is a higher degree of resources expenditure.

Table 5.1 summarises the findings after ranking the primary and secondary source material and the evidence that emerged from the fieldwork on the basis of the definition given to the established indicators. It clearly emerges that administrative capacity is weak in Sicily. leading to low SFs implementation, but much more developed in Basilicata, accounting for higher SFs expenditure. The key findings are strong enough to corroborate the hypothesis that a set of administrative preconditions must be in place at the regional level for implementation to succeed in a MLG framework.

5.6.1 Management

Well developed management abilities seem to have been absent in Sicily during the first two periods and have only recently started to appear. The weaknesses of management arose from an ineffectual central coordination

Table 5.1 Administrative capacity overall score

Key determinants of administrative capacity	Indicators	Score per programming period						Overall score	
		Sicily			Basilicata			Sicily	Basilicata
		1989–1993	1994–1999	2000–2006	1989–1993	1994–1999	2000–2006		
Management	(a) Clarity in the definition of roles	0	0	1	1	2	3	0.3	2
	(b) Coordination and cooperation among *assessorati*	0	1	2	1	2	3	1	2
	Overall score	0	0.5	1.5	1	2	3	0.65	2
Programming	(a) Programme design	0	0	1	1	2	3	0.3	2
	(b) Programme approval	0	0	1	1	2	3	0.3	2
	Overall score	0	0	1	1	2	3	0.3	2
Monitoring	(a) Introduction of a system of indicators and of monitoring procedures responding to national agreed standards.	0	1	2	1	2	3	1	2
	(b) Guaranteeing the availability of financial, physical and procedural data	0	1	1	1	2	3	0.6	2
	Overall score	0	1	1.5	1	2	3	0.8	2
Evaluation	(a) Production of evaluation reports	0	1	2	1	2	3	1	2
	(b) Integration of the evaluation method and culture in the implementation system	0	0	1	1	2	3	0.3	2
	Overall score	0	0.5	1.5	1	2	3	0.65	2
	Overall score for administrative capacity							0.6	2

that left each department to act on its own and did not allow an integrated approach to develop. Most of the time, the lack of effective coordination led to the duplication of activities and a slowing down of the implementation process due to the absence of clarity in the roles and responsibilities of the administrative personnel. An opposite situation emerged in Basilicata, where progressive improvements in management took place and it reached a high level of performance. Here, a strong and efficient central coordinating level organised the actions taken by the various departments involved, giving the personnel a clear vision of their duties and ensuring significant administrative outputs.

The fieldwork highlighted the contribution of regional organisational structure and size to the low capacity of management in Sicily *vis-à-vis* Basilicata. The organisation of the Sicilian regional administration was characterised by a strong vertical and compartmentalised administrative hierarchy, which did not favour exchanges between different assessorates and made management an individual concern. Interviews confirmed that this lack of collaboration has always been part of the administrative culture in Sicily and is still very persistent. Each department has always had its own decision-making, political and organisational autonomy. Once an administrative culture is implanted, it is very difficult to dismantle. In Sicily, there was a prevailing tendency for each department to keep its activities within the boundaries of the department itself and to avoid any sharing of knowledge or information. Furthermore, the regional administration had the disadvantage of being divided into 12 assessorates and 22 departments, which appeared to be a further obstacle to overall coordination of activities. This situation was made worse until recently by the absence of a central coordination structure.

In Basilicata the vertical hierarchy was weaker and this facilitated a horizontal coordination of activities that eased management and programming activities. Moreover, the region had the advantage of being divided into only six assessorates, which corresponded to an equal number of departments – i.e. each assessorate had only one department. It appears that the reduced number of internal departments and the limited number of people involved encouraged a more effective coordination of activities.

5.6.2 Programming

The second component analysed in this chapter was programming, in terms of the ability to design an efficient programme and to begin the implementation without delays. In Sicily both these features appeared to be absent in the first two periods and only started to emerge during the 2000–2006 planning period. Indeed, it was only in this planning period that the ROP was based on a clearer SWOT analysis and was linked to empirical regional needs; before this it had been based on the 'thoughts and suggestions of a few people'. Similarly, it was only recently that there were shorter delays in having the programme approved, compared to the previous periods when it had taken up to two years for the programme to be agreed upon with the Commission. Naturally, the lack of coherence between the programme and the territorial needs and the delays in beginning implementation were serious impediments to the smooth implementation of the policy and to spending the available resources.

Once again, the situation in Basilicata was completely the opposite. Here, the regional administration was always very thorough in analysing the strengths and weaknesses of the regional territory and in formulating policy strategies that could improve the circumstances. This allowed the region to achieve a considerable level of expenditure, overcoming the first period of delays in programme approval.

5.6.3 Monitoring and Evaluation

The last two components of administrative capacity to be analysed were monitoring and evaluation. Although these two components have been ranked separately, they are closely interconnected. Indeed, deficiencies in monitoring activities compromise the possibility of carrying out a complete evaluation. The importance of these two components in improving the implementation of resources is demonstrated by the fact that, where performed correctly, they allow the regional administration to identify possible future problems and to intervene to correct the problems in due course.

In Sicily, as with the other components, monitoring and evaluation have only recently begun to improve, whereas they have been given a high priority in Basilicata since the beginning of the 1980s. Furthermore, for these activities to work it is essential that there is a high level of coordination and cooperation between a number of different actors. This is further confirmation of the validity of the loop that represents administrative capacity (Figure 3.1). Indeed, in Sicily there seems to have been a disjunction between the gathering of data for monitoring purposes and the management of programmes and projects. In the latest programming period, 2000–2006, monitoring systems satisfied the accountability needs of the system (in particular the need for the Commission to report on the proper use of public funds). However, they did not feed back sufficiently into the management process. In Sicily, 60 per cent of civil servants judged monitoring and evaluation as an 'extra workload, which is time consuming and will add little improvement to programme administration'. This latter opinion was shared by only 25 per cent of respondents in Basilicata. As regards the perception of the political class, 90 per cent of respondents in Sicily answered that the political class perceived monitoring as a mere bureaucratic requirement through which to access EU funding. In Basilicata, on the other hand, 80 per cent answered that the political class perceived monitoring and evaluation as a very useful instrument for implementation (question 6). Undoubtedly the results of the questionnaire confirm that in Sicily, unlike in Basilicata, the practice of monitoring and evaluation still needs to be improved, and to become instrumental in enhancing the implementation of the resources.

5.6.4 *Overall Administrative Capacity*

The above findings confirm the connection between the various components of administrative capacity. A first observation is that poor management leads necessarily to a poor quality of programming. Indeed, a development programme that covers the whole territory needs to include the contributions of each department, assembled by the central management body. The absence of the latter leads to a lack of coordination and effective management in the decision-making and policy implementation system. The ROP, conceived as a knowledge-based programme (Barca, 2001b), refers to a 'knowledge' that is often tacit and distributed among various levels of government (Anselmo and Raimondo, 2000). Strong horizontal cooperation is therefore necessary to establish the knowledge-sharing process and enable the programme to function and reach the stated goals.

Second, monitoring data needs to be collected to provide feedback of necessary information to the MA so that problems can be solved. Third, evaluation reports should be produced to support not only the actual planning process but also the future programming activities.

At this point, a second question arises: why are the activities of management, programming, monitoring and evaluation not performed as efficiently in Sicily as they are in Basilicata? In other words, why does administrative capacity vary at the regional level? In Chapter 6 I test the second part of the central hypothesis and second set of preconditions, which investigates the role of political factors in influencing the features acquired by the key component of administrative capacity.

6

THE SECOND SET OF PRECONDITIONS FOR MULTI-LEVEL GOVERNANCE

6.1 Explaining Administrative Capacity Variation

The previous chapter tested the first set of preconditions for implementation to succeed. It assessed administrative capacity and provided evidence to suggest that the observed variation between regions in the implementation of SFs is positively correlated with the degree of regional administrative capacity. Therefore, it is related to the activities of managing, programming, monitoring and evaluating development programmes.

This chapter continues the analysis by testing the second set of preconditions and answering the second question, which asks what it is that determines the degree of administrative capacity.

The established literature suggests four competing explanations. The first identifies the degree of education and training as the important intervening variable in determining capacity (North, 1992; Berg, 1993): data gathered at the individual level regarding the educational level of administrators show that substantial similarities exist between Sicily and Basilicata in this respect. The second explanation looks at the centralisation of policy by the government, which allegedly impedes the development of capacity at the regional level (Gualini, 2004; Marks *et al.*, 1996b). This explanation cannot be used in the case of southern Italian regions because all were subject to a centralised approach that ended in the same year, 1992. Conversely, this reinforces the hypothesis that the intervening variable accounting for the variation in administrative capacity must be found within the region. The third explanation advocated by the literature focuses on a mafia component (Mauro, 1998).The existence of criminal organisations has been identified in both

Sicily and Basilicata, although there is a more established literature on the Sicilian mafia. However, we do not have any systematic measures of the level of corruption or the penetration of the regional administration by organised crime. Therefore, it is difficult to establish any causal relationship between corruption/organised crime and administrative capacity. I suggest that we should find an alternative explanation that can be quantified and measured in both regions. The fourth explanation considers social capital (Putnam *et al.*, 1993) as a variable accounting for regional capacity variation. The analysis by Putnam *et al.* reveals that, in accordance with their definition of social capital, civic tradition over the period 1860–1920 and civic community in the 1970s appear to be similar in both Sicily and Basilicata (Putnam *et al.*, 1993: 150–1) – ruling out this explanation as well.

Given the lack of a satisfying explanation, the second part of my central hypothesis suggests that the features acquired by the four key components of administrative capacity, as exemplified by Sicily and Basilicata, might be influenced by three political factors, namely political interference, government stability and political accountability

I believe that each of these political factors affects not only administrative capacity in general but also specific key components (cf. Figure 3.2). I therefore want to test the following three corollary relationships, in which:

1   Weak/strong management performance is influenced by a high/low level of political interference.
2   Low/high programming coherence, in terms of strategy continuity and time taken for approval, is attributable to an unstable/stable government subject to frequent/infrequent changes in leadership.
3   The existence and functioning of a monitoring system and the spreading of an evaluation culture within the regional government is related to political accountability.

These relationships are examined in the three main sections of this chapter. It would appear that while a relationship may be identifiable, the political and administrative factors will not be so neatly correlated. Certainly political interference affects mainly the management system, but it also appears to influence programming performance. Similarly, government instability affects programming coherence and approval, but seems also to have some bearing on management performance. Finally, both political interference and government instability characterise a political class that appears not to be accountable.

6.2 Separation of Political and Administrative Powers

6.2.1 Privatisation of Civil Service and the 'Spoils System'

Recognising that a major source of delays and inefficiency was to be found in the working methods and general attitude of the civil service, Italy embarked in 1993 (D.lgs. 29/1993), and more emphatically in 1998 (D.lgs. 80/1998), on a series of reforms with three aims: (1) to de-politicise the civil service; (2) to separate the political sphere from administrative tasks; and (3) to instil new management practices across the Public Administration system (PA).

As mentioned in Chapter 4, the set of policies, which contained an assortment of measures to reach the three goals, was dubbed by both proponents and critics of the reform as the 'privatisation of the civil service'. The D.lgs. 29/1993 *Razionalizzazione dell'organizzazione delle Amministrazioni pubbliche* (Rationalisation of the Organisation of the Public Administrations) introduced into the PA a new merit-based payment system and performance evaluation system whose aim was to improve the efficiency of the PA by linking the duration of the contract to performance indicators.[1] This was a tremendous innovation in the Italian PA, and changed the perception of the civil service. Indeed, previously a civil service job had been considered a 'job for life', whereas following the changes it was no longer a certainty and pay scales were determined by performance indicators.

As with every new process, the change was not immediate. Indeed it took several years, during which various amendments were made to the original D.lgs. 29/1993, which reached its final form in 2001 with D.lgs.165/2001. Among other innovative changes, D.lgs. 29/1993 ratified a clear demarcation of duties and responsibilities between the administrative and the political spheres: government exercises the functions of providing political and administrative direction, by defining objectives and programmes to be implemented, whereas managers are solely responsible for administrative activity, management and the consequent outcomes.

This latter point is made explicit in D.lgs. 165/2001, which achieves the goal of full responsibility for the managerial class in the administration of programmes. Article 14 states that: 'the political class cannot, in any circumstances, revoke, reform, reserve to themselves, move to a higher level, or otherwise adopt provisions or actions which are the competence of the administrator'.

The above laws eliminated any residual form of interference between politics and management by placing the latter exclusively in the hands of the administration. Nevertheless, the bureaucracy did not always fully use its newly acquired powers, because of the distorted effects of the 'spoils system' which was introduced in Italy in 1998 (Cerbo, 2002). The political system (the government) had the power to appoint top-level executives (or general managers), a power intended to create a relationship based on trust between the politician and his top bureaucrats, and to ensure the that the political class was still in a position to maintain control over decisions (Cerbo, 2002). In reality, the political class used its powers to appoint personnel in order to interfere with and control implementation rather than to put capable people in charge of the administration (Checchi and Garibaldi, 2002). Fortunately this was not a general trend, and some regions, such as Basilicata, were able to enjoy the benefit of a separation of powers between managers and politicians, and the advantages for the politician of selecting trusted and capable general managers.

In conclusion, the PA reform initiated in 1993 was the beginning of a series of innovations at both the central and regional levels which aimed at the modernisation of the whole system and improvement of the administrative machinery by giving more space for manoeuvre to the managerial class. Although there were some distorting effects which limited the real separation of powers, this did not halt the progression towards an entirely de-politicised administrative system.

PA reform, which was first implemented at the national level, was not immediately adopted in all regions. One reason for this difference in response may be the desire of the political class to retain power and to limit the responsibilities transferred to the administrative class. This view is supported by the opinions expressed by some of the politicians interviewed in Sicily, who unanimously expressed their unease at witnessing such a restriction of power and responsibility. As revealed in the following sections, an opposite situation emerged in Basilicata, where the political class had always worked in full cooperation with the administrative class, even before the introduction of D.lgs 29/1993 and its successors.

6.2.2 *Sicily Dominated by Disruptive Political Interference*

The investigation into management activities in Sicily presented in section 5.2 revealed that the introduction of novel financial instruments such as the SFs was not accompanied by any radical change in the regional administration structure. Notably, civil servants and managers of the different departments declared during interviews that since the introduction of SFs they had been subject to even greater interference from the political class.

In Sicily, the dominant party (and its internal factions) was able to use the administration to support its clientelistic style of politics by creating a 'political market' based on the exchange of political support for either the procurement of posts within the administration itself, or benefits for clientele and 'friends' (Cassese, 1984). Thus, politicians, in order to increase their influence, typically would either fully infiltrate the administration, down to the lower levels, or bypass it altogether by carrying out directly tasks that should have belonged to the administration (Melis, 1996; Ferrera, 1984). Civil servants were willing to accept politicians' intrusions into the administrative sphere in exchange for privileges and benefits (D'Amico, 1992).

As mentioned earlier, the process of power separation started in Italy in 1993 with D.lgs 29/1993. In reality, it was not until 2000, with LR 10, that a proper separation of powers and responsibilities between the political and administrative spheres was formalised in Sicily, whereas in Basilicata this process had been put in motion much earlier, in 1996. Again, this opposite reaction to implementation at the regional level for such an important decree reveals the extent to which the political class in Sicily tried to retain ultimate power over the whole regional administration for as long as possible.

It should be acknowledged, nevertheless, that before Sicily's implementation of LR 10 there had been previous attempts to organise the two spheres of action; however, these had failed to achieve a clear separation of competences, leaving a lot of room for political intervention. L.R. 6^2 was approved in 1997 specifically to regulate the responsibilities of the regional cabinet in the area of SFs management, by simplifying the approval procedure for tendered proposals. Until then, the procedure had been greatly politicised, as it came under the combined responsibility of the cabinet and the relevant *assessorato*.[3] LR 6/1997 changed the procedure in order to limit political intervention from the centre of the regional government by shifting responsibility for the implementation of measures from the political to the administrative level – the division manager competent in the field of each measure was appointed as responsible for the implementation. However, we should not forget that a strong political influence persisted inasmuch as the *assessore*, being appointed by the president of the region, maintained a significant connection to the main political leader.

Another step forward in this direction was made by LR 10/1999, which gave the division manager responsibility not only for the implementation of the measures but also for their overall management. Nevertheless, the introduction of this limitation did not seem to be very effective. Indeed, when asked to describe the strength of political power in SFs management before the implementation of LR 10/2000, 85 per cent of those interviewed answered that 'it was strong and more influential than the administration'.

Even though there was a move toward a more independent and 'productive' relationship between bureaucrats and politicians, the basis of their relationship was still an exchange of power and prestige for job and career security. The two parties reached a *modus vivendi* based on a policy of reciprocal self-restraint; it is symptomatic of this that overt conflicts between politicians and higher bureaucrats were very rare (Leopoldo, 2000).

Politicians, as mentioned above, also bought the acquiescence of senior bureaucrats by granting additional benefits that could double or triple their income, such as the substantial remunerations deriving from being nominated as a member of the board of public bodies, which imply little additional workload and much more power (Morisi, 1993).

6.2.3 Interaction between Politicians
and Bureaucrats after LR 10/2000

In Sicily the real recognition of the administrative responsibilities was tied to LR 10/2000. It is only with this law that a clear demarcation of spheres of actions was traced, establishing that the technical management and implementation of the Funds was up to the administration, whereas the general strategic guidelines for programming were in the hands of the political leaders. Indeed, 50 per cent of questionnaire respondents felt that only recently had the relationship between the MA and political class become 'collaborative with respect to each other's role', although 30 per cent still believed that there was 'major interference by the political level in the MA's role' (question 1). Furthermore, according to 62 per cent of responses, the separation of powers had made a positive impact on SFs management (question 2). But while 50 per cent of respondents felt that political interference was now quite limited compared with the past, 40 per cent declared instead that there was still political interference in administrative responsibilities (question 5). However, respondents seemed to agree that successful implementation requires balanced collaboration between the two levels, and not the dominance of one over the other: both components have distinct roles and capacities that can produce positive results only when they work together (question 4).

In addition to the questionnaire, I conducted interviews to investigate further whether the political class interfered in the management of SFs and, if so, what was the impact of such interference. The interviews covered the opinions of general managers as well as those of politicians, in two separate focus groups.

The general managers agreed with the statement that less interference from the political side makes management more efficient. Political interference, moreover, serves to disincentivise the general managers, who, in turn, 'abdicate' their powers to the politicians and do not fulfil their own roles.

An opposite point of view emerged from the interview with the political class. The politicians shared the opinion that politicians have to be involved and have the last say in management activities – as well as in the other steps of the implementation process – because they have been empowered through elections to take decisions and make sure that they are executed whereas the administrative class has no such authorisation.

In summary, it can be said that in Sicily friction still exists between the political and administrative levels of management. The relationship has improved over the years, but a balance between administrative and political powers and responsibilities has not yet been reached. This ultimately affects management, which becomes unclear in terms of its role and prerogatives. Furthermore, political interference serves to delegitimise the role of the managerial class.

6.2.4 A More Technocratic Type of Government in Basilicata

The analysis of management features in Basilicata reveals that SFs programmes, and the IMPs previously, succeeded in introducing into the regional administration new ways to employ the instruments for economic development; this led to significant innovation in the management of ordinary development programmes and in the overall regional administration.

The principles underlying SFs management contributed to the initiation of a cultural innovation process. The new model of management was based on horizontal coordination and clear definition of roles, which is possible to achieve if there is agreement between the administrative and the political class with respect to their responsibilities.

The interviews carried out and the documentation examined[4] reveal that the region of Basilicata, albeit with some initial difficulties, has been able to separate the political and the administrative powers.

In order to fully implement the aims of D.lgs. 29/1993, Basilicata initiated, with LR 12/1996, a process of overall reorganisation inspired by the principle of responsibility and the definition of demarcation lines between the two roles in management. Indeed, Resolution 11 of the Regional Cabinet, dated 13 January 1998, differentiated the responsibilities of the political sphere from those of the administrative. Furthermore, an additional decision, 600/2002, set criteria and parameters for evaluating the general performance of administrators.

According to this scenario, the technicians in charge of managing the programmes were given more room to experiment with technical solutions for overcoming daily problems, free from political interference. Moreover, the role and power of the political class was restricted to political direction and excluded technical intrusion. This model of governing the regional administration delivered good results not only with regard to the implementation of the SFs, but also with regard to public policy delivery in general (Ecosfera *et al.*, 1999: 80).

6.2.5 *Interaction between Politicians and Bureaucrats after LR 12/1996*

The picture that emerges in Basilicata is opposite to the one we observe in Sicily. Indeed, in Basilicata, the regional government had always recognised administrative responsibilities and the technical benefits in terms of efficiency and effectiveness of public action that could develop from a proactive relationship between the administrative and political spheres. Indeed, 60 per cent of respondents felt that even before LR 12/1996, which formally separated the administrative and political spheres of action, the weight of political power in SFs management was in equilibrium with the administrative power (question 3). Following LR 12/1996, there was a further improvement in the collaborative relationship between the two bodies, as declared by 95 per cent of the respondents (question 1). In addition, three-quarters of the sample declared that the separation of powers had a positive impact on SFs management (question 2). Similarly to the respondents in Sicily, however, they still felt overall that a successful implementation requires a balanced collaboration between the two levels (question 4). In contrast to Sicily, this balanced collaboration has always dominated the Basilicata government and can be identified as the determinant variable for the successful management of SFs. Indeed, 60 per cent of the sample answered that there was no political interference, while 40 per cent stated that political interference was very limited (question 5).

6.3 Government Stability (1988–2006)

6.3.1 *A History of Government Instability in Italy*

The literature on government instability generally treats this factor as economically destructive (Alesina *et al.*, 1996; Fosu, 1992) and a hindrance to growth (Londregan and Poole, 1990; Barro 1991, 1996; Easterly and Levine, 1997). It is hypothesised that government instability destabilises economic rules on resource allocation, governing effort and expected outputs. Such destabilisation is likely to reduce efficiency of the production process and, hence, restrict economic growth (Fosu, 1992). Kuznets (1966: 451), for example, writes: 'Clearly, political stability is necessary if members of the economic society are to plan ahead and be assured of a relatively stable relation between their contribution to economic activity and their rewards.'

In the European context Italy has experienced one of the highest levels of government instability. In the past, the prime minister was appointed through a competitive multi-party electoral system.[5] Despite recent changes (cf. section 4.2.2),[6] political deadlock and government instability have defined Italian politics over the past fifty years. Between the first election in 1946 and the most recent in 2006, there have been 58 governments appointed in Italy. This means that on average there has been one government per year, and only one has lasted for the full five-year term.[7] Similarly, regional governments have also experienced high instability. Indeed, as mentioned in Chapter 4, the Regional Assembly (in Sicily) and Regional Councils (in other regions) elected the President until 2001, when the law, L.cost. 2, was changed. Now the Regional President is elected by direct universal suffrage along with the Regional Councils (and Regional Assembly in the case of Sicily). This change in the election procedure seems to have had a positive effect on government stability.

In fact, before L.cost. 2/2001 the President could be removed by a majority vote of no confidence (*mozione di sfiducia*) from the Regional Council (and Regional Assembly in the case of Sicily). If this happened, the Council (or Assembly) would have to appoint a new President. The motion of no confidence was used frequently until the new law introduced the direct election of the President. It would be interesting to investigate the reasons for government instability, but my aim here is to investigate the effect of such instability on administrative capacity in the region, especially on the programming functions. Besides the impact on economic growth, which is pointed out by the existing literature, are there other consequences of instability? In this section, I want to test the hypothesis that government instability is accountable for poor programming performance, in terms of weak development of programme design and delays in programme approval, leading ultimately to low expenditure of resources. Furthermore, I will try to highlight the destabilising effect government instability also has on management activities.

6.3.2 Sicily: 14 Governments in 20 Years (1986–2006)

Sicily has a long history of government instability, having experienced the highest level of all Italian regions. Indeed, the data on regional governments show a high level of instability since the creation of the region in 1947 – i.e. 55 governments in 54 years. Table 6.1 shows the changes in government during the period of my analysis, 1988–2004, which covers the entire 10th, 11th, 12th and 13th legislatures. Indeed, over these 20 years, there was an

Table 6.1 Legislatures and governments in Sicily 1986–2006

Government	Period	President
X Legislature (31 July 1986 to 10 August 1991)		
41°	31 July 1986 to 6 August 1987	R. Nicolosi (DC)
42°	6 August 1987 to 12 January 1988	R. Nicolosi (DC)
43°	12 January 1988 to 14 December 1989	R. Nicolosi (DC)
44°	14 December 1989 to 10 August 1991	R. Nicolosi (DC)
XI Legislature (12 August 1991 to 16 July 1996)		
45°	12 August 1991 to 16 July 1992	V. Leanza (DC)
46°	16 July 1992 to 26 April 1993	G. Campione (DC)
47°	26 April 1993 to 21 December 1993	G. Campione (DC)
48°	21 December 1993 to 16 April 1995	F. Martino (PLI)
49°	16 April 1995 to 16 July 1996	M. Graziano (DC)
XII Legislature (18 July 1996 to 11 July 2001)		
50°	18 July 1996 to 29 January 1998	G.Provenzano (FI)
51°	29 January 1998 to 21 November 1998	G. Drago (CCD)
52°	21 November 1998 to 9 November 1999	A. Capodicasa (DS)
53°	9 November 1999 to 26 July 2000	A. Capodicsa (DS)
54°	26 July 2000 to 11 July 2001	Temporary Commissioner
XIII Legislature (11 July 2001 to 27 April 2006)		
55°	11 July 2001 to 27 April 2006	S. Cuffaro (UDCC)

Source: Author's elaboration on regional government data, Sicily

average of 1.5 governments per year, rather than having governments lasting for the five-year term. As the table shows, with the beginning of the 13th legislation, which corresponded with the new L.cost. 2/2001, governments became more stable.

I will argue that this constant level of instability partly accounts for the lack of coherence in the development policies put into place by each government. This hypothesis is supported by other authors, such as Piattoni and Smyrl (2002), who carried out a comparative study of two northern regions, Tuscany and Liguria, along with two southern regions, Puglia and Abruzzo. Their results showed that some regions were able to use the funds efficiently, while others failed. Piattoni and Smyrl argue that 'the explanation for this differential policy efficiency lies in the different capacity of the regional political class to allocate the cost and benefits of economic development, in turn explained by its stability and commitment' (2002: 136).

In Chapter 5, I measured programming capacity with regard to two indicators, programme design and rate of programme approval, and found that both indicators were weak in Sicily. The analysis of documents, evidence drawn from the questionnaires and interviews, and my own personal observations combine to suggest that the significant instability of the Sicilian government was primarily responsible for (1) the absence of a coherent policy strategy for the creation of endogenous development and the investment of resources in long-term projects; and (2) accumulating long delays in the approval of programmes due to the incoherence and constant revisions of the programmes.[8]

These findings are confirmed by the responses given to the questionnaires. When asked about the effect of government instability on SFs, the interviewees gave a very clear answer: 100 per cent agreed that the effects are generally negative (question 1). In particular, 54 per cent held the opinion that government instability influences 'the continuity of the programme', and 46 per cent believed that it influences 'the strategic coherence of the programme' (question 1). As far as programme approval is concerned, the majority (90 per cent) believed that the delays were due more to government instability than to any administrative deadlock (question 2). Lastly, most agreed that since 2001 the government had been more stable and that remarkable improvements in the coherence and continuity of the programming activities had been made (question 2).

Further interviews with civil servants revealed that after 2001 there was a change in the approach of the political class towards programming economic interventions and resources expenditure, which became oriented towards the long term rather than a short-term horizon of one year, as had been the case previously. Many speculated that the ability to engage in long-term planning was linked to the fact that the political class knew direct election of the regional president guaranteed a more stable government and that they would therefore be held accountable for the results of the development programmes after five years. There is, I believe, a strong relationship between government instability and political interference. Indeed, if a politician knows that he has only a short period to 'exploit' his power, then it is very likely that he will use his time in power to gain maximum personal rewards. The only way for him to do this is by interfering in administrative activities and imposing his own will on the administration. The features discovered so far in Sicily, where both political interference and instability are present, confirm this hypothesis. A further confirmation comes from Basilicata, where I have not discovered strong political interference in administrative matters, and where, as shown in the next section, there has been no political instability.

6.3.3 *Basilicata: a Government* per legislature

The situation in Basilicata was very different from that of Sicily: each government lasted for the whole five-year period of the legislature. This was the case not only between 1970 and 1985, but also during the period of my analysis (Table 6.2). This stability guaranteed that the programme was approved on time and that the strategy planned at the beginning of the legislature remained coherent for the entire period. Government stability enabled the political class to develop a system of governance for the SFs based on the coherence between the development plan, territorial needs and the concrete implementation of the strategy, which has been continually reinforced over the years.

Further endorsement of the importance of government stability to successful implementation of the SFs can be drawn from the answers to the questionnaire. The same questionnaire used in Sicily was circulated among bureaucrats and politicians in Basilicata. In response to the question about the effects of political instability on SFs programming, 100 per cent of the Basilicata respondents believed that high instability produces negative effects on the programming actions (question 1). Furthermore, half of those interviewed considered government stability to be a determining factor for the coherence of the programme; the other half considered it was so for the continuity of the programme (question 2). Finally, none answered the last two questions regarding approval delays and change in governments because the problem had never arisen in Basilicata

A further important element that emerged during my research is that during the changes of government in Basilicata the politicians tried to maintain as much continuity as possible in the roles covered by the administrative

Table 6.2 Legislatures and governments in Basilicata 1985–2006

Government	Period	President
IV Legislature (20 June 1985 to 10 July 1990)		
5°	20 June 1985 to 10 July 1990	G. Michetti (DC)
V Legislature (11 July 1990 to 15 June 1995)		
6°	11 July 1990 to 15 June 1995	A. Boccia (DC)
VI Legislature (16 June 1995 to 16 April 2000)		
7°	16 June 1995 to 16 April 2000	R. Di Nardo (PPI)
VII Legislature (17 April 2000 to 17 April 2005)		
8°	17 April 2000 to 17 April 2005	F. Bubbico (DS)

Source: Author's elaboration of regional government data, Basilicata

staff. Therefore, even if there was a reshuffle of general managers, or a new manager was appointed, there was always an attempt to keep key people in their positions to ensure programme coherence and continuity.

6.4 Political Accountability

6.4.1 *The Cause and the Impact of Low Political Accountability*
Schmitter (2004: 47) described political accountability in the following terms:

> Generically speaking, political accountability is a relationship between two sets of persons or (more often) organisations in which the former agree to keep the latter informed, to offer them explanations for decisions made, and to submit to any predetermined sanctions that they may impose. The latter, meanwhile, are subject to the command of the former, must provide required information, explain obedience or disobedience to the commands thereof, and accept the consequences for things done or left undone. Accountability, in short, implies an exchange of responsibilities and potential sanctions between rulers and citizens, made all the more complicated by the fact that a varied and competitive set of representatives typically interposes between the two. Needless to say, there are many caveats, loose linkages, and role reversals in this relationship, so that its product is almost always contested. Information can be selective and skewed; explanations can be deflected to other actors; sanctions are rarely applied and can be simply ignored.

Moreover, in terms of political accountability, each citizen has the same rights and obligations, that is, to be informed (with limited exceptions) about official actions, to hear justifications for them, to judge how well or poorly they are carried out, and to act accordingly – electorally or otherwise. It has been shown that the growth and welfare of citizens is enhanced by governments that function well; that is, governments that abide by the rule of law, and whose administrative machinery delivers goods and services in an efficient manner (Knack and Keefer, 1995; Mauro, 1995; Easterly and Levine, 1997).

An extensive literature on the sources of political accountability describes the machinery of government as a game between a principal – the public – and an agent – the politician or policy-maker – in which the former delegates to the latter a given set of instruments with which to carry out certain goals. In the game, the interests of the parties may be at odds: in the case of self-interested politicians, the delegation of decision-making and policy implementation responsibilities automatically opens up the possibility of significant inefficiencies. As shown in seminal articles by Barro (1973) and Ferejohn (1986), the solution to this delegation problem, where politicians may be tempted to exploit the lack of information that citizens have about policies and their consequences to pursue their own agenda, lies in the public establishing a control mechanism, such as regular elections, to discipline the policy-maker. If electors vote retrospectively – that is, if they look back to the results achieved by the incumbents before casting their vote – elections should make policy-makers accountable to the public.

If we apply the above argument to the case of the Italian regions, then we can suggest that the regional political class lacked an important element of accountability because, as previously discussed, until 2001 the president of the region was elected by the council and not by the public. In general, this was a further motive for the political leader to disregard accountability to the citizens. To this purpose, the national constitutional reform that introduced the direct election of regional presidents aimed to strengthen the accountability of political leaders towards the electorate.

A second element of the argument of Barro and Ferejohn concerns the lack of information available to the citizens. As regards this, information and publicity are at the heart of SFs procedures because the final beneficiaries of their implementation are the citizens. Indeed, one of the main principles of SFs implementation is monitoring and evaluation practices, where the results are provided to the public, the socio-economic actors, the national government, the EU Commission and other third parties involved in programme implementation or simply interested in the policy process. Therefore, a political class which wants to decrease the amount of information available on the activities of the Funds and the utilisation of their budgetary resources will be reluctant to submit to any form of monitoring and evaluation procedure: the higher the willingness to mismanage the resources, the lower the inclination towards a functional monitoring and evaluation system.

I would argue that the lack of accountability is strongly related to government instability. This assumption is supported by other studies that have found stable political regimes to have some form of accountability to their constituencies (Adserà *et al.*, 2003; Schmitter, 2004). According to my hypothesis I expect to find that in Sicily, where there is strong government instability and persistent political interference, the degree of accountability will be low. On the other hand, I expect to find the opposite in Basilicata.

It should be mentioned that the study of political accountability and its outcomes is mainly based on my own personal observations and on the results produced by the questionnaires and interviews.[9] In my case study, I concentrate on two features: (1) how the political class is perceived by civil servants; and (2) whether the political class has obstructed or manipulated the activities of monitoring and evaluation procedures regarding the SFs. My aim is to determine whether the political class is considered accountable and whether there is any link between the latter and the performance of the monitoring and evaluation activities.

6.4.2 Accountability and the Quality of Monitoring Procedures in Sicily

The bulk of the literature on Sicily during the last forty years agrees that the political class is not accountable (Boissevain, 1966; Giner, 1982; Viesti, 2003; Finocchiaro Castro and Rizzo, 2006). According to some authors, the priority of the regional political class in Sicily is to reinforce itself, and the easiest way seems to be to build strong preferential linkages both with the administrative class and with the local government level (Piattoni, 1997). The latter, in exchange for guaranteeing the support required, demands increasing resources for strengthening clientelistic networks.[10] Therefore, in order to 'buy' consensus from local political leaders, regional political leaders use additional funding, and there is no economic development logic behind this allocation of resources (Trigilia, 1992). The distorted mechanism of private bargaining between the regional and the local political class is increased by the local politicians' desire to preserve their unequal power position *vis-à-vis* the citizens (Chubb, 1982). Eventually, the clientelistic network substitutes the citizens as the relevant point of reference for regional politicians.

My study supports this proposition, and adds two further elements which lead to low accountability: political instability and the electoral system. Regarding the first factor, as examined in section 6.3.2, Sicily has experienced a high rate of changes in government – i.e. a new government almost every year. Therefore, government officials may make decisions that are not purely development-oriented because their policy horizons are limited to their time in office. The shorter the timescale, the more likely it is that they will take actions that do not provide an overall regional gain. The goal, instead, is short-term political gain.

Until 2001, the second factor, the electoral system, provided for the president of the regional government to be elected by the Council and not by the citizens, thereby undermining the basic control system that would guarantee accountability. With the new policy of direct election of the president, it is possible to foresee a growing accountability of the president *vis-à-vis* the voters.

Responses to the questionnaire confirmed this hypothesis. When asked their opinion on the accountability of the political class, 42 per cent of interviewees answered that they considered the political class to be partially accountable (question 1); 40 per cent said that there was no procedure in place to ensure accountability (question 1), and an impressive 85 per cent of those interviewed declared that the poor accountability of the political class was due to high government instability (question 2). On the other hand, the hypothesis that the political class obstructed the practice of monitoring and evaluation was not validated by the results. Indeed, there was not enough evidence to support such a hypothesis. When asked about a clear connection between the political will and the performance/improvement of monitoring and evaluation activities, the answers clearly denied a link between these two aspects (question 3). Furthermore, in answer to the question of whether the political class supported or obstructed the monitoring and evaluation of SFs, 85 per cent declared that the political class was indifferent to and distant from these activities (question 4). In addition, almost all of those interviewed defined the political class as 'far too interested in their own activities to consider monitoring and evaluation as an instrument of improving management or as manipulative tools' (recorded interview). One respondent added: 'our political class is far too negligent to understand how powerful these instruments could be!' (recorded interview).

Based on the interviews, questionnaire responses, and my personal observation, I can conclude that a political class which is negligent of the importance of monitoring and evaluation activities can be held responsible for the lack of performance of these two instruments in a regional setting where they are crucial for the good management of the SFs.

6.4.3 *Is the Political Class Accountable in Basilicata?*

Analysis of the political model in Basilicata presents a significantly different picture to that of Sicily. Two main features have so far characterised the Basilicata regional government: (1) a balanced relationship between the political and the administrative classes; and (2) strong government stability. Consequently, if my hypothesis and the model of analysis are correct, I would expect to find that the political class is more accountable in Basilicata than it is in Sicily.

The main sources of information on the accountability of the political class in Basilicata are, first, the field research carried out by Leonardi, Putnam and Nanetti in 1976, 1981 and 1983 for the completion of the book *Il Caso Basilicata* (1987); and, second, the field research I carried out, using interviews and questionnaires, in June 2006.

Leonardi interviewed 35 people who had regular contact with the political class (mayors, NGO representatives, representatives of economic associations), and 58 per cent defined it as honest (Leonardi *et al.*, 1987: 30). The general opinion that emerged from the interviews was that people were trustful of the political class (Leonardi *et al.*, 1987: 95-116). Clearly, this analysis of the first 15 years of the regional government produced a positive picture of Basilicata's political class.

In a similar way, I interviewed a sample of civil servants and politicians about political accountability. Here, 65 per cent of the sample felt that the political class was accountable, compared with a smaller percentage (42) in Sicily (question 1). In the same vein, 50 per cent declared that there were procedures in place to ensure accountability (question 1), and an impressive 90 per cent declared that the accountability of the political class was related to government stability (question 2). During an interview, the former general manager of the MA said:

> Political stability forces the political class to be accountable because they know they will be seen as responsible for the results of their actions and their names will be correlated to any success or failure. On the other hand if a politician knows he will soon be gone, then he will act irrespective of the consequences.

Clearly, the responses confirm the validity of the findings of Leonardi *et al.* (1987) and suggest that we can define the political class in Basilicata as accountable.

Analysis of the second set of questions, which focused on understanding whether the political class had obstructed or encouraged monitoring and evaluation activities, substantiates the belief that the political class in Basilicata was supportive of those activities. When asked whether there was a connection between the political will and the performance/improvement of monitoring and evaluation activities, 75 per cent of those interviewed identified a partial connection (question 3). Furthermore, in answer to the question of whether the political class supported or obstructed any form of monitoring and evaluation of SFs, 85 per cent declared that the political class had supported those activities (question 4). At the same time, 90 per cent said that the political class had contributed to the spread of a culture of evaluation within the regional organisation (question 5). In contrast to the image of political indifference and disregard towards monitoring and evaluation that emerged in Sicily, it appears that in Basilicata the political class considered these activities to be useful instruments in improving its own political strategies (question 6).

6.5 The Relationship between Administrative
Capacity and Political Factors

Following my second question – why does administrative capacity vary at the regional level? – the primary and secondary sources, and, most significantly, the interviews with policy-makers both in the administrative and political arenas, have supported the second part of my central hypothesis, which is that three main political factors – i.e. political interference, government stability and political accountability – influence the features acquired by the four key components of administrative capacity.

The findings that emerge from my study can be summarised under two main headings.

6.5.1 Correlations Between Political
Factors and Administrative Components

*Deficiency in Management Correlates
with Strong Political Interference*

A weak management system can be attributed not only to the skills and training of the administrative class, as the existing literature suggests, but also to the existing institutional structure and, more importantly, to the practice of power-sharing between the political and the administrative layers. The analysis demonstrates that this is the case for Sicily, where a poor management system, measured in terms of the lack of clarity of role among personnel and the lack of coordinated activities within each *assessorato,* can be traced back to the blurring between administrative and political responsibilities.

Indeed, the results of the empirical investigation undoubtedly support my first hypothesised relationship, which was that between management of SFs and political interference. Indeed, to improve the management of SFs it was necessary to have better coordination among the different departments of the regional administration and a greater clarity of roles. Such conditions are strongly determined by the separation of powers and responsibilities between the political and the administrative classes. This scenario is exemplified in Basilicata. Here, the data revealed that successful implementation of the SFs depended on the existence of a strong centre of coordination for the formulation of strategy and management of the Funds. These conditions were supported by a healthy alliance between the political and administrative spheres in Basilicata. In fact, the creation of the Cabin of Direction, composed of a 'Mixed Committee' representing the political level and the Interdepartmental Technical Commission, which incorporates the technical staff, was the key factor in achieving successful management because it created an arena for discussion and exchange between the political and technical levels of management. The two levels have worked together with a full recognition of their respective roles, powers and responsibilities, and this has led to a constructive relationship. The absence of interference in each other's spheres has allowed the administration to consolidate its role as the ultimate 'implementor' of the policy. The reason for this outcome can be clearly traced back to the support provided by the political class, which saw in the EU Funds an opportunity to restructure the regional economy and innovation with regional programme.

Poor Programming Performance Correlates with Government Instability

The empirical research brought to light substantial evidence to support the suggestion that government stability has an important bearing on programming performance. Regional governments that change constantly have more difficulty in maintaining a strong commitment to multi-annual programmes. In addition, unstable governments are more likely to witness changes not only in the political class but also in the civil servants responsible for the implementation of development programmes.

Bureaucrats facing continual change in political leadership have no incentive to make decisions in terms of programming which might then be reversed by an incoming wave of new politicians. In such a situation the safest way to avoid a potential conflict with the political class is not to decide, and to postpone decisions indefinitely (Cassese, 1984). Such behaviour is likely to cause significant discontinuity and delay in the overall administration of programmes. A multi-annual programme takes years to deliver results, while a cabinet that lasts for less than a year can only deal with short-term matters.

In the case of Sicily, the frequent changes of government had repercussions on the programming activities in terms of the two indicators I investigated: programme design and programme approval. Indeed, programme design was robbed of coherence and continuity. A high degree of political instability allowed each government to act regardless of any long-term plan, because it 'knew', according to past experience, that it would last no longer than a year. Since 2001, with the change in the electoral system, Sicily has witnessed its first government to remain in power for the entire five years of the legislature. This has been identified as one of the reasons for the improvements recently registered in programming performance.

The case of Basilicata is unlike the situations described above. Here, the regional governments have always been stable, and this has guaranteed the ability to implement long-term plans, to ensure coherence and continuity in the planning strategy, and to avoid delays in programme implementation.

Monitoring and Evaluation Practices are Affected by Political Accountability

The evidence for this correlation is based mainly on the results of the data collected through questionnaires and interviews, and on my personal observations. In Sicily an overall agreement on the existence of weak political accountability has emerged. As far as the eventual correlation between the latter and the under-utilised practice of monitoring and evaluation is concerned, the link seems to exist. However, in Sicily this link is not as strong as the one that emerged in Basilicata.

Indeed, in Sicily it seems that the political class has not been interested in supporting monitoring or evaluation activities. It cannot be said that the political class has actually obstructed those activities; however, it can be speculated that the indifference shown by the political class might have contributed to the slow spread of an evaluation culture within the regional administration.

Conversely, it is apparent that in Basilicata the political class is perceived as accountable, and that there is a correlation between the improved monitoring and evaluation activities and the supportive actions taken by the politicians. Such a result confirms the hypothesis that if the political class is accountable it will be supportive of forms of monitoring or evaluation. On the other hand, if the political class acts in a clientelistic fashion, then it will have no interest in publicising its activities.

6.5.2 *Correlations Between the Three Political Factors*

Investigating the correlation between the political factors and the administrative key components has also revealed that not only does a correlation exist between these two areas, but also that a political model can be anticipated by looking at the features acquired by the three political dimensions.

Indeed, in Sicily the high degree of government instability appears to have been responsible for the following features: (1) the strong intervention of the political class in the administrative arena; and (2) the lack of accountability of the political class. An opposite situation emerges in Basilicata. Here government stability seems to foster (1) mutual respect for respective roles within the political and administrative arenas; and (2) a more accountable political class (cf. Figure 3.2).

PART III

THE EFFECT OF MULTI-LEVEL GOVERNANCE IN AN OLD AND IN A NEW MEMBER STATE

7

EVIDENCE FROM STRUCTURAL FUNDS IMPLEMENTATION IN TWO SPANISH REGIONS

FABIOLA MOTA AND ANDREA NOFERINI[1]

7.1 Administrative and Political Systems in Spain: EU Membership and Adoption of European Regional Policy

Across Europe, empirical evidence for the SFs expenditure rate in Objective 1 regions shows that, along with Ireland and Portugal, Spain's overall performance has been extremely positive during all periods. Indeed, Spain's CSFs rates of absorption were 87 per cent and 82 per cent respectively in 1989–1993 and 1994–1999, and reached 98 per cent in the 2000–2006 period (Eurostat, 2008). However, when considering individual Spanish Objective 1 regions, we observe that not all regions have followed the same general trends, with some regions showing below average expenditure rates (see Table 2.3, Chapter 2). Andalusia and Galicia – the two most recipient regions – present different performances, Galicia's rate of absorption being higher than Andalusia's for all the periods considered here. Why then do regions show different absorption capacity in the implementation of SFs? And what are the determinants of these differences?

By comparing two Spanish Objective 1 regions, this chapter tests the relevance of administrative capacity and political factors in explaining the observed variations. The following sections are the result of an in-depth case-study of the two regions. Data collection was based upon document analysis (official reports published by the EC and other EU institutions as well as documents by Spanish ministers, regional departments and external evaluators) and semi-structured interviews with regional public officials. The selection of these regions was made to ensure that two contrasting performances were represented. Also, Andalusia and Galicia share the same institutional conditions and arrangements within the Spanish constitution. Since the beginning of the decentralisation process they acceded to regional self-government through the special constitutional *via* and they are both considered *historical* regions within the multinational Spanish state.

7.1.1 *The Autonomic State within Spain's Political System*

Spain's current political, institutional and administrative arrangements are the consequence of the interplay between three developments which began in the late 1970s and came to fruition during the 1980s and 1990s. These are the transition to democracy which was initiated with the promulgation of the 1978 political constitution; the consequent process of political and administrative decentralisation that gave birth to the regional system; and, finally, becoming a member of the EU in 1986.

At the end of the Franco regime, the 1978 Spanish Constitution had to cope with many simultaneous demands. On the one hand, the central administrative apparatus was asked to embrace modernisation and be more effective and efficient. On the other, the Spanish multinational question required political accommodation. With the creation of the so-called 'Autonomic State' (*Estado autonómico*), the new constitution provided a process of extensive decentralisation of powers and the constitutional recognition of some specific features of some regions. This latter aspect meant that four of the 17 regions (Catalonia, the Basque Country, Andalusia and Galicia) attained, from the beginning, the maximum power competences available at that time, and the capacity to hold regional elections separately from the electoral schedule imposed on the remaining regions. Furthermore, by 1983, following the adoption of all the autonomy statutes, two groups of *Comunidades Autònomas* (CA – Autonomous Communities) had emerged. According to their level of authority and autonomy from the central state, seven were in the higher tier (the four quoted above plus Navarre, the Valencian Community and the Canary Islands) and the remaining ten in the lower tier. Nevertheless, despite the asymmetry of the system, all regions possessed similar institutions and enjoyed a single constitutional status (Aja, 2001: 234). As a result, although it is not a fully federal arrangement, Spain is today one of the most (unitary) decentralised countries in Europe.

However, given the open-ended nature of the Spanish Constitution (Section VIII), the political institutional setting is in 'permanent movement' between centralised and decentralised styles of governance (Dudek, 2005). In recent years, moreover, intergovernmental relations have been affected by the political weight that some nationalist regional parties have acquired within the national arena.[2] Nevertheless, relations among the CAs, by means of either formal agreements or other horizontal cooperation instruments, are still relatively underdeveloped. As Aja (2001: 237) has pointed out:

> Although region–state relations are far more intensive, the entire field of intergovernmental relations (especially sectoral conferences) is regulated on a rather shaky basis, because of the absence of an explicit constitutional foundation and the predominance of bilateral relations between the different governments.

From a functional perspective, it is possible to separate national and regional competences into *exclusive*, *concurrent* and *shared* competences. Exclusive competences are those that may be exclusive for the state or may be exclusive for regions. Foreign affairs, defence, coordination of economic activity and defence of competition are some examples of exclusive competences that belong to the central state. Conversely, agriculture, transport, urban planning, social services and tourism all fall within the exclusive remit of regional powers.

Concurrent competences occur when the central state promulgates the basic legislation (*legislación basica*), but regions are able to supplement this basic legislation with developmental legislation (*legislación de desarollo*).[3]

With shared competences legislative functions are retained by the central state but the implementation of legislation is the responsibility of the CA. Many EU-related issues are, for example, introduced in regional context via shared competences. Initially, EU policies belonged to the domain of foreign policies. In this sense, the central state was responsible for them. Given that Community politics were intended to belong to foreign affairs, regions remained therefore excluded. Later on, the Spanish Constitutional Court reversed this interpretation by recognising European Law as not pertaining to any concrete matter and allowing regions' participation.

7.1.2 *The Administrative System in Spain*

Starting in the mid 1970s, Spain's transition to democracy coincided with the beginning of the process of political and administrative decentralisation.[4] All regions have now established parliamentary systems in which regional governments are politically accountable to regional parliaments and have adopted proportional representation. Over three decades, regions have come to manage more than 35 per cent of public expenditure; they employ more than one million civil servants (50.4 per cent of the total public servants in Spain compared to 21.7 per cent of the central state government employees);[5] and they implement and monitor more than 3,000 laws and regulations (Ramió and Salvador, 2002). Regarding the delivery of public goods and services – health care, active labour market policies or education – all regions in Spain have gained autonomy as the regional share in total public spending rose from 14 per cent in 1985 to 35 per cent in 2005 (Gil-Ruiz and Iglesias, 2007). Finally, as a consequence of the process of adaptation and Europeanisation of regional policy-making, participation of regional actors in the design of regional strategy has progressively increased.

Regarding organisational structure, all CAs have demonstrated a noticeable pattern of institutional isomorphism in which the formation of regional administrations has followed the structures of central administration. In this sense, for some critics, regional bodies did not fully exploit the potential for institutional creativity that was available to them at the beginning of the reform. Political uncertainty stemming from the process of democratic transition and the urgent need not to lose European structural aid are usually considered the two main reasons for this adoption of similar organisational structures at the regional level.

Broadly speaking, the current Spanish organisational structure of regional administrative bodies relies on the presence of a (limited) number of *Consejerias* (a form of regional ministry), each one usually dedicated to a specific area (or a group of strictly interlinked areas). Each regional department (*Consejeria*) usually contains a general secretariat (*Secretaria General*), charged with the common functions across the department (human resources, external representation, financial accountability), and a variable number of general directorates (*Direcciones Generales*). It is relevant to observe that the responsibility for both the general secretariat and the general directorates is assigned by criteria of political accountability with respect to the regional government.[6]

7.1.3 *The Institutional Framework for Cohesion Policy in Spain*

Despite its obvious traditional and historical regional disparities, Spain did not pay serious attention to regional policy until the second half of the 1980s.[7] With accession to the EU in 1986 Spain took its first steps to intervene in regional policy. At the same time, at the European level, the 1988 reform of Structural Funds created a completely new approach, based on pluri-annual integrated programmes that were no longer centred exclusively on the national level (Leonardi, 2005). Spain is the country which has benefited the most from Structural and Cohesion funds in absolute terms, although Ireland, Greece and Portugal have benefited more in per capita terms. EU funds represented 0.82 per cent of Spain's annual GDP between 1986 and 2006, peaking at over 1 per cent in 2001–2003. In other words, since 1986 every Spanish citizen has received around 130 euros a year from Brussels (Torreblanca, 2005). In total, EU structural aid for regional convergence in the 1989–2006 period amounted to about 97 billion euros (at 1999 prices).[8]

Since 1989, one of the ten Spanish Objective 1 regions, i.e. Cantabria, has lost this status, and five more – Asturias, Castile and Leon, Valencian Community, Canary Islands and Murcia – plus the autonomous cities of Ceuta and Melilla, are set to lose theirs in 2007–2013, in some cases due to actual rising GDP per capita levels (phasing-in) and in others due to statistical effects (phasing-out) (see Table 7.1). Unlike some parts of Europe, there is no sharp north–south divide in the Spanish regional distribution of wealth. However, regions differ according to many variables and economic convergence has not occurred at the same pace everywhere. Andalusia in the south and Galicia in the north-west, for example, have remained relatively poor areas after successive periods of European financial aid.

From the institutional perspective, within the Spanish Objective 1 CSF, all main activities related to the management, implementation, and monitoring of SFs are coordinated by the Ministry of Economy.[9] Within the latter, the Directorate General for Community Funds and Regional Finance (*Dirección General de Fondos Comunitarios y Financiacion Territorial, DGFC*) is designed as the Managing Authority (MA). For the drafting of the ROPs, the DGFC has regular contact with the regional departments of economy which manage the process at the regional level. The DGFC works together with other SFs administration units in the Spanish government, while also working on a basis of cooperation and shared responsibility with the authorities in the regions.

Historically, the involvement of the regions in the design and implementation of ROPs has developed in line with successive versions of SFs, covering the financial periods 1989–1993, 1994–1999, 2000–2006 and 2007–2013. The first plan, drafted solely by the central government in Madrid, was judged a complete failure due to its excessive politicisation and the lack of any implementation strategy (Closa and Heywood, 2004). The succeeding Regional Development Plans (RDPs), in contrast, paved the way for wider participation by the regions, whose involvement was rather

Table 7.1 Structural Funds breakdown for CCAA 1986–2005

Region*	Structural Funds 1986–2006		EU27 GDP *per capita*		
	Million euros	%	1995	2000	2005
Andalusia	25,568.8	23.3	68.6	71.9	80.4
Aragon	3,280.9	3	99	102	109.5
Asturias	4,711.4	4.3	81	81.5	90.2
Balearics	854.1	0.8	111.4	120.2	113.7
Basque Country	2,894.2	2.6	109.6	119.6	130.8
Canarias	6,110.7	5.6	88.7	92.5	93.7
Cantabria	1,398.9	1.3	85.5	91.2	100.9
Castile-and-Leon	11,096.7	10.1	88.3	88.3	97
Castile-La Mancha	7,935.4	7.2	75.4	76.7	81.8
Catalonia	7,313.3	6.7	111.6	118.9	122.1
Extremadura	6,074.6	5.5	58.9	62.1	69.7
Galicia	12,894.8	11.7	75	75.8	84.2
La Rioja	328.7	0.3	105.2	111.1	110
Madrid	4,254.4	3.9	120.1	132.7	133.9
Murcia	3,567.9	3.2	76	81.9	87.7
Navarra	695.5	0.6	115.7	124.2	129.2
Valencian Community	10,360.8	9.4	87.5	94.1	94.8
Spain	109,931.5	100	91.9	97.6	103
EU27			100	100	100
Objective 1 regions			77.2	80.4	86.7

Source: J. F. Armesto (2008)
* Objective 1 regions in bold

more effective in the 1993 and 1999 planning periods. It was some years before the regions could actively participate in framing the regional strategy. In some cases, the central administration deliberately aimed to limit the autonomy of the regions.[10] In other cases, the regions were not all equally successful in demanding and promoting greater participation.

Many analysts agree that the EU's regional policy had a dual impact in Spain. First, it was an essential factor for the development of a regional policy. Prior to accession, Spanish regional policy was indeed limited to a series of *ad hoc* initiatives, guided by political priority. Second, as was the case with central administration, EU membership has also led to changes in the organisational structure of Spanish regions. Nowadays, almost all CAs have adopted the so-called 'threefold' organisational model, which involves (1) each department having a focus on EU affairs; (2) a body dedicated to

Table 7.2 The institutional framework of European Structural Aid in Spain

Position	*Institution*	*Functions*
Managing Authority and Payment Authority	• General Directorate for Community Funds and Territorial Finance (Dirección General de Fondos Comunitario y Financiación Territorial, DGFC) • UAFSE (Ministry of Labour) • Ministry of Agriculture and Fisheries	The institutional link between the Commission and the regional government. Functions also as payment authority
Intermediate Organism	• Regional Departments of Economy	Represents the regional government and is charged with linking the national Managing Authority and the regional managing units
Monitoring Unit	• General Directorate for Community Funds and Territorial Finance (Dirección General de Fondos Comunitario y Financiación Territorial, DGFC)	Controls the financial circuit and accounting
Managing Units	• Regional departments • Development Agencies • Other institutions	Have the legal competences for spending activities
Final beneficiaries	• Firms • Families • Citizens	

formulating general policy and orientation; and (3) coordination mechanisms (Perez Tremps *et al.*, 1998).

In absolute terms, Spanish regions have benefited from SFs since they have received funds from the EU without contributing directly to the EU budget. Nevertheless, European funds have not always been at the free disposal of regional governments but rather have been managed through the Spanish national budget. The latter factor has imposed serious constraints on regional financial autonomy. Regional governments have often complained of the low

Table 7.3 Objective 1 CSFs, 2000–2006: distribution of Funds for management by central government and CA

Regions	Central government		Regional government		Total		Regional control over Funds
	Million euros	%	Million euros	%	Million euros	%	%
Andalusia	7,660	31.1	4,291	28.8	11,951	30.2	35.9
Asturias	1,243	5.0	598	4.0	1,841	4.7	32.5
Canaries	1,666	6.8	1,077	7.2	2,743	6.9	39.3
Cantabria (phasing out)	111	0.5	250	1.7	361	0.9	69.3
Castile-Leon	2,973	12.1	1,729	11.6	4,702	11.9	36.8
Castile-La Mancha	2,067	8.4	1,067	7.2	3,134	7.9	34.0
Extremadura	1,926	7.8	1,169	7.9	3,095	7.8	37.8
Galicia	2,933	11.9	2,475	16.6	5,408	13.7	45.8
Murcia	1,149	4.7	536	3.6	1,685	4.3	31.8
Valencian Community	2,781	11.3	1,607	10.8	4,388	11.1	36.6
Ceuta	73	0.3	44	0.3	117	0.3	37.6
Melilla	80	0.3	37	0.2	117	0.3	31.6
Total	24,662	100	14,880	100	39,542	100	37.6

Source: Ministry of Economy

degree of autonomy shared with respect to central government in managing EU SFs (Table 7.3). If compared, however, to the situation in the early 1990s, when regions only controlled around 10 per cent of EU structural aid, the relevance of regional finance in SFs management today has notably increased.

7.2 Contrasting Implementation Performance: Administrative Capacity in Andalusia and Galicia

7.2.1 Regional Administration: From Creation to Modernisation (1982–2005)

The administrative structures set up in Andalusia (since the Law of Government and Public Administration of 1983) and Galicia (since the Law of the Xunta and Presidency of 1983) are not very different from those of other CAs or of the implicit central state reference. During the decisive period of competence transfer (1982–1986) the recently created regions decided to create parallel structures with the central administration in order to facilitate the negotiation process as well as the subsequent 'take-up' of competences and civil servants.[11] As a consequence, a basic regional structure arose among the 17 CAs. This model, which continues today with few variations, comprises around 10 to 15 *consejerías* or *consellerias* (regional ministries or departments) organised into central services and provincial delegations in each of the provinces (eight in Andalusia and four in Galicia). Nevertheless, the political will and efforts aimed to 'straighten' the administration take it along a modernising path that varies between CAs, which, in turn, achieved different degrees of success.

According to Bouzas (1999, 2004),[12] the creation of the Galician administrative apparatus occurred in a period of 20 months characterised by both political instability and administrative uncertainty. It was only later that the regional administration could begin a process of increasing development and consolidation in the supportive context of a more stable political environment. The number of modifications and alterations of the administrative apparatus decreased considerably while coordinating and administrative support units increased, thus contributing to the articulation of the regional administrations. However, the complexity of the decentralisation process at the central level made it difficult to set up a policy of regional civil service immediately. For example, there were problems in transferring human resources from Madrid to the new emerging CAs at that time. The second legislature brought a period of stabilisation. Despite the first two years of political instability and governmental change, the process of regional administration development still continued positively. The provincial level of the regional apparatus was also fixed and there was growth in the public sector. The 1990s and the first years of the new century have been characterised by the four consecutive mandates held by the former Francoist minister Manuel Fraga, supported by an absolute majority in the Galician parliament. During this period, the focus has moved from configuration of the administrative apparatus to improving regional management by the introduction of the modernisation programme. The programme included the rationalisation and simplification of procedures, the definition of some formal models of communication, the computerisation of administrative activities and the setting of some citizen's attention. Regarding human resources, the programme introduced the regulation of civil service, continuous professional training and some mechanisms for evaluating managerial performance.[13]

Andalusia presents a very similar administrative structure, characterised by a highly politicised institutional environment, where the absolute electoral majorities gained by the PSOE in the regional elections of 1982, 1986 and 1990 reinforced a mechanism of bureaucratic recruitment characterised by clientelistic selection. The first period of the Modernisation Plan of the Public Administration started in the 1980s with the aim of improving information dissemination and communication with citizens. Decree 57/1983, with the creation of information offices, marked the beginning of this modernization process. Some years later, decree 260/1988 launched new government interventions aiming at more efficient delivery of public services through programmes of administrative rationalisation and simplification of administrative procedures. The implementation of the new administrative procedures was so slow that it resulted in an overlap with the modernisation programmes carried out by the central administration from 1992. Although the Andalusian administration was moderately successful in implementing a modern public style, it was not the same as regards the measures for the rationalisation of the civil service and improvements in the efficacy of Public Administration (Law 6/1985 for Organising the Civil Service of Andalusia).[14] Indeed, as Porras (2005: 478–9) summarises:

> The potentially original experiences of management and innovation had very little accomplishment in practice [...] The continuity of a traditional bureaucratic culture, the use of traditional legal instruments and the persistence of obsolete models of organisations, all that has contributed to produce the immediate effect of a constant deficit of performance. (Author's translation)

7.2.2 Regional Administrative Response and Adaptation to EU Regional Policy

As occurred for the national central administration, accession to EU membership in 1986 also prompted relevant and specific changes in the organisational structure of regional administration regarding the external actions of the regions and relations with EU institutions. In 1988, for example, Galicia – following the example of some pioneer CAs – created the *Fundación Galicia Europa*, a private law institution located in Brussels that was politically dependent on the President of the Xunta.[15] A decade later, in 1997, a new secretariat – within the Presidency's Secretariat – was also created: *Secretaria Xeral de Relacións con Union Europea e Acción Exterior.* This public body represents the support organism of the President of the Xunta, with competences in all European issues affecting regional government. One of its basic aims is to facilitate coordination among the sectoral departments belonging to the Xunta.

Likewise, in 1990, Andalusia set up its Delegation of the regional government in Brussels, which initially had to belong to the *Instituto de Fomento Andaluz* (IFA: Institute for the Promotion of Andalusia, belonging to the Department of Economy) until 1994. Later on, the office was placed directly under the responsibility of the regional Presidency. Its initial economic goals were complemented by a representative role in which it acted as an institutional intermediary between the regional government and the European institutions.

Following two decades of development, we can see that in Galicia and Andalusia today the coordination and management of European policy are competences of two basic regional departments: the Presidency's Department on the one hand, and the Department of Economy on the other. With respect to Cohesion policy, these latter departments – especially the Galician *Dirección Xeral de Planificación Economica e Fondos Comunitarios* and the Andalusian *Dirección General de Fondos Europeos* – are charged with the management of SFs within the region that dialogues with Madrid and Brussels. It is worth noting that both regional departments were created at the same time in 1996. The large amount of SFs received by Galicia and Andalusia as Objective 1 regions has heightened the relevance of their respective Departments of Economy, and their units for SFs management in particular have been endowed with great authority regarding regional policy. More generally, after two decades national and regional governments today share a similar approach to European cohesion policy, and to EU policies overall. Institutional and political representation is endowed upon (national and regional) executives, directly to the President's private office or via the Ministry of Foreign Affairs. Economic and programming responsibilities rely, instead, upon the (national or regional) department of economy. The structure reflects the classical dual perspective of political and economic re-vindication (Cienfuegos, 2000). In regional organisational structure, the institutional proximity of the President to EU policies shows an evident will for political control over European issues. The dominance of the departments of economy in the SFs policy process reveals, instead, the centrality of planning and programming activity for any policy intervention.

7.2.3 Assessing Administrative Capacity in Andalusia and Galicia

Being historically among Spain's least developed regions, Andalusia and Galicia have been the two greatest recipients under Cohesion policy. In the last two decades, the overall amount of SFs received by Galicia reached approximately 11,000 million euros, corresponding to 11.8 per cent of the total financial assistance assigned to Spain. Andalusia received 25,568 million euros between 1986 and 2006, accounting for 25 per cent of the total amount, and is the largest recipient region. In both territories economic convergence has occurred, although it has followed different patterns. Convergence in Galicia, for example, has occurred at a slower pace with respect to the national average. In the 1995–2005 period, Galicia's economy reduced the gap with the EU27 by only 9.2 percentage points (from 75 to 84.2 per cent of the EU27 GDP per capita),[16] while the overall Spanish reduction was 11.1 per cent. Andalusia, on the other hand, performed above the national average by achieving a reduction of 11.8 percentage points (from 68.6 to 80.4 of the EU27 GDP per capita).

We have investigated the key components of administrative capacity mainly for the first four years of the last financial period 2000–2006, but with constant reference to the past programming periods. The first essential element of administrative capacity is *management*, which refers to correct implementation of the ROP by ensuring clarity of roles and coordination among regional departments. In Galicia, as well as Andalusia, correct management of EU funds is guaranteed by the leading role performed by the regional department of economy, which is the MA at the regional level. In both regions since 1994–1999 – as a consequence of an evident learning process – the definition of roles has increased in clarity and effectiveness, along with an improvement in communication and coordination among regional departments. Within the regional government, communications are today absolutely institutionalised and information flows smoothly through official and formal channels. When some administrative departments act in an uncoordinated fashion, or try to increase their autonomy, this is mainly for political reasons rather than due to any lack of coordination mechanisms.[17]

Programming refers to the defining of the correct regional strategy to help reduce socio-economic disparities. According to EU regulations, this is based on a multiannual interval and should indicate which interventions should guarantee the achievement of objectives and goals. The design of any strategy usually relies on background analysis of the socio-economic context, which is today performed through traditional SWOT analysis. In neither Galicia or Andalusia were SWOT analyses carried out during in the 1989–94 period and these were only partially implemented in the 1994–99 period. However, from the outset of the planning phase for the 2000–2006 period, SWOT analysis was fully accepted and used as the main tool for defining the regional development strategy. Regarding the approval of the ROP, it is relevant to notice that the process is also influenced by the attitude of both the EU and national government. In this sense, the 1994–99 and 2000–06 OPs for both regions were officially approved within the year without reporting relevant delays or incidences.

The correct implementation of any ROP requires a strict *monitoring* activity that must include coherent data-gathering and some clear methodology for analysis of the results and outcomes. Central and regional public administrations here are equally responsible and coordination mechanisms between the two levels matter. In both Andalusia and Galicia, monitoring provisions for the 1994–1999 period were very weak and only financial monitoring was really performed. Indicators for the physical measurement of the results of SFs interventions were not fully developed in Andalusia and they were not properly functioning in Galicia. The lack of results for monitoring activities, combined with a weak capacity for evaluation, meant that evaluation activity during the programme period was limited. For the 2000–2006 financial period, however, both regions seriously committed to the definition of an effective monitoring system that includes physical and financial variables. Throughout this latter period, the monitoring system has worked properly in Andalusia as well as in Galicia and has constituted the most reliable instrument for measuring the improvement in the implementation of ROPs.

Finally, *evaluation* is the fourth component of administrative capacity and, in general terms, assesses how the execution of OPs is respected in accordance with the programmed timetable. Given that some specific evaluations are mandatory as requested by the EC, the two regions behaved in almost the same way. Both *ex-ante* and *in itinere* evaluations have been carried out and evaluation reports have been assigned to independent consultants. Given the 20-year inclusion of Spain in European Cohesion policy, a dense network of specialised private and public firms has emerged in the field of SFs evaluation. For this reason, in both our selected regions, evaluation reports are equally detailed and extensive. As far as the culture of evaluation is concerned, our field-work shows that, although with some isolated problems, the introduction of evaluation methodology is becoming much more accepted today in both public administrations.

As Table 7.4 shows, both Andalusia and Galicia present very similar results in terms of administrative capacity as we define and measure it. The two regions are, indeed, similarly endowed regarding the capacity and the skill of their respective regional administrations in the overall management of SFs according to their rules and procedures. What we observe in both regions is an incremental learning process from the 1994–1999 period onward that moved administrative capacity from *developing* to *consolidated*. The result is not surprising if we take into account the common process of

Table 7.4 Band of scores for overall administrative capacity degree

Key determinants of administrative capacity	Indicators	Galicia		Andalucia		Overall score	
		1994–1999	2000–2006	1994–1999	2000–2006	Galicia	Andalucia
Management	(a) Clarity in the definition of roles	2	3	3	3	2.5	3
	(b) Coordination and cooperation among *assessorati*	2	3	2	3	2.5	2.5.
	Overall score	2	3	2.5	3	2.5	2.7
Programming	(a) Programme design	0	3	0	3	1.5	1.5
	(b) Programme approval	2	3	2	3	2.5	2.5
	Overall score	1	3	1	3	2	2
Monitoring	(a) Introduction of a system of indicators and of monitoring procedures responding to national agreed standards.	1	2	0	2	1.5	1
	(b) Guaranteeing the availability of financial, physical and procedural data	1	3	1	3	2	2
	Overall score	1	2.5	0.5	2.5	1.7	1.5
Evaluation	(a) Production of evaluation reports	2	3	2	3	2.5	2.5
	(b) Integration of the evaluation method and culture in the implementation system	2	3	2	3	2.5	2.5
	Overall score	2	3	2	3	2.5	2.5
Overall score for administrative capacity						2.1	2.1

decentralisation and regional apparatus-building that involved all the 17 Spanish regions and that was led – at least during the first years of the transition – by the central administration.

7. 3 The Role of Political Factors in Implementation Outcome

There are conspicuous similarities and differences between the political conditions for SFs performance in Galicia and Andalusia. First of all, both are special regions according to the constitutional *via* of accessing political autonomy. However, whereas Galicia was declared a *historic nationality* by the Constitution, in Andalusia the self-governing process was somewhat more conflicted since it required a popular referendum. The referendum process triggered a huge social and political mobilisation in the region, led by the left-wing parties (notably by the PSOE-A, Partido Socialista Obrero Español de Andalucía, which at that time started the campaign for the national elections of 1982). These founding circumstances dramatically politicised the entire process of institution-building in the region and contributed to the socialist party maintaining regional power to date.

Basically, the initial political support for the left in Andalusia is explained by the socio-economic structure of the region: a typically underdeveloped society, mostly agrarian, characterised by large estates (*latifundios*) that employed huge numbers of agrarian workers. The start of a political movement demanding political autonomy for the region during the first quarter of the twentieth century – and, at the same time, helping to shape an identity as a political community – is closely linked to the demand for agrarian reform and the aspirations for economic development (Jimenez, 1977). Although a regionalist political party emerged during the democratic transition (Partido Andalucista, PA), with a leftist ideology, it never came to challenge the leadership of the PSOE-A. Instead, the latter succeeded in the symbolical integration of left-wing ideology and regional political identification (Montabes and Torres, 1998).

Contemporary Galicia, on the contrary, is usually depicted as a bastion of the conservative right and it is well known that the conservative government is strongly embedded in the region. The traditional productive structure of the Galician agricultural sector, based on *minifundios* (as opposed to *latifundios*), the lack of transport infrastructure, and the absence of a strong industrial base, all explain the conservative and locally-oriented political preferences in Galicia. Since democratisation, the national conservative party (the Partido Popular, PP) has dominated the region.[18] From 1990 to 2004, regional government – the Xunta de Galicia – was presided over by the PP under Manuel Fraga. The highly political fragmentation of the Galician left-wing, along with the crosscutting nationalist cleavage, hindered the possibilities of a left-wing electoral turnover (Rivera *et al.*, 1998). Only recently has the socialist party (Partido Socialista de Galicia-Partido Socialista Obrero Español, PSdG-PSOE) been able to seduce the traditionally conservative Galician society. In the 2005 elections the PP lost its overall majority – while remaining the largest party in the parliament – and a new coalition formed by the PSdG and the BNG (Bloque Nacionalista Galego) took joint control of the regional government, with the PSdG's leader, Emilio Perez Touriño, serving as Galicia's new president. Finally, it is worth mentioning that, compared to other nationalist and regional movements in Spain, Galician nationalism is often considered a rather weak movement, despite the presence of a strong regional identity. Currently, the only nationalist party of any electoral significance, the BNG, is a conglomerate of left-wing parties and personalities who lay claim to Galicia's political status as a nation.

7. 3.1 *Political Stability*

In order to compare the degree of political stability in Andalusia and Galicia we have measured four essential characteristics: (1) the effective number of political parties in the regional parliament as an indicator of the number of political veto players; (2) the type of government, according to the degree of independence from the parliament (from the most independent in the case of homogenous majority to the most dependent in the case of minority coalition; (3) the number of cabinets per legislature; and, finally, (4) the number of presidents of the regional executive (see Table 7.5).

Although we find similarly high levels of political stability in both regions, the Andalusian scenario is striking due to the extraordinary stability of regional governments. In fact, the most unstable political legislature lasted only two years, from 1994 to 1996, when the regional political scenario was labelled 'the pincer' (*la pinza*) because of the political opposition coming as much from the left (IU party) as from the right wing (PP) of the parliament. At that time, the regional President, Manuel Chaves, decided to dissolve parliament ahead of time and call for elections. The Andalusian government during the two following legislatures was formed by a majority coalition between the PSOE-A and the regionalist Andalusia Party (PA). Since then, the regional party system has evolved once again towards a practical two-party system, with the PSOE-A acting as the leading political party in the region. Moreover, the permanence of Manuel Chaves as chief of the executive during five consecutive mandates and the formation of four homogeneous majority governments in seven legislatures has increased the perception of a predominant party system.[19]

Table 7.5 Political stability in Andalusia and Galicia

Legislatures	EPPN[a]	Type of government[b]	Number of governments[c]	Presidents	Total score
Andalusia					
1982/1986	2.4	Homogeneous majority PSOE/A (1)	2	1 Rafael Escuredo	
				2 José Rodríguez de la Borbolla	
1986/1990	2.5	Homogeneous majority PSOE/A (1)	1	José Rodríguez de la Borbolla	
1990/1994	2.5	Homogeneous majority PSOE/A (1)	1	Manuel Chaves	
1994/1996	2.9	Homogeneous minority PSOE/A (3)	1	Manuel Chaves	
1996/2000	2.6	Majority coalition PSOE/A; PA (2)	1	Manuel Chaves	
2000/2004	2.4	Majority coalition PSOE/A; PA (2)	1	Manuel Chaves	
2004/2008	2.3	Homogeneous majority PSOE/A (1)	1	Manuel Chaves	
Mean values	2.51	1.57	1.14	0.42	5.64
Galicia					
1982/1986	3.3	Majority coalition AP/PP, UCD (2)	5	Gerardo Fernández Albor (AP/PP)	
1986/1990	2.8	1 Homogeneous minority AP/PP (3)	2	Gerardo Fernández Albor (AP/PP)	
		2 Quasi-majority coalition (PSOE-PSG,PNG-PG,CG) (4)		Fernando González Laxe (PSG)	
1990/1993	2.5	Homogeneous majority PP (1)	1	Manuel Fraga (PP)	
1993/1997	2.4	Homogeneous majority PP (1)	1	Manuel Fraga (PP)	
1997/2001	2.4	Homogeneous majority PP (1)	1	Manuel Fraga (PP)	
2001/2005	2.5	Homogeneous majority PP (1)	3	Manuel Fraga (PP)	
2005/2009	2.6	Majority coalition PSOE/PSG, BNG (2)	1	José López Touriño (PSG)	
Mean values	2.6	1.87	2	0.57	7.04

a NEPP: 1–1.8 'single party'; 1.8–2,4 'two party'; 2.5–2.8 'multi-party with moderate polarisation'; 2.8–3.5 'polarised multi-party'. Effective number of political parties (Laakso and Taagepera 1979)

b Type of government has been measured according to the following values: (1) homogeneous majority (2) majority coalition (3) homogeneous minority, and (4) minority coalition.

c Number of governments refers to cabinet reshuffle per legislature.

In Galicia, on the other hand, we can distinguish two different periods which depict the political scenario in the region. The first is characterised by rather high political fragmentation within the Galician parliament, which, during the first and second legislatures, experienced a somewhat polarised party system. The fragmentation was basically due to the split and disappearance of the centrist party UCD (Unión de Centro Democrático) and the re-organisation of the conservative party AP/CP/PP (Alianza Popular, Coalición Popular, Partido Popular), on the one hand, and the atomisation of the left-wing and nationalist parties, on the other (Diz *et al.*, 1998). During the first legislature, five governmental crises were experienced and it was a vote of censure in 1987 against the conservative government of Fernández Albor that, finally, forced the first government overturn in Galicia. However, the electoral results of 1990 established the first Galician homogeneous majority government, which would stay in power until 2005. During this second political period the Galician party system moved from polarisation towards a moderate multi-party system and even a two-party system.

Taking into account all regional legislatures since 1982 until 2009, the overall measurement of political stability (actually, political instability) is somewhat higher in Galicia (7.04) than in Andalusia (5.64). We might therefore conclude that conditions for governance are more favourable in Andalusia, whereas in Galicia the higher number of veto players (political parties in parliament, and factions within them) is likely to have reduced the government's autonomy for making any other decision than to maintain the status quo (Tsebelis, 2002).[20] Therefore, according to our hypothesis, the rate of SFs absorption should be higher in Andalusia due to a more stable political environment that could have favoured long-term planning strategies. Nevertheless, if we consider the periods of SFs policy under consideration – from 1994 to 2006 – we find that the conditions of political stability are very similar in both regions. Indeed, the average total score for stability during the four legislatures after 1994 is 5.8 in Galicia and 5.72 in Andalusia. We then have to conclude that, for our selected case, political stability does not play a relevant role in explaining why rates of absorption vary.

7.3.2 *Political Interference*

Given that politically the two regions can be classified as equally stable, we have also investigated conditions of political interference in both regions in order to explain why the SFs absorption rate might vary. Basically, political interference refers to restrictive or disruptive and invasive actions of the political class towards the administrative sphere, thus reducing its independent capacity to perform effectively and for the general interest. As is well known, Spain has a continental model of PA whereby, like France, the strict separation between politics and PA is unknown. Within this framework, upper-level positions within the administrative structure are appointed at the government's discretion, which means that those positions do not belong formally within the civil service career structure. The reform of national PA in the early 1990s – Law 30/1992 on Public Administrations – as well the further legislative developments – Law 6/1997 on Organisation and Functioning of the General Administration of the State (LOFAGE) and Law 50/1997 on Government – were aimed at introducing principles of efficacy, professionalism and accountability into the PA, as well as some monitoring mechanisms for evaluating civil servants' performances. For instance, the LOFAGE made it obligatory for General Directors – who are politically appointed – to be recruited from the PA or civil service career. There is some empirical evidence, however, that the enforcement of this principle has been rather limited, given the numerous exceptions to this rule.[21]

At the subnational level, CAs present similar conditions to the central state regarding the weak separation between the regional political realm and regional PA. Nevertheless, in Andalusia, as opposed to Galicia, there has not been any serious and coherent political attempt to keep the administrative sphere away from political interference. Unlike central state administration – and the majority of other regional administrations – in Andalusia the administrative position of *general sub-director* – a linking position between the political hierarchy and the strictly administrative level – is missing. As a consequence, 'an evident gap between the more directly political level, represented by the General Director, and the strictly administrative level, represented by the Chief of Service' characterised the entire process of institution-building (Olvera, 2003: 473). Some historical reasons can explain the direction of such a process. On the one hand, the haste of regional institution building imposed a human resources policy that was strongly dependent on political recruitment rather than on objective requirements and professional skills. On the other hand, there was the wilful disposal of as much as possible of the previous dictatorship's bureaucracy by the socialist party in government.[22]

The Galician PA structure is also very similar to central state organisation, and links between PA and politics, although considerably relevant, are apparently more regularised than in Andalusia. In Galicia, for instance, there is the administrative position of the *general sub-director*, the mere existence of which may represent, at least, a first formal obstacle for those regional politicians who seek to capture administrators. Due to some historical circumstances, the first conservative regional government in Galicia was supposedly more tolerant of former Francoist public officials than was the left-wing Andalusian government (Márquez, 1993). Thus, at the beginning of the democratic transition, top-level positions in the civil service – e.g. assistant director – were more likely to be occupied by civil servants whose careers had developed under the dictatorship. As a consequence, the older functionaries who had been socialised into their government position under the authoritarian regime were less disposed to act under strict, rational, merit-based bureaucratic guidelines. All of these circumstances 'favoured the spread and maintenance of clientelistic behaviour in Galicia, especially since functionary positions were linked to party affiliation and clientelistic networks' (Dudek, 2005: 120). Nevertheless, the Galician PA reform of the early 1990s was intended to modernise and professionalise the regional civil service as a protection against the politicisation of the PA. For example, from 1991 a managerial training diploma became an obligatory eligibility requirement for administrative positions directly appointed by the government. The rationale of the reform was to restrict the arbitrary appointment of civil service's highest positions as well as guaranteeing that appointed officials had acquired certain specific knowledge and capabilities for carrying out their tasks as public administrators.

Although the disruptive and invasive action of the political class seems as important in Andalusia as in Galicia, in Galicia some normative efforts and policy interventions have been implemented in order to restrict political interference. However, the apparent failure of the Andalusian government to regularise the regional civil service has hindered the formation of a professional public class devoted to serving the general interest. Accordingly, we may observe the dominance of a form of political dependence that conditions all public action. Regional administrative activity is strongly correlated with the main political variables as well as being sensitive to the electoral cycle. This generates inconvenient ups and downs (electoral periods, effects of internal conflicts within the dominant party) and situations of relative paralysis in policy-making. Some evidence of higher political interference in the administrative structure of Andalusia compared to Galicia is, for example, reported in the mid-term evaluation of the Regional IOP (Integrated Operational Programme) 2000–2006: whereas in Galicia it is observed that there is a scarcity of specialised staff for the implementation of the SFs, in Andalusia it is considered that the excessive turnover of the public officials responsible for SFs management is an obstacle for good implementation performances.[23]

7.3.3 Political Accountability

The absence of political accountability in Andalusia and Galicia is usually attributed to practices of political clientelism. But whereas in Galicia a somewhat traditional clientelism has occurred, based on hierarchical interpersonal relations which are mostly held at the local level, in Andalusia traditional clientelism has been replaced by party clientelism (Cazorla, 1994). In the former region, there has been a tradition of clientelism embedded in the local branches of the conservative AP/PP party that has clearly challenged the political accountability of the ruling political class. One of the best known cases of clientelism was in the town of Lalín, which serves as a perfect example of how road construction becomes a reward for clients (Dudek, 2005). Since EU funds are used for financing a major portion of road construction, such expenditure suggests that EU funds may be used to reinforce expensive clientelistic networks. Conversely, clientelistic networks may serve to perform high rates of SFs absorption. Indeed, the lack of transparency in governmental action in Galicia has long been criticised by the parliamentary opposition. As a result, Galicia was the first Spanish region to approve a law against citizen misinformation about the actions carried out by the regional administration, Law 4/2006 on Transparency and Good Practices in Public Administration. That law intended, among other goals, to increase the information concerning the government and administration in order to favour transparency and accountability. The creation of this law was one of the main electoral promises of the Socialist Party of Galicia during the electoral campaign of 2005.

We observe in Andalusia a different pattern of political clientelism: on the one hand, the process of bureaucratic class selection that shaped the regional administration was defined by a clientelistic form of designation; on the other hand, a process of party electoral loyalty was established, especially among the rural electorate, which constitutes the most stable support for the majority force. This process of fixing loyalties to the majority party, especially in the countryside, was related to the rural subsidies stemming from the *Plan de Empleo Rural* (PER: Rural Employment Plan) (Cazorla, 1994).[24] The PSOE-A demonstrates a major capacity for the development of welfare and social assistance policies along with effective mechanisms for using the rural population as electoral support. In summary, in both Andalucia and Galicia there are clientele systems that are not negatively perceived in public opinion.

7.4 Constraints on the Implementation of Cohesion Policy

In general terms, Spanish regions have performed somewhat satisfactorily regarding the rate of absorption of SFs. At the end of 2006, the average rate of absorption for Objective 1 regions was 85.17 per cent. Nevertheless, some regions perform better than others in implementing SFs. From 1989 until 2006, Galicia, for example, steadily performed better than Andalusia.

Throughout this chapter we have tried to answer the question of why the rate of absorption of SFs varies between Objective 1 regions. Following mainstream literature, we have considered the traditional institutional variables – regional administrative capacities and political stability – which may directly or indirectly affect the performance of regional governments. Given the pronounced asymmetry of the Spanish state model (the most decentralised among the unitarian states of the EU), we selected autonomous communities that were most similar from the constitutional and institutional perspectives (Andalusia and Galicia) in order to maintain the comparability of our case study.

We found that both regions developed similar administrative structures to deal with SFs management and, more generally, to keep in touch with European institutions. In considering the four components of regional administrative capacity (programming, management, monitoring and evaluation), we found no specific difference that could explain or justify variance in the absorption capacity of the two regions. Basically, ROP financial effectiveness is guaranteed in both regions by the relevant role played by the regional departments of economy. It is highly likely that the early adoption of the European cohesion policy as regional state policy, along with the territorial decentralisation of the state and the devolution of regional policy, can explain, to a large extent, similarities in the administrative building process. Moreover, the decentralisation of regional operative programme management, although always driven by the central state, served to seriously involve regional government as well as other public (and non-public) actors in SFs policy management. In both regions, incremental learning accumulated during the preceding programming periods (1989–1993 and 1994–1999) has been very useful in this respect. Finally, cooperation between the central, regional and local administrations, as well as the participation of civil society's actors, in the programming phase has also improved over time and permitted the commitment to long-term management strategies.

Political conditions are also very similar in the two selected regions, at least as regards the political dominance of the socialist party in Andalusia and the leadership of the conservative party government in Galicia. In Andalusia, for example, the constant permanence of a single majority political party since the transition has meant the lack of any *de facto* political turnover in the region. In Galicia, even in the presence of some turnover, the political environment was extremely stable throughout the 1990s. It is most likely that both phenomena have decreased the degree of autonomy of regional PA with respect to the political sphere. As a consequence, political interference is indeed considerably developed in both regions and is basically manifested through clientelistic recruitment and the appointment of civil servants and upper-level positions within the regional administration. In the 1990s, some reforms were introduced in order to restrict political interference by means of regularising and professionalising the regional civil service. In Galicia some normative efforts and policy interventions partially succeeded in improving the transparency of the PA. In Andalusia, on the other hand, all attempts to develop a professional civil service were frustrated. Despite some difference in intensity, it is relevant to note that the invasive action of the political class seems as important in Andalusia as in Galicia. Finally, despite some relevant progress in the modernisation of the regional apparatus, both public administrations suffer from a clear deficit in accountability. Given the widespread diffusion of clientelistic behaviours, government action has not always been transparent and democratic political accountability is equally weak in the two regions.

According to our analysis, therefore, differences in implementation performance seem to be more dependent on political factors rather than on administrative ones. Andalusia and Galicia are equally endowed regarding regional administrative capacity in the management of SFs, but Andalusia's more invasive political environment might explain why its implementation of SFs presents a less positive record than that of Galicia. However, and significantly, the impact of administrative and political variables is less intense than expected. We therefore believe that regional political conditions do not provide the only explanation for why the rate of absorption of SFs varies. After all, both Andalusia and Galicia can be depicted as extremely stable political arenas, such that some more pronounced interference (or a different kind of clientelism) in the latter region can only partially explain differences in SFs implementation records.

We therefore believe that in order to evaluate regional performances some missing political and institutional variables should be included in the analysis. How SFs management activities are distributed among national and regional governments, who controls SFs financial flows, and how relevant the level of the national co-financing is in regional programmes, are matters that should indeed be considered with much more attention. Within the institutional framework of the Spanish Autonomic State, for example, difficulties regarding intergovernmental relations and coordination between centre and periphery, as well as differences in political agendas, might indeed explain to some extent the uneven SF absorption capacity of the regions.

8

THE IMPACT OF POLICY IMPLEMENTATION IN POLAND

Centralisation, Decentralisation and Recentralisation

Justyna Glusman

8.1 EU Cohesion Policy and Multi-level Governance in the New Member States

The adoption of the EU cohesion policy constituted a major challenge for the EU's new Member States and was at the same time the driving force of the regional reforms carried out in these countries. From the first day of accession Poland and the other new Member States became eligible for regionally-oriented financial assistance of a volume far exceeding the funding available from the national budgets. However, an entirely novel approach to both policy planning and management had to be undertaken for EU funds distribution, which put considerable strain on Poland's administrative structures at all levels. The multiannual development plans became the basis for programming regional investments, while their implementation required the involvement of multiple regional, local and social actors in order to realise the partnership principle.

Poland had already conducted a series of regional reforms in the 1990s, in an attempt to rationalise its territorial structures and regional policy-making, and with a view to prepare for challenges related to membership in the EU. The reforms aimed for the introduction of self-governance at local and regional levels as well as the endowment of regional authorities with sufficient powers and competencies to conduct regional development policies at the subnational level. While the first goal was realised, the ability of the subnational authorities to effectively carry out development actions in their territories remains debatable. There were very limited resources available for this purpose from both regional and national budgets, and it remained a largely theoretical problem until the moment of accession to the EU. It was the anticipated inflow of EU SFs to Poland after 2004 that was to put the new administrative structures to the first real test.

Nonetheless, concerns about the inadequate administrative capacity of the regional governments resulted in the decision to centralise the EU funds' distribution system in Poland. In effect, the majority of responsibilities related to funds disbursement in the 2004–2006 budgetary perspective were eventually handed over to the central administration units.

Like the subnational structures, however, the central administration units had to thoroughly reorganise themselves and modernise the management structure in order to prepare for the reception of such volumes of assistance, which were in addition hedged with a high number of procedural conditions. The new obligations required a considerable increase in the number of public administration officials as well as the reorganisation of the internal structure of governmental departments. Most of the adaptation efforts in this respect fell in the period immediately preceding accession or even after the entry into force of the key programme documents. In spite of that, the first budgetary perspective 2004–2006, subject of this analysis, represented a period of practically permanent systemic evolution. It was marked by a major redesign in 2006 in response to the unsatisfactory absorption level, which resulted in the creation of an entirely new institution, the Ministry of Regional Development, thus centralising administrative forces in charge of the EU funding.

The novelty and mutability of the administrative structures in charge of processing the EU funding and the centralisation of their management have significant consequences for the analysis of Poland's performance in the regional policy field. In particular, the instability of the institutions responsible for the Funds' absorption forces the structure of the current chapter to depart from the analyses carried out in the former sections of this book. In the context of the features of the Polish system outlined above, the major limitation is the unfeasibility of qualifying the administrative capacity in line with the criteria outlined in the Introduction. The novelty of the framework created to process EU assistance does not allow for reliable measurement of such features like the political culture of cooperation, political accountability or transparency. Although the procedural rules for the Funds' disbursement formally meet the criteria outlined in the *acquis*, in practice the standards with respect to the notions listed above still remain considerably low when compared with the Western European norms. A few years after accession to the EU, Poland's regional policy system is still undergoing a learning process and it is simply too early to examine the indicators based on political stability.

The second challenge lies in carrying out a comparative analysis of the administrative structures in charge of different programmes in conditions of systemic centralisation. Since most of the programming phase documents as well as the monitoring and evaluation procedures have been designed within the Ministry of Economy,[1] the value of indicators defining the level of administrative capacity will be similar across the operational programmes. For this reason, current analysis focuses on the implementation phase of the regional policy, in which various governmental departments were entrusted with responsibilities to carry out the concourses for applications and choice of the projects to receive the co-financing. In line with the theoretical framework used in this book, I will argue that variation in the administrative capacity of the governmental units in charge of the particular operational programmes does explain differentiation in Funds' expenditure level. I will demonstrate that the rate of absorption in the areas where administrative capacity has been traditionally weak is the lowest and that the most serious problems with policy adaptation occur in those areas.

Nonetheless, the largest problems pertaining to the system of Funds distribution in Poland seem to be horizontal and go across various programmes. Arguably, they result from the poor administrative capacity in general, a lack of clear division of competencies across the government and governmental agencies, an inadequate legal framework, and the incompetency of personnel dealing with the funds.

Similarly, centralisation of the system makes it no longer feasible to refer to political stability as an explanatory factor for differences in the performance of various programmes. In the centralised framework, it is rational to expect that the political shifts will affect absorption in various programmes in similar ways.

This chapter examines how Poland has adapted to the MLG system. At the core of the analysis is an investigation of the successes and failures of Poland's authorities in implementing the EU cohesion policy through the scrutiny of the performance of the two Sectoral Operational Programmes (SOPs), Fisheries and Increase of Competitiveness of Enterprises. The proxy is the rate of absorption of the Structural Funds achieved in the first EU budgetary period applicable to Poland, 2004–2006. While a comprehensive measurement of the effects of the funding should involve more complex analysis of the type and geographical distribution of projects, the rate of absorption seems the most reliable and quantifiable indicator available for such a short time span.

Moreover, this paper discusses the possible consequences of the centralisation of the EU Funds' distribution system on Poland's governance. Arguably, this decision has politically reinforced the central administration *vis-à-vis* the regions. Although formally centralisation of funding was solely a technocratic decision to make certain that Poland is able to actually utilise the assigned funds, it may have far more long-lasting political consequences.

The following section will briefly outline the key points of debate in the literature on EU enlargement and its consequences for the shape of the regional policies of the Central Eastern European Countries (CEECs). The Polish path to regional reform is analysed in the context of external pressures, which came mostly from the European Commission (EC). The following section illustrates the institutional features of the EU Funds distribution system in Poland and examines the link between administrative capacity and success in programme implementation. The conclusions summarise the findings.

Comparing the volume of SFs available for Poland with resources from the national budget assigned for regional development leaves no doubt about the potentially huge impact of the former on the country's whole system of regional assistance. From 2004 the legal basis for distribution of regionally-oriented funds was the National Development Plan for 2004–2006 (NDP 2004) approved by the EC as the Community Support Framework (CSF).[2]

The aggregate resources for the projects completed within the CSF would amount to around 17.5 billion euros.[3] The bulk of this, 12.9 billion euros, came from the EU budget and the remainder, about 3.8 billion euros, constituted public (from national or regional budgets) and private co-financing. In contrast, the entire domestic financing of the regional development not attached to realisation of the CSF (in the framework of the so-called 'regional contracts')[4] amounted to only 856.6 million euros (Ministry of Economy 2005a: 49). Thus, it represented merely around 5 per cent of the resources available from the day of accession. In consequence, the EU Funds were to become the basic source of financing for Poland's regional policy and the principles of the EU cohesion policy were extended to practically all regionally-oriented actions.

8.1.1 *The Anticipated Impact of the EU*
Cohesion Policy on CEE Members

There is a spate of literature focusing on the EU cohesion policy and its impact on the governance of the countries participating in aid programmes (Keating, 1995b; Kohler-Koch, 1996; Keating, 1998; Goetz and Hix, 2000; Hughes *et al.*, 2001), particularly its potential 'regionalising effects'. And yet access to SFs is seen as producing varied political outcomes across the EU. Authors on the one hand state that cohesion policy has empowered the regions *vis-à-vis* the member countries' central governments (e.g. Goetz and Hix, 2000), or, on the other, affirm that paradoxically the centre has been empowered and reasserted (e.g. Keating and Hooghe, 1996). The literature on the impact of the EU on the CEECs regional policies remains equally discordant.

Scholarly opinions on the role of EU cohesion policies in regionalisation processes in CEECs are invariably linked to authors' general perceptions of the effectiveness of the EU conditionality regime applied to the candidates for EU membership. While some scholars see it as a strong causative power guiding CEE reforms (e.g. Grabbe, 2002), others question this assumption and claim that domestic idiosyncrasies were equally important or even more significant than external pressures in structuring the reform processes in the applicant countries (Dimitrova, 2002; Hughes *et al.*, 2003; 2004). The studies in the second stream agree about the mixed results of the application of the EU pressures for change across CEE, although they assign them to a variety of factors. Hughes *et al.* (2001; 2003; 2004), in their detailed policy-tracing analyses of the regional reforms in CEE, see the varied degrees of decentralisation as a consequence of the incoherent demands of the Commission, which were not firmly ingrained in the *acquis communautaire*. Dimitrova (2002), in turn, links such variation to the different starting conditions and degrees of misfit between candidates and the 'Community model' of regional governance as well as institutional veto points.

A pertinent controversy that arises in the context of policy transfer to CEE in the regional field is whether the EU has tried to impose a regional policy and administrative blueprint upon the candidate countries or whether its demands for adaptation were purely technocratic and embedded into the *acquis communautaire*. Hughes *et al.* (2001) claim that in the early years of the pre-accession process the Commission actively promoted a policy model anticipating reconfiguration of CEE subnational administration tiers by establishing elected regional institutions with decentralised powers.

The imposition of the reforms from the top has been equally a concern of Hughes *et al.* (2001: 2), who argue that a Europeanized regionalization is being pursued 'from above' by national governments anxious to meet the EU conditionalities, while on the other hand, the Europeanization of regionalization has received a mixed reception 'from below' by more pragmatic local elites within the CEECs.

Paradoxically, while one of the main integration concerns of the EU was the involvement of regional and local governments, the EU marginalised the participation of subnational elites in the pre-accession strategy (Hughes *et al.*, 2001: 9). As a result, there was a perception among CEE policy-makers that the EU was trying to 'foist' a regionalisation policy model upon them in a rather non-consultative fashion, which resulted in relatively little engagement with and knowledge about the EU among local elites. This poverty of awareness affected both the regional and local prerequisites for EU membership, and the potential benefits deriving from the funding of regional development programmes (Hughes *et al.*, 2001: 34). This view is shared by some CEE scholars, such as Grosse, who points out in a study on Poland's adaptation to the EU regional policy that regional self-governments had far too little knowledge about the shape of the funds' distribution system (Grosse, 2004), which impeded their ability to cope with the challenges related to the funds' absorption.

The policy-tracing analysis of the regional processes taking place in Poland since the early 1990s demonstrates the prevalence of domestic over international sources of the regional reforms. Although the reforms were carried out with a view to future participation in the EU cohesion policy, the key trigger was the mounting need to detach from the 'democratic centralism' and democratisation of the governance system to accompany the sweeping changes in the economic and political spheres. The EC, which since the Madrid European Council of 1995 increasingly focused on the administrative capacity issue, did, however, undertake attempts to pressure Poland to adopt particular systemic solutions. In line with Hughes *et al.* (2003; 2004), this paper argues that the Commission's incoherent demands, which were not firmly anchored in the *acquis*, had less causative power than in the policy areas with detailed and legally binding prescriptions for adaptation. Thus, regionalisation of the Polish governance system in the late 1990s resulted from domestic path-dependency rather than external pressures.

The EU remains, however, a strong causative force in determining the shape of Poland's regional policy after enlargement. Because of the disproportionate disparity between the regional resources from the EU and from national budgets mentioned above, the CSF remains the key programme document based on which Poland's regional policy is conducted. Its policy assumptions, agreed with the EC, constitute the guiding principles for the majority of territorial and public-investment actions carried out in Poland after 2004.

Paradoxically, however, despite the Commission's initial zeal for regionalisation and promotion of the MLG system, the accession to the EU structural policy seemed to empower the central authorities rather than the regions. The increasing concerns of European institutions and member countries alike regarding Poland's ability to carry out an effectively decentralised regional policy resulted in the increasing preference for a centralised Funds distribution system. The issue is that the adoption of centralised and sectorally-oriented Funds distribution structures might bring about a gradual re-centralisation of the Polish governance system in the future, despite the decentralising reforms conducted by Poland's authorities in the 1990s. The following section demonstrates how, despite carrying out a major administrative reform described by Hughes *et al.* as 'exemplary adaptation' (2001: 41), post-accession Poland ended up with a centralised regional policy system opposite to the MLG system.

8.2 Constructing the Multi-level Governance System in Poland

Poland's regional reforms commenced at the beginning of the 1990s, well before accession to the EU. The direct trigger was concern that the regional deficit may impair the positive results of the sweeping changes taking place in the economic and political spheres since 1989. Although the formulation of Poland's regional policy assumptions took place largely 'with a view' of accession to the EU and future adaptation to the European regional policy, its direct impact on the reforms trajectory was limited. The pace and shape of the regional changes implemented in Poland throughout the 1990s coincided more closely with a domestic timetable rather than with international political events, the key influence being the election calendar. Should the post-Solidarity forces have lost the 1998 elections, realisation of the reform in its present shape would probably have been postponed indefinitely (see Glusman, 2008).

Nonetheless, by the year 2000, when the accession negotiations on the regional policy chapter commenced, Poland's administrative system was certainly unprepared to benefit from the EU cohesion policy in a way that could ensure respect for its rules and principles. Incapacitated territorial structures and the inadequate financial resources of the voivodships, as well as poorly demarcated competencies between various administrative tiers, did not provide sufficient fund absorption capacity. In other words, it was uncertain whether the authorities would be able to manage the programmes as well as transfer and account for expenses from the EU cohesion policy budget.

8.2.1 The Origins of Poland's Regional Policy Reform

The communist regime left behind a fragmented territorial administrative structure based on 49 'voivodships' and sectorally-oriented public finance flows. The 'national councils' governing these small regions remained entirely subjugated to communist party rule and did not play any role in designing structural policies in their areas. The concept of regional policy understood as a bulk of territorially-oriented policy actions[5] appeared, in this institutional context, redundant.

Nevertheless, the political and economic challenges that Poland faced in the wake of systemic transformation put regional and administrative reforms back on the political agenda. Rising regional differences and unemployment levels, and the abrupt impoverishment of large sections of society, reinforced the debate on regional policy as a remedy to the negative effects of the 'shock therapy'. An additional stimulus for change came from the national councils, which, as the repository of the old communist elites, seemed at best unsuitable partners for putting the modernisation reforms into effect.

The post-communist government of Tadeusz Mazowiecki took the first modest step towards devolution of some central government powers and democratisation of Poland's governance. The Local Government Act adopted in March 1990 introduced a two-tier administrative system, restoring self-governing municipalities. Although around 2,500 *gminas* (communes) were too small to conduct any regional policy, the reform lent importance to the notion of local interest and created nascent structures willing to pursue it. At the same time, the 49 voivodships remained the repository of the state's powers in the regions.

Although the 1990 reform fell far short of a fully fledged democratisation of the governance system, it constituted an important advance in the direction of the institutional model advocated by Poland's academics since the 1970s. The leading experts in the regional policy field, Jerzy Regulski[6] and Michał Kulesza,[7] initiated in 1978 the 'Experience and the Future' seminar, which eventually formulated the key principles of the self-governance reform to be carried out in Poland.[8] They anticipated splitting from the 'democratic centralism' of the single state authority and conferring legal status upon the communes (Emilewicz and Wołek, 2002). The systemic change in the late 1980s presented a tremendous opportunity to put these theoretical postulates into practice.

Rationalisation of the territorial policies by transfer of some state powers to the subnational structures was the key objective of the awaited reform. A country the size of Poland, with almost 40 million inhabitants, simply could not be managed effectively from the central level only. On the one hand, the territorial reform was expected to facilitate economic growth and increase Poland's attractiveness to foreign capital (Szomburg, 2001: 12). On the other, decentralisation was seen as potentially contributing to further democratisation by mobilising social energy and activating local communities (Grosse, 2003: 9). The advocates of change, in particular academics, representatives of the newly created local units and some politicians, emphasised the positive effects of institutional reform spilling over to the political and social domains.

Yet the political turmoil of the 1990s impeded further progress on the territorial issues involving decentralisation of the state's power. The incumbent governments focused on restoring economic equilibrium and putting the country on the path of economic growth,[9] while regional development was seen as having secondary importance (Hausner and Marody, 2000: 97). Furthermore, decentralisation was frequently perceived as a threat to the unity of the country and thus remained a politically contested topic. None of the major political forces showed any particular resolve regarding broader application of the self-governance principle, the key component of academics' proposals.[10] The attitude of the political heirs of the Solidarity movement[11] was, however, generally more pro-reformist. On the other hand, post-communist parties, such as the Democratic Alliance and the Polish Peasants Party,[12] which formed the governing coalition in 1993–1997, overtly opposed power devolution and territorial decentralisation. There was thus no chance for progress in this sphere until there was a shift in political representation to the benefit of the anti-communist forces in October 1997.

The reinstatement of political activities in the regional policy field became feasible with the coming to power of the post-Solidarity Jerzy Buzek government.[13] It won the elections on the premise of systemic changes, which would complete the country's transition efforts.[14] These included reform of the health system, pensions and insurance, education and territorial administration. Earlier, the post-Solidarity environments had managed to ensure the insertion of provisions on self-governance into the Constitutional Act (1997).

After much political wrangling over the size and number of provinces, which dominated political discourse on the territorial issues, the government adopted a compromise solution assuming the division of Poland into 16 self-governing provinces, known as voivodships (Table 8.1). The key premises of the reform were the introduction of a tri-level territorial administrative system, devolution of central government's powers to the voivodships and the introduction of self-governance at all levels of territorial administration.[15] The voivodship marshals appointed by the elected regional

Table 8.1 Territorial division of Poland after the 1998 reform.

Number of units	Level	EU nomenclature
1	Country – Poland	NUTS I
16	Provinces – voivodships	NUTS II
44	Subregions – macroregions	NUTS III
373	Counties – *poviats*	NUTS IV
2489	Municipalities – *gminas*	NUTS V

Source: *Reply to the Common Position of the EU from July 2000* (PM Chancellery 2000)

parliaments were to assume a substantial part of the competencies thus far executed by central administration. In each province the Minister of Internal Affairs also appointed the voivod, in charge of guarding the 'national (central government's) interests' in the region. In practice, the voivods' offices formed parallel regional bureaucratic structures.

The territorial division adopted in 1998 was assigned prior to accession the Nomenclature of Territorial Statistical Units (NUTS) categories. In the course of the accession negotiations on Poland's membership in the EU, the Eurostat accepted Poland's territorial units in their original shape and number.

Although seen by both domestic policy-makers and the EC officials as a great achievement, the reform suffered from a number of difficulties and did not address all the deficiencies of Poland's territorial policies. The general shortcoming was that policy implementation had not led to realisation of its ambitiously defined goals, namely the introduction of the rational division of public tasks and competencies between the central and regional administration, and the enhancement of social integration by strengthening local communities and citizens' participation in public life at the local level.[16] Strong provinces were expected to facilitate pro-developmental actions in the regions but they were also expected to become future players at the EU level (Klasik, 2001: 183). However, the capacity of regional self-governments to act was constrained by weak financial safeguards based on their own limited financing (Gilowska and Misiąg, 2000; Gilowska, 2001). The regional contracts, designed as the key instruments for the regional policy, also did not meet the expectations of reform authors (Pyszkowski *et al.*, 2000: 120; Grosse, 2003b: 17). Experts argue that the Law on the principles of support for regional development (2000) set the model of the subtle steering of self-governments' expenditures and that regional contracts substituted the factual decentralisation of public finances (Gilowska, 2001: 145). The poor demarcation of competencies between governmental and self-governmental administration in the regions provided yet another platform for conflict. The unwillingness of the voivods to relinquish their role in the regional development process was its main source (Hausner and Marody, 2000: 100). This exacerbated the conflict with the self-governmental administration, in particular in those regions where the leaders had differing political affiliations.

The largest deficiency of the Polish regional reform, pointed out by practically all academics in the field as well as the very authors of the regional reform themselves[17] (Hausner, 2001: 174; Gilowska, 2001: 159; Kulesza, 2002: 202; Grosse, 2003: 10) was the excessive centralisation of the public finance system. As Kulesza (2002: 202) argues, there is a visible gap between centralisation of the financial management and decentralised organisation of local and regional authorities, their constitutional and statutory position, and the broad scope of responsibilities. Such systemic design has undermined the autonomy of the regions in making decisions about regional development while confirming the longstanding tendencies of the centre to dominate the subnational governmental units. The increasing concern of the EC that the weak Polish regions lacked the administrative capacity to conduct their role in regional development policies and effectively absorb large volumes of EU assistance corroborated domestic critiques of Poland's reforms.

8.2.2 *EU Pressure for Domestic Change in Poland's Regional Policy*

The involvement of the EU in the domestic processes and scrutiny of applicants' progress in adaptation increased considerably after 1997 and the publication of the opinions (Avis) (CEC, 1997) on the candidate countries. The opinions included a requirement from the applicants to demonstrate the possession of sufficient capacity to function within the EU MLG system (Verheijen, 2000), first made explicit during the Madrid European Council. The Avis (CEC, 1997) in a sub-section of 'Administrative capacity to apply the *acquis*' devoted to the regional policy and cohesion stipulated that the applicant should demonstrate the 'existence of appropriate and effective administrative bodies, in particular a high degree of competence and integrity in the administration of Community funds' (CEC, 1997: 107). The Commission, although without pointing to any concrete systemic solutions, noted that the current arrangements in Poland with the Ministries of Economy and Central Affairs dealing with regional policy did 'not yet work entirely adequately'; while with respect to financial control, the effective administration of the *acquis* would require improvements in organisation and coordination 'to create the necessary administrative and budgetary control framework' (CEC, 1997: 107).

The general tone of the EU monitoring documents with regard to Poland's territorial reform was positive, however. Underlining Poland's good chances for membership, *Agenda 2000* summarised that 'Poland … should be able in the medium term to … establish the administrative structure to apply [the *acquis*]' (CEC, 1997b: 63). Also, in the 1999 Regular Report on Poland's progress towards accession (CEC, 1999d: 13) the Commission described the administrative reorganisation undertaken so far as an 'impressive' and 'fundamental' reform of the state administration, which ought to provide significant opportunities for economic and democratic developments at all levels of Polish society. This positive outlook seems, however, to gradually fade away in subsequent Commission Reports.

The following pre-accession documents signalled some problems with Poland's adaptation in the regional policy and administrative fields. In the Accession Partnership (CEC, 1999e: 10) the EC asked Poland's government to prepare the 'national policy for economic and social cohesion', clarify the division of competencies between institutions responsible for carrying structural policies, organise efficient inter-ministerial coordination and improve the budgetary system according to SFs standards (CEC, 1999e: 10). These recommendations followed the Commission's observation in the 1998 Regular Report that Poland's 'regional development strategy is still at a conceptual stage' with weak fiscal procedures and inadequate financial instruments for regional intervention (CEC, 1998: 34).

In the context of financial arrangements for Funds distribution, early pre-accession documents noted in particular the need for 'adequate allocation of financial revenues and of revenue raising powers' to the new administrative structures (CEC, 1999d: 13). Nonetheless, analysis of subsequent Regular Reports suggests that the position of self-governments in this system was gradually less ascertained, pointing to shifts in the Commission's preferences noticed by Hughes *et al.* (2004a). Contrasting with the 1999 Report, more than a year after opening the negotiations in Chapter 21, the 2001 paper (CEC, 2001d: 79) explicitly called for 'careful consideration' of the role of the regions in Funds management in the period up to the end of 2006. This subtle attitudinal change seems to reflect the increasing concerns of the EC about the administrative capacity of the newly established regional structures to process vast volumes of regional funding from the EU budget. The 2001 Report expressed it directly by pointing out that 'above all, the administrative capacity of the units within the ministries and/or other bodies which will be designated as future managing authorities …

needs to be considerably strengthened', so they would be able to take on the responsibility for 'the efficiency and correctness of the management and implementation of the Structural Funds' (CEC, 2001d: 80). In this way the document openly suggested that the managing roles should be taken up by the central, rather than subnational, administrative structures.

The EC officially refrained from giving specific advice on the division of competencies in the Funds allocation system between different administrative tiers, and only monitored 'compliance with the *acquis*'.[18] It also asserted that 'for Structural Funds key issues concerning the distribution of responsibilities remain open' (CEC, 2001d: 79). However, while the initial recommendations advocated endowment of the regional authorities with appropriate fiscal tools for regional policy conduct, the Commission seemed gradually to recognise its misconceptions about Poland's regional reform. The officials appointed in the Delegation in Warsaw rather openly expressed their doubts about the capability of regional authorities to ensure Funds absorption. The basis for such concerns was apparently the inconsistent performance of the regions in the context of PHARE institution-building projects.[19] These views were also known to the Polish officials, in particular from the Office of the European Integration Committee (UKIE).[20] Similarly, academic accounts on adaptation in the regional policy area pointed to the Commission's preference for a centralised funds distribution model (see e.g. Hausner and Marody, 2000: 103; Grosse, 2003: 67), in which the Ministry of Economy would have ultimate responsibility for the programming and implementation of aid programmes. The Commission considered the single structure for Funds disbursement more trustworthy, transparent and easier to monitor.

The decision to centralise the management of the EU Structural and Cohesion funds, which far exceeded in volume any previously available resources for regional development, seemed the rational answer to the weaknesses of the reform indicated above. Endowment of the financially weak regions and their inexperienced authorities with such responsibilities could lead to a serious implementation gap and put in question adaptation efforts in the regional policy field. At the same time, securing an appropriate absorption level of EU funds was a political priority during the first years of Poland's membership in the EU. On the one hand, access to EU cohesion assistance was presented as one of the key reasons to join the EU in the first place. On the other, an inability to utilise available resources could position Poland as a net payer to the EU budget, which was politically unacceptable. Thus, it was the absorption logic that guided all decisions undertaken with respect to the design of an institutional system of funds management. It suggested superiority of the centralised over decentralised systemic solutions.

8.3 The Institutional System of EU Funds Distribution in Poland

The concerns of the EC and Polish politicians about the absorption level were not unfounded when one considers the scope of demands attached to the EU funds disbursement. Successful implementation of EU structural assistance requires a massive administrative workload. Even though no specific institutional solutions were outwardly imposed by the *acquis*, the framework Council Regulation (EC) 1260/1999,[21] laying down general provisions on the Structural Funds (1999),[22] demanded that the member countries benefiting from EU funds set up number of institutions that would fulfil certain roles.

Thus, apart from introduction of the geographical division according to the NUTS, the countries benefiting from aid need to draft multiannual development plans, based on which funding would be disbursed and appraised by the Commission, and to assure realisation of the complementarity and partnership principles as well as coordination between various funds. The key institutions involved in funds distribution are the managing authorities responsible for the efficiency and correctness of the management and implementation of assistance, and the monitoring committees overlooking their realisation. The beneficiary countries need to set up a system allowing the gathering of reliable financial and statistical information, carry out the monitoring by reference to physical and financial indicators

Table 8.2 The management structure of the Operational Programmes

Operational Programme	Managing Institution
SOP Increase of Competitiveness of the Enterprises	Ministry of Economy
SOP Human Resources Development	Ministry of Labour and Social Policy
SOP Restructuring and Modernisation of Agriculture and Development of the Rural Areas	Ministry of Agriculture and Rural Development
SOP Fisheries and Fish Processing Industry	Ministry of Agriculture and Rural Development
SOP Transport	Ministry of Infrastructure
Integrated Regional Development Operational Programme	Ministry of Economy
Technical Support	Ministry of Economy

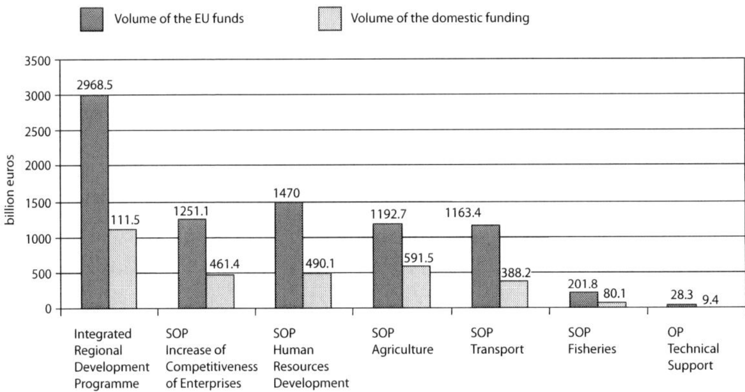

Figure 8.1 Budgetary appropriations for the operational programmes (in billion euros in prices as of early 2010) (CSF, 2003)

specified in the operational programme, and submit periodical implementation reports with its results to the EC.

The system of distribution of EU funding in Poland for the 2004–2006 perspective has been almost entirely centralised. The NDP/CSF divided the funding from the SFs into six single-fund sectoral programmes (the Sectoral Operational Programmes – SOPs) and one multi-fund (ERDF and ESF) Integrated Regional Development Programme (IRDP).[23] The centralisation of management concerned all stages of the policy-making. The programming is initiated by the Managing Authorities (MA), which for all programmes are central government ministries (Table 8.2). Most of the responsibilities, however, fell on the Ministry of Economy,[24] as the MA of the CSF and MA for three sectoral programmes.

The operational functions related to the Funds' disbursement are carried out by the government's specialised agencies, such as the Polish Agency for Entrepreneurship Development or the Agency for Restructuring and Modernisation of Agriculture. Solely in the case of the Integrated Regional Programme, the implementation functions were transferred to the regional authorities, the Marshal Offices. However, even in this latter case they have to share the responsibilities with the Voivodship Offices, representatives of the central governments in the regions. The Ministry of Finance (Paying Authority) is responsible for executing the payments in all the programmes (Figure 8.1).

8.4 Policy Implementation and Administrative Capacity: Is there an Implementation Gap?

The absorption of the SFs in Poland in a manner consistent with the *acquis* encountered difficulties at practically all stages of policy-making. The biggest problems appeared, however, following the programming of the policy, which also affected realisation of the projects. Poland's government committed itself during the accession negotiations (PM Chancellery, 2000) to establish an efficient system of programming, monitoring and financial control of structural instruments by the end of 2001, to adjust regional statistics by the end of 2002, and to complete works on the National Development Plan (NDP) by the end of 2001. Due to the slow progress of the negotiations these dates had to be, however, revised. The eventual agreement anticipated that Poland should implement the legislative arrangements for provision of co-financing in the multiannual horizon by 2002, create an institutional system (defining the target structure of the institutions involved) by the beginning of 2003, and prepare the layout of the NDP together with the number and type of the Operational Programmes (OPs) by the end of February 2002 (Ministry of Economy, 2002). Despite the extension of the deadlines, Poland did not submit its NDP to the Commission until the end of 2002, but it was formally endorsed by the Act on the National Development Plan (2004) only on 24 May 2004, after accession to the EU. Eventually, the first concourses for the projects co-financed by the EU funding were opened at the end of 2004, nearly one year later than anticipated, but some programmes did not operate before the end of 2005.

The key reason for these delays was understaffing of the governmental units endowed with the roles in Funds management. As Żuber pointed out in 2002 (Żuber, 2002: 6), in order to assure appropriate servicing of the tasks related to absorption of the assistance, the number of officials employed by PA should have risen sixfold within less than two years (until 2004). Thus ministries, central government agencies and marshal offices should employ around 1,300 personnel, while another 1,800 should join the units implementing the OPs and the Cohesion Fund. Such a steep increase was very difficult to achieve due to organisational and financial problems. By the end of September 2003 the PA (central and regional) reached the level of around 65 per cent of the target employment to be achieved by January 2004 (Ministry of Economy, 2003: 7). Figure 8.2 presents the dynamics of the employment level in the PA units involved in EU funds management.

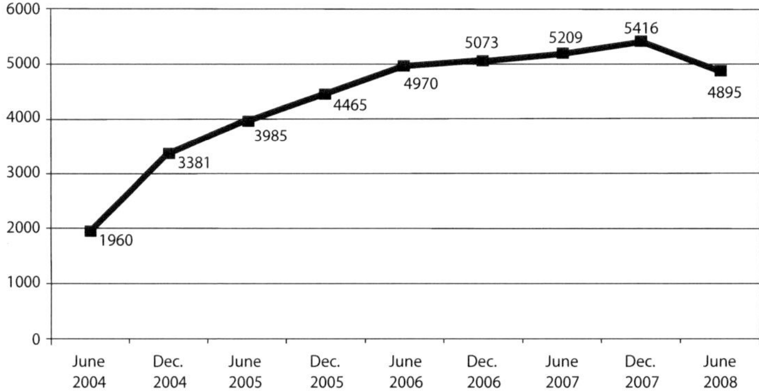

Figure 8.2 The dynamics of employment in public administration units involved in the management of the EU structural and cohesion funds from 1 June 2004 to 1 July 2008 (Ministry of Regional Development 2008: 13)

Whereas the implementation of the framework legal acts establishing the overall administrative structure and rules for the policy conduct proceeded with some delays, the actual enforcement of the EU-financed programmes posed a true challenge. To grasp the complexity of the task one needs to consider that there have been 179 legal acts, ordinances to the Law on the NDP for 2004–2006,[25] which regulated in detail the mode of distribution of the EU structural assistance. Another consequence of permanent delays with the programming stage was the lower quality of these documents. The OPs had to be prepared in parallel, which impaired the coordination of works and synergy between various programmes. In consequence of the mistakes and contradictions in the programming documents, the rules governing the distribution of money had to be permanently amended. For instance, there were 14 amendments of documents guiding the distribution of grants in the framework of the SOP Increase of Competitiveness of Enterprises (the measure for Small and Medium Enterprises-SMEs) during the first year of programme operation. The unstable legal environment presented a serious procedural barrier for the potential beneficiaries of the funding. It constrained its availability since the interested entities had to keep up with all the changes and invest considerable administrative resources to prepare applications. The enterprises encountered procedural barriers to the most serious deficiencies of the system of SFs allocation (FSME, 2006: 9).

The complex institutional system managing the EU Funds and the high number of agents involved in processing the applications also led to serious prolongation of the application process. The average timing from the moment of submission of application for assistance until the payment was nine months during the first year of the Funds' operation. In light of these difficulties and growing complaints about the way the system operated, but also the initially very low absorption levels in the majority of the OPs, the government decided to implement in 2006 the 'Renovation programme', aimed at simplifying the procedures for absorption and its improvement. As a result the Ministry of Regional Development was set up and endowed with the leading role in Funds management. It became the MA for all programmes apart from Agriculture and Fisheries. The reform anticipated simplification of the application for funding procedures, amendment of the Act on the NDP and the Law on Public Procurement.

The 'Renovation programme' was also to remedy for one of the major systemic setbacks, that is, the operation of the IT system for the SFs management (SIMIC). Although it was supposed to start working before Poland's accession to the EU (and construction began in 2002), the system has never become fully operational. The incompleteness of the data input in the system has hindered the monitoring and evaluation processes, since the data needed to be collected manually by each institution (around 120 in total) involved in the Funds' disbursement (Wojtuch, 2006). Despite nearly PLN (Polish Zloty) 20 million spent on the programme, the managing institutions decided to abandon it in the new budgetary perspective and process the applications using simpler and more reliable IT tools. In May 2007 the Supreme Chamber of Control assessed that the electronic system of the monitoring of EU funding represents an example of 'failure in introducing information technology'.[26]

One year after accession, in May 2005 there were still serious concerns about Poland's ability to use the SFs since the average absorption rate, that is funds actually committed and disbursed, was only around 9.3 per cent of the programmes' budgets (Ministry of Economy, 2005: 51).[27] However, thanks to the procedural amendments and institutional changes implemented in the midst of the budgetary perspective, by the end of 2008 the absorption of the EU funds seemed assured.

According to the government report on the implementation of the NDP (Ministry of Regional Development, 2008), at the end of 2008 the value of the submitted applications for co-financing from the EU funds amounted to around PLN 74 billion (around 18.5 billion euro), which constituted more than 230 per cent of the allocation for the whole programming period

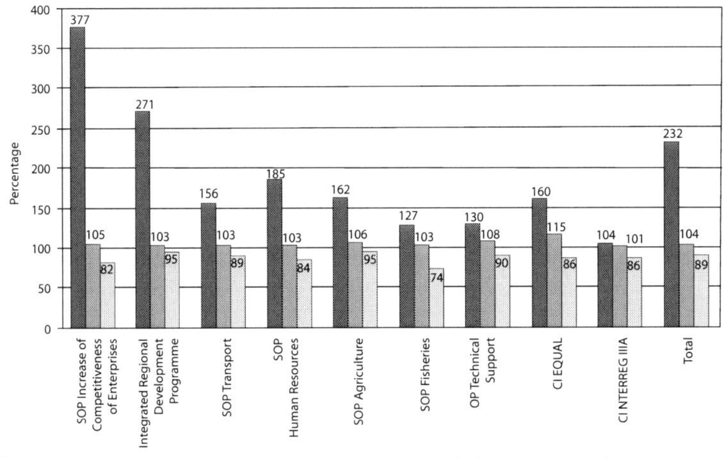

Figure 8.3 Value of the submitted applications, signed contracts for co-financing and executed payments as a percentage of realisation of commitments for 2004–2006 at the end of October 2008 (Ministry of Regional Development 2008: 21)

2004–2006. During this period, the beneficiaries of funding signed the contracts for more than PLN 33 billion (106 per cent of the allocation) and the paying authority executed payments for around PLN 26 billion, which amounts to around 83 per cent of the whole allocation.[28]

As Figure 8.3 demonstrates, despite initial difficulties with programming and management of the programmes throughout their operation, Poland's government has almost managed to utilise all the available resources. There were, however, considerable differences between performances of the particular OPs, discussed in the following section.

8.4 Administrative Capacity and the Pattern of Funds Absorption in the SOP Fisheries and the SOP Increase of Competitiveness of Enterprises

Although most of the problems that Poland's PA encountered regarding the EU-financed assistance system were common to all the programmes, the implementation of some OPs was particularly difficult. As discussed above, delays of the programming and legal adaptation as well as problems with the IT system for monitoring assistance concerned practically all fields covered by the OPs. The systemic centralisation of the policy-making and endowment of one institution, the Ministry of Economy, with most of

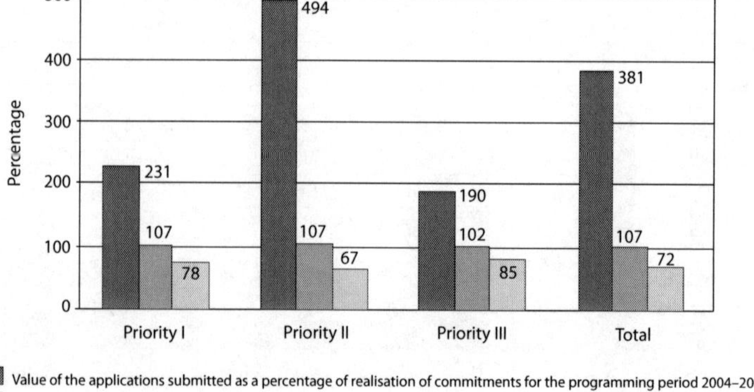

Figure 8.4 Value of the submitted applications, signed contracts and executed payments in the SOP Increase of Competitiveness of Enterprises as a percentage of the 2004–2006 allocation. (Ministry of Regional Development 2008: 27)

Note: Priority I – Development of enterprise and increase of competitiveness through business support institutions, Priority II – Direct support for enterprises, Priority III – Technical assistance.

responsibilities related to programming assistance, monitoring and evaluation, precluded large differences between the programmes. However, the management of the OPs and their operation was handed over to a number of institutions (around 120 entities were involved in one way or another in implementation of assistance), which coped with these tasks with varying degrees of success. It may be assessed through the observation of the pattern of funds' absorption, which varied across the OPs.

In line with the analytical framework outlined in the initial chapters of this volume, the administrative capacity is seen as a precondition for the system to work. Irrespective of the volume of funding, some programmes seemed to operate more smoothly than others, which is demonstrated by the consistently high level of applications for assistance, their timely processing and the disbursement of payments to all programme priorities. Analysis of the indicators of administrative capacity in two of the programmes, Sectoral Operational Programme Increase of Competitiveness of Enterprises (SOP ICE) and SOP Fisheries will allow for determining the factors standing behind the ability of the public authorities to assure absorption.

While the general level of Funds' absorption in the end of the programming period 2004–2006 seems satisfactory, a number of problems

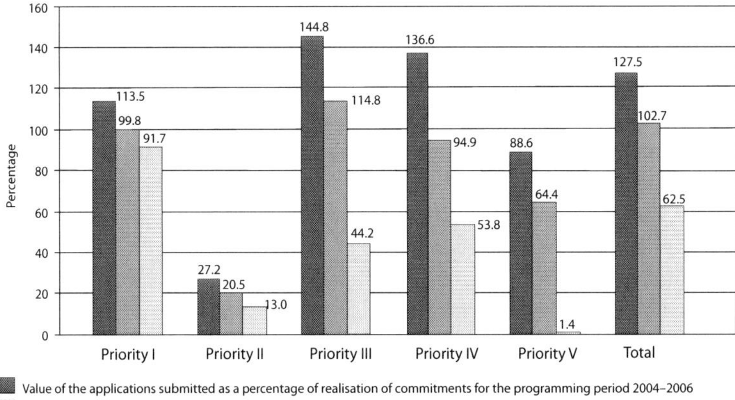

Figure 8.5 Value of the submitted applications, signed contracts and executed payments in the SOP Fisheries as a percentage of the 2004–2006 allocation (Ministry of Regional Development 2008: 41)

Note: Priority I – Adjustment of the fishing capacity to the fishing resources, Priority II – Modernisation of the fishing fleet, Priority III – Protection and development of the maritime resources, fish farming, harbour infrastructure, fish processing, inland fishing, Priority IV – Other activities, Priority V – Technical assistance.

contributing to delays in processing the payments occurred during the programmes' operation. As Figure 8.3 demonstrates, the SOP ICE enjoyed the highest value of the submitted applications and executed payments (with the Integrated Regional Development Programme next in line), while the lowest results were observable in the programme with the smallest budget and thus theoretically easiest to process, the SOP Fisheries. The analysis of the expenditure rates within the programmes' priorities shows that all priorities covered by the SOP ICE were equally popular among the potential beneficiaries (Figure 8.4). On the other hand, there were high discrepancies in this respect between various priorities within SOP Fisheries. Thus the managing institution of the latter needed to put considerable efforts in promotion of the programme despite the benefits to the sector offered within its framework.

As Figure 8.5 demonstrates the SOP Fisheries appeared to be the most differentiated programme in terms of the absorption level, with record low applications for assistance in some measures, such as support for vessel modernisation (Priority II). The governmental report from June 2005 pointed out that applications for assistance in some measures oscillated only at the level of around 1 per cent of the assigned budget (Ministry of Economy, 2005: 61).[29]

In order to improve the overall absorption rate in the programme, the Monitoring Committee decided in 2008 to reallocate the funding from the vessel modernisation objective to the fish processing industry.[30] The need for such actions demonstrated the poor correlation between the programme design and the real needs of its potential beneficiaries, as was admitted by the Ministry of Regional Development Report (2008: 42). Poor results were also shown in the low level of applications for the technical support component of the programme, available for the authorities in charge of its implementation. While submitted applications in all other OPs exceeded the available budgetary allocations, in the SOP Fisheries the applications came to less than the allocation. These results suggest that notwithstanding relatively low absorption levels in the Fisheries programme, the officials in charge were either unwilling or unable to utilise available assistance for improvement of this record.

The analysis of content of the SOP Fisheries already suggests the likelihood of occurrence of some problems at the implementation stage. The programming phase, as mentioned above, had been centralised by the Ministry of Economy (the Department of the Structural Policy Coordination), in charge of monitoring the preparations for Funds' reception, among others, through the monthly reports from the managing institutions of particular programmes (Ministry of Economy, 2003: 2). However, the content of the programmes had to be worked out by the latter. In case of the SOP Fisheries this role was handed over to the Department of Fisheries in the Ministry of Agriculture while the Department of Managing the SOP ICE in the Ministry of Economy was in charge of the second programme. The former, however, was still not operational in September 2003 (Ministry of Economy, 2003: 3).

Apart from the institutional delays, there were serious problems with enactment of the laws necessary for disbursement of some types of funding. Absence of the Act on the fish market as well as unfinished work on the Act on structural assistance in fisheries[31] indicated inability of the Fisheries Department in the Ministry of Agriculture to fulfil its programming functions. Moreover, the quality of the SOP Fisheries programme, implemented by the ordinance of the Minister of Agriculture in August 2004, remains questionable. The programme overlooked a number of problems which Poland's fisheries encountered after accession, did not make a clear linkage between those and the choice of priorities, did not prioritise actions, and did not include the SWOT analysis (2004). These weaknesses were recognised by the Fisheries Monitoring Committee, which even in 2005, during the programme operation, was making serious revisions to the text.

Although a number of scholars, potential beneficiaries and the consulting companies pointed to the deficiencies present in all OPs (see e.g. Grosse, 2003a; 2004), the quality of particular documents differed. For instance, the SOP ICE, adopted one month earlier than the SOP Fisheries, addressed the problems it aimed to tackle in a more accurate and comprehensive way. The programme included the SWOT analysis of the competitiveness of the Polish economy and linked the programme objectives and the priorities with the defined weaknesses. Thus it had from its inception more chances to address the real needs on the ground. Although there were numerous revisions of the programme documents throughout its operation, no major revision of the text of the programme itself needed to be conducted.

At the management stage of the Funds' absorption, the SOP ICE seems equally superior to Fisheries. Although far more complex due to the much larger volumes of funding in its budget, the rate of expenditure in the former has been consistently higher. The key advantage seemed the location of the MA of the SOP ICE within the Ministry of Economy, which played the role of the MA of the CSF, and as such possessed considerable organisational and human resources for dealing with the EU funds. The Ministry, as the leading institution in charge of the EU funds, employed the highest number of qualified staff, and its departments were able to pool resources from other units. In particular, during the first programming period there were a high number of interdepartmental meetings, which resulted in the consolidation of the information transfer channels and the possibility to work out common solutions.

In contrast, the staff of the Department of Fisheries, placed in the Ministry of Agriculture, was detached from the core institutions dealing with EU funds. Additionally, the Department of Fisheries remained understaffed and underfunded. Inadequate human and operational resources (there were only 12 officials dealing with fisheries in 2003) prevented it from tackling effectively the mounting problems in the industry. Additionally, it seemed marginalised within the structures of the ministry, which dealt with agricultural problems of much larger political importance. Some fishermen's organisations claimed that the weak position of the Department of Fisheries within the ministerial structures hampered its ability to conduct the reforms and contributed to legislative delays in adaptation (Gzel, 2002). In the opinion of fishermen, but also some administration officials, the government was intellectually, technically and financially unprepared to carry out a reform of such scope as adaptation to the CFP (Common Fisheries Policy).[32]

Moreover, the political turbulence concerning the administration of the sector at the central executive level, and the repeated transfer of responsibilities for fisheries, first from the Ministry of Transport to Agriculture, then to the Ministry of Maritime Economy and then back to Agriculture, all over the course of a few years, hampered development of an efficient policy management system. Furthermore, in 2006 the new Minister of Agriculture, Andrzej Lepper,[33] dismissed the majority of key employees of the Department of Fisheries. The structure lost its intellectual capacity to prepare good quality programming documents, such as the OP Fisheries in the 2007–2013 budgetary perspective.

The complexities related to Funds' management within the PA resulted in the level of absorption of the EU Funds in the SOP Fisheries at the level of around 70 per cent, the lowest of all OPs realised within this budgetary perspective. The Ministry of Regional Development identified the key problem as the persistently low level of contracting and payments, in particular concerning the funds for temporary suspension of fishing and vessel modernisation. In the latter priority, the level of absorption reached only 18 per cent of available allocation and only four agreements were signed (Ministry of Regional Development, 2008). As representatives of fishermen agree, due to the weakness of the PA, the funds for the Fisheries programme were either not spent or devoted to goals of secondary importance, which was likely to hinder the policy outcome of EU Funds' operation in the field.[34]

The centralisation of the monitoring and evaluation of Funds has not been sufficient to remedy the problems with their administration which occurred at the implementation phase. The ability to introduce serious improvements to the programmes, even though they did include the system of indicators and monitoring procedures, was hampered by their short lifespan. The first budgetary perspective that Poland participated in lasted only two years. Additionally, the monitoring was hindered by problems with the IT system, which has never become fully operational. The ineffective SIMIC prevented the monitoring committees from fulfilling their functions as it impeded both the full analysis of the data and the possibility of an early reaction to the signals of risks.

8.5 Conclusion: How Long can Centralisation Last?

The administrative system in Poland in the wake of accession has been characterised by the unclear division of competencies between administrative tiers, insufficient financial resources of the regional authorities, weak administrative capacity, and competition with government administration in the regions (voivodship offices). These systemic failures called into question whether implementation of a MLG system during the first years after accession was the optimal choice. Following such arguments, the European Commission promoted a centralised system for Poland in the first post-accession years. This decision further reinforced the position of the central government in regional policy-making.

As the above data demonstrate, if assessment of the results of the implementation of the EU Structural Funding was constrained solely to the absorption level, the centralised management system has appeared to produce desirable outcomes. Although the policy output of the Funds application in Poland is still uncertain, the centralised structure for their distribution in the first years of membership allowed for securing a reasonably high absorption level. This outcome raises a question about the unconditional desirability of MLG which is often pointed out in the literature on EU cohesion policy. Administratively weak regional authorities and a volatile political system create contextual conditions in which MLG may fail to assure social representativeness and effective Funds distribution. Thus a decision to centralise EU Funds management may have been the best first choice when guided by the premise of securing sufficient level of funds absorption.

However, the demonstrated variation in performance of the two centralised OPs may also be interpreted as proof that the degree of decentralisation is not the most important factor in assuring appropriate expenditure level. Rather, as the cases of the two analysed programmes have showed, the administrative capacity of the units involved in the Funds' implementation, no matter whether at the central or subnational level, does make a difference for the achieved expenditure rate.

Nonetheless, the maturing of Poland's democracy and the experience acquired in the implementation of regional policy will probably lead to a gradually shifting governance paradigm. The cohesion policy of the EU, by endowing the regions with a substantial role in the Funds management, does seem to encourage the emancipation of subnational structures and demands for democratisation (Goetz and Hix, 2000). This has been confirmed in Poland during the working out of the subsequent 2007–2013 budgetary perspective, where the Polish regions took a much more active position. As a result, the new system anticipates endowing the voivodships with responsibilities for absorption of around 25 per cent of the appropriated assistance. It remains to be seen, however, whether this systemic solution will prove equally effective in both delivering absorption and solving problems that persist from the first budgetary perspective.

9

IMPROVING IMPLEMENTATION PERFORMANCE IN THE EU MULTI-LEVEL GOVERNANCE FRAMEWORK

9.1 Are the Two Sets of Preconditions Valid Across the EU27?

This research began by observing some puzzling empirical evidence. Retrospective data on SFs implementation rates over the past 16 years, presented in Chapter 2, show very different performance levels among Member States; in particular, Italy's performance has constantly lagged behind that of other EU Member States, while Spain's performance has been among the highest. However, an analysis of Italy's and Spain's Objective 1 regions clearly reveals that not all regions follow the national trend. Retrospective data suggest that SFs implementation over previous planning periods has differed markedly between regions within the same Member State. The performance spectrum ranges from a very low implementation rate in Sicily and Andalucía to a high rate in Basilicata and Galicia.

Having observed that variation exists at the regional level, and having established that, within the new MLG framework, regional governments play a fundamental role in the success of policy implementation we have tested the relevance of two sets of preconditions in determining implementation output.

These two sets of preconditions are (1) administrative capacity in terms of management, programming, monitoring, evaluating; and (2) political factors in terms of political interference, stability and accountability. Our further suggestion was that a relation might exist between the two sets.

Analyses of the three Member States – Italy, Spain and Poland – were carried out to varying degrees of depth, and show contrasting evidence regarding the relevance of the two sets of preconditions and their interconnections.

In Italy variation in implementation seems to be strongly dependent on differences in administrative capacity, so that higher administrative capacity in Basilicata has favoured higher implementation while lower administrative capacity in Sicily seems to be accountable for its poor performance. Furthermore, political factors seem to have had an important influence on the evolution of the four actions of administrative capacity measured in both Sicily and Basilicata.

In Sicily the following characteristics were revealed:

1   A disruptive political interference, where the political class dominates the administrative sphere, thus restricting the latter's ability to implement the programmes, interfering with management activities and ultimately increasing the uncertainty of 'who does what', and leading to an uncoordinated set of actions and a confusion of roles.
2   A high level of government instability with constant changes of leadership has caused a significant amount of discontinuity and delay in the overall administrative system and has had repercussions on programme coherence and delays in approval of the programmes.
3   A lack of accountability of the political class has led to its closed attitude to any form of evaluation or monitoring of programmes.

The opposite situation emerged in Basilicata, where we found that:

1   There is a supportive political class, which has seen the EU Funds as an opportunity to reinforce the region's social and economic structure and renew programmatic interventions. The two levels, political and administrative, have been able to work together, each fully recognising the other's role, power and responsibility in creating a constructive relationship.
2   The governments have always been very stable. This has enabled the implementation of a long-term plan, and has ensured coherence and continuity in the formulation of the development strategy, and the avoidance of undue delays in programme preparation or authorisation.
3   The political class is perceived as accountable and favours the development of monitoring and evaluation practices.

In Spain differences in implementation performance seem to be more dependent on political factors than on administrative ones. Both Andalusia and Galicia are indeed equally endowed regarding regional administrative capacity in the management of SFs. However, Andalusia's more intrusive political environment might explain why its implementation of SFs presents a less positive record compared to that of Galicia.

In Poland, where subnational government was very weak, a centralised approach to SFs implementation has been beneficial in guaranteeing the prompt absorption of the Funds, where an initial MLG division of responsibilities might well have delayed SFs implementation, given the lack of capacity at subnational level coupled with a volatile political system.

9.2 The Efficiency of Multi-level Governance as a System for Policy Implementation

The findings of this research on the key components of administrative capacity and on the relevance of political factors in influencing the variation in capacity between the regions have solid implications for questioning the efficiency of MLG as an implementation system.

In this respect, MLG provides a framework for policy-making and policy implementation and can deliver great results. However, it requires that all the actors involved at different levels possess adequate capacity to administer the policy. A process of decentralisation within the Member States is deemed necessary in order that the subnational regions may emerge in the EU arena. However, this is not sufficient to develop administrative capacity. Two different but complementary arenas, political and administrative, constitute regional government. They need to find an equilibrium in their mutual interactions, where each respects the other's roles and responsibilities without limiting or interfering in its arena. It is through proactive cooperation between the administrative and political bodies that regional institutions can achieve the goal of effectively implementing their policy, and therefore deliver results. Based on this, the following recommendations emerge for EU, national and regional policy-makers.

For EU Policy-makers

EU policy-makers have stressed the relevance of administrative capacity for improving levels of implementation of cohesion policy. Although administrative and institutional capacity were highlighted as vital elements with regard to this, neither a clear definition of administrative capacity nor a strong and coherent assessment model is to be found in the existing literature. The first accomplishment of this research is to have provided a definition of administrative capacity that can be replicated in other regions or Member States.

Indeed, EU policy-makers seem to repeat the same mistakes. The new Council regulation for cohesion policy over the period (2007–2013) continues to be extremely vague. The aim of SFs for the new Objective 1 regions is laid out as follows:

> In the case of regions and Member States eligible for support under the Convergence objective, the aim should be to stimulate growth potential, so as to achieve and maintain high growth rates, including addressing the deficits in basic infrastructure networks and strengthening institutional and administrative capacity. (Council Decision 18/08/2006: 5)

In subsequent pages we read that

> an appropriate amount of the European Social Fund (ESF) resources shall be allocated to capacity-building, which shall include training, networking measures, strengthening the social dialogue and activities jointly undertaken by the social partners. (Council Decision 18/08/2006: 42)

Still there is no sign of a more concrete and operational definition of administrative capacity.

For Cohesion countries and regions under the Convergence Objective (Objective 1), increasing productivity and quality at work in the public sector – especially in the economic, employment, social, educational, health, environmental and judicial areas – is essential in order to pursue and accelerate reforms, to raise productivity and growth in the wider economy and to promote social and territorial cohesion and sustainable development. The SFs can play an important role in supporting effective policy design and implementation, which involves all relevant stakeholders, in a broad range of fields. Thus, Member States are invited to conduct a comprehensive analysis to identify the policy areas requiring the most support with regard to administrative capacity (Council Decision 18/08/2006).

In conclusion, the EU policy-makers call upon Member States and regions falling under the Convergence Objective to build up public administrations and public services at national, regional and local levels, but still they do not give any specific definitions or indicators by which eventual progress may be benchmarked. This research has attempted to fill this gap, first by providing a model of administrative capacity that can be applied by Member States to any region, irrespective of its administrative tradition; second, by suggesting objective indicators which would not only make it possible to measure improvements in a specific country over time, but also to make cross-country comparisons.

For National Policy-makers

The experience of Member States of the management and implementation of SFs demonstrates that there is no single, universally applicable model that holds true for all cases and situations, as demonstrated in the accounts of Italy, Spain and Poland given here. The context of regional administrative structures and political culture has a significant bearing on the actual model that is adopted in a particular location. It would therefore be a mistake to study the efficiency of SFs implementation without taking full account of this diversity of context.

According to EU policy-makers, Member States should ensure that the need to increase efficiency and transparency in public administrations and to modernise public services is adequately addressed. Guidelines for action under this heading are the following:

> (i) Support good policy and programme design, monitoring, evaluation and impact assessment, through studies, statistics, expertise, and foresight, support for interdepartmental coordination and dialogue between relevant public and private bodies; (ii) Enhance capacity building in the delivery of policies and programmes, especially through mapping of training needs, career development review, evaluation, social audit procedures, implementation of open government principles, managerial and staff training and specific support to key services, inspectorates and socio-economic actors. (Council Decision of 6 October 2006: 18)

As already stated, these guidelines appear to be very generic. What in practice do national governments have to do? How can they enhance capacity building? Once again, questions arise that have been central to part of this research. To which capacity are we referring? How do we measure the progress of these capacities?

Close reading of the EU official documents helps us deduce what the Commission means by the phrase 'administrative capacity'. In general terms, the Commission has sought the following reforms in the public administrations of the applicant states: legislation, specifically that regarding the civil service; the establishment of a civil service career; political neutrality of the civil service; and pay reform designed to bring public sector pay closer to that in the private sector. Behind, and below, these broad horizontal measures the Commission has now routinely reviewed the capacity of applicant states to implement the *acquis* in different areas.

New Member States, which have dealt with the issue of administrative capacity since the negotiations started, have been trying to implement actions to promote administrative capacity at the national level and also to assist the sub-national level in doing so, following the above EU guidelines. The EU15 Member States, however, started their programmes of capacity building more recently. Some countries, such as Spain, England and Italy, invested in capacity building activity during the period 2000–2006. National policy-makers play an important role in this area because they can allocate part of the budget to implement programmes of regional assistance for improving capacity. To do this, however, they need a clear idea of which capacity aspects to be improved. National policy-makers aware of the specific regional deficiencies could suggest more effective and targeted interventions.

For Regional Governments

The extensive fieldwork conducted allows us to provide the regional governments with some useful indication of how to improve SFs implementation. Regions need to carry out the following actions:

1   Set up a structure for improving centralised management that guarantees horizontal coordination and clarity of role among personnel, mainly when several departments are involved. This will support the programming, monitoring and implementation process for the whole period by maintaining a constant vision of the whole process.
2   Develop a programme based on a coherent SWOT analysis whose strategy of development responds to the real territorial needs. It should be possible to carry out the development plan within the time period set out by the multiannual European time span. Both an effective programme design and efficient programme approval time will allow the implementation process to be speeded up.
3   Provide a punctual and accurate monitoring system which directly feeds information into the management unit, in order that interventions may be made where necessary. This will allow the management unit to intervene when monitoring data indicates that problems have appeared.
4   Support the spread of evaluation activities within the regional administration, so that programming of future interventions can be improved.

An evaluation carried out in three stages — *ex-ante, in itinere* and *ex-post* — will highlight qualitative problems, which not always are captured by the monitoring indicators.

My research revealed that administrative activities are mostly influenced by some political factors. Therefore, bearing this in mind, the regional government should aim to do the following:

1   Reduce political interference in the administrative arena. This has been the subject of both national and regional legislation that aims to differentiate the two spheres of action. However, the formal legislation can only do so much; it is up to the political class to respect the administration and to give it space to operate. It is the responsibility of these two spheres to work together in order to promote the successful implementation of development programmes.

2   Promote government stability, not only in terms of keeping the same President for the entire legislation, but also in not reshuffling members of the council midway through the government's tenure. Regional governments that change constantly have more difficulty in maintaining a strong commitment to multiannual programmes. Unstable governments are also more likely to witness change in the civil servants responsible for sustaining development programme as well as in the political class. This is likely to cause a significant amount of discontinuity and delay in the overall administrative system.

3   Increase political accountability, so that monitoring and evaluation activities are not perceived as a threat but as supportive elements of any decision-making process.

The above implications for administrative and political actors, although deduced through a thorough investigation of SFs policy implementation, could also be expanded to other policy areas which are expected to be implemented within a MLG framework.

NOTES

Chapter 2

1   The reform was achieved through five Council Regulations: the framework Regulation (2052/88) and the implementation Regulations (4253/88, 4254/88, 4255/88, 4256/88). It became effective on 1 January 1989.

2   All of these regions have a number of economic signals/indicators 'flashing red': a low level of investment; a higher than average unemployment rate; a lack of services for businesses and individuals; and poor basic infrastructure.

3   The Community Support Framework (CSF) is a document approved by the European Commission, accordingly with the Member State, on the basis of the evaluation of a Development Plan presented by the State itself. The CSF contains a summary of the existing socio-economic context, the strategy planned to improve the context, the priorities, the specific objectives, the division of the financial resources, and the conditions for implementation. The CSF is implemented through an Operational Programme (OP), which is elaborated by each Region and approved by the European Commission. The OP describes in detail the priorities set by the CSF and it comprises operational interventions implemented through pluriannual measures.

4   The ten new Member States are Malta, Cyprus and eight Central and Eastern European Countries: the Czech Republic, Estonia, Hungary, Latvia, Lithuania, Poland, the Slovak Republic (Slovakia) and Slovenia The only exception to this rule is Cyprus which, given that only the Greek part has entered, has a GDP per capita of 77.8 per cent (EU15) and 85.4 per cent (EU-25). See European Commission, 2004: 200. In 2007 two new Member States joined the EU, Bulgaria and Romania, and their GDP per capita levels were also below the 75 per cent threshold.

5   In all EU countries 'regions' exist as geographic and statistical entities. However, they do not necessarily exist as administrative or political entities. With the exception of Germany, Austria and Belgium, which had federal structures (in Belgium's case since 1995), other European Member States started this process of institutional adjustment from different points. Of these, we can identify

three groups according to their governance structures in 1988: (1) those with no regional tier of governance (Greece and Ireland); (2) those with some form of subnational institutions (UK, Portugal, and the Netherlands); and (3) Spain, Italy and France with a full system of regional bodies but with varying responsibilities for regional policy.

Chapter 3

1   The relevance and part of the definition of the four key components are suggested by Council Regulation n.1260/99, n.2052/88, n.2081/93.

2   Documentation used includes the evaluation reports of other EU Objective 1 regions. I have been working for a consultancy firm appointed by the European Commission to carry out the Assessment of Mid-Term Evaluation Report of Spain, UK, and Ireland. This appointment has allowed me to familiarise myself with the problems encountered by these countries in administrating the funds.

3   The Member States submit programming documents to the Commission following its general guidelines. Programming documents can take the form of Community Support Frameworks (CSFs) translated into Operational Programmes (OPs), or Single Programming Documents (SPDs), comprising a single document approved by the Commission, which combines information on the overall plan and the indication of how the OP will be implemented. For Objective 1 regions a CSF is required at the national level which is then translated into operational programmes at the regional level, i.e. Regional Operational Programmes (ROPs).

4   The three monitoring types are as follows:

i   Financial data: monitoring of the financial indicators concerning the effective costs incurred by final beneficiaries. The data, collected for each project and gathered by measure, are benchmarked with the financial plan (as detailed in the priority axis and measure) of each OP, both Regional and Sectoral, and Programme Complement. The financial indicators of performance are monitored on a quarterly basis.

ii   Physical data: monitoring of the project physical data, collected into a grid of shared indicators as stated by the CSF Managing Authority. Monitoring activities concern implementation, performance and impact indicators reported in the OPs and Programme Complements.

The performance and impact indicators are estimated during the evaluation on the basis of monitoring data available for each project and measure. The physical indicators of performance are monitored on annual basis.

iii   Procedural data: Monitoring provided for all OPs, both Regional and Sectoral, up to the launch round of projects, and implemented through the definition of survey sheets by activity type and measure-based data-collection models. Data collected at project level (through a significance limit and the choice of the procedural pathway to be monitored). The procedural indicators of performance are monitored twice a year, on a six-monthly basis.

5 Contextual factors are socio-economic development; political culture; and social stability. Endogenous factors are: conflict within the regional government (*giunta*); conflict within the regional legislative body (*consiglio*); and external conflict with the national and local government.

6 Government stability is measured in terms of the number of different cabinets installed in each region during the period of legislature.

7 I have made some changes to the original IDFM in order to adapt the methodology to my study. The four stages of the IDFM are: Start up, Development, Consolidation, and Sustainability. In my analysis the four stages start from a lower level – i.e. Absent – because after performing the fieldwork it was clear that many capacities were not present in the regional administration when the cohesion policy was introduced.

8 The same external evaluator, namely, Ernst & Young, carried out the intermediate evaluations for Sicily and Basilicata.

Chapter 4

1 Law 646 of 1950 established the *Intervento straordinario* (Extraordinary intervention) as the legislative framework for the regional policy, operating through a special fund managed by a specific state agency, the *Cassa per il Mezzogiorno – Casmez* (Fund for the South). From 1950 to 1984, the *Casmez* was in charge of national regional policy implementation in favour of the South. The origins of the *Intervento Straordinario* are consistent with a policy tradition that, since the early stages of the Italian unitary state, has been characterised by a '[s]tate-centric, supply-oriented pattern of interventionism in economic development measures' (Gualini, 2004: 81).

2 The long cycle of reform was introduced mainly by the governments led by Amato and Ciampi (1992–1994) and by the centre-left coalitions (1996–2001).

3 The criteria were: (1) inflation – no higher than 1.5 per cent above the average inflation rate of the lowest 3 inflation countries in the EU; (2) interest rates – the long-term rate no higher than 2 per cent above the average of interest rates in the three countries with the lowest inflation rates; (3) budget deficit –no more than 3 per cent of GDP; (4) national debt – no more than 60 per cent of GDP; (5) exchange rates – currency within the normal bands of the ERM with no re-alignments for at least 2 years (Talani, 2004).

4 On Europeanisation see also Börzel and Risse, 2000; Fabbrini and Della Sala, 2004; Page, 2003.

5 Law 59/1997 is also known as the Bassanini reform and encompasses the re-designation by government of the duties and powers of regional and local governments; the reform of the public sector bargaining system; the reform of the macrostructure of government; the introduction of the annual law on de-legislation and simplification (to enforce this delegating law more than sixty legislative decrees were needed).

6 What these reforms accomplished was to formally put the national and regional levels on a more equal footing *vis-à-vis* the Constitutional Court and in the

allocation of primary powers in a variety of policy making sectors, including regional policy, to the regions.

7 The two main political parties in Italy were the DC (Christian Democrats) and the Partito Comunista Italiano (Communist party – PCI). With the development of the Cold War the PCI was permanently excluded from government because of its 'anti-system' nature, and this principle became the lowest common denominator in the formation of governing coalitions. It meant that the DC indefinitely governed in alliance with the smaller parties of the centre and with the Partito Socialista Italiano (Socialist Party – PSI). The failure to achieve alternation in government has been regarded by many scholars as being at the heart of Italy's problems (Bull, Newell, 1993).

8 Newell (2000) identifies two other factors as accountable for the transformation of the party system: (1) the sudden occurrence of judicial investigations unveiling and prosecuting the structure of political corruption; and (2) the change in electoral behaviors, and the rise of the Northern League, a regionalist party that built its fortunes on a populist critique of the traditional political class. This Populist Party proved able to capitalise on the discontent of the richest and most developed part of the country. The southern part of the country was accused of inefficiently consuming resources produced in the north, and the traditional parties were held responsible for the consequent spread of corruption. The diffusion of corruption in Italy was fuelled by two concurring factors. First, in the southern regions the State was historically weak, and resources were mainly allocated through personal links. Second, the political system never underwent an alternation in power. In 1992, a number of major investigations hit all of the major governmental parties, including their top leaders and officials.

9 The term 'spoils system' originated in Anglo-Saxon systems and indicates the right given to the winning political party in elections to make key appointments in the bureaucratic system. Many consider this practice to be justified when capable persons are appointed to senior policy-making positions. They hold that the party in power must craft policy to meet its constituents' needs (Peters, 1997). On the other hand, it is unwarranted when political leaders dismiss able persons from non-policy-making positions. They do this to bring on board others who are qualified only by loyalty to the party, thus compromising governmental effectiveness.

10 Law n. 59/1997 originally previewed the spoils system for the communal and provincial level. Law n. 145/2002 significantly upgraded the previous law by extending the system to all the administrative leaders of the public administrations – i.e. regional and ministerial general managers. Furthermore, it has established (1) that all the managing assignments are temporary, lasting for a maximum duration of three years for the general manager and five for the others; (2) 10 per cent of the positions of general manager and 8 per cent of the places for division manager can be appointed from outside the administration (Cassese, 2002).

11 In 1996, the Financial Act (Law n. 662/1996) realised a further step in the institutionalisation of this policy approach, extending the rationale of negotiated area-based agreements to a comprehensive set of development tools. In particular, the Act introduced two new forms of institutional agreement. The first was *intesa istituzionale di programma* (institutional protocol of understanding), aimed at realising inter-governmental coordination between State, regional and provincial governments. *Intese istituzionali di programma* are called in particular to outline programmes and related objectives and joint actions, to define the listing and scheduling of operational agreements (*accordi di programma quadro*), and to set criteria for monitoring and evaluation and periodic revisions of objectives. The second was *contratto d'area* (area-based contract), a peculiar collective agreement put together by the 1996 national central accord to foster employment within Objective 1 areas.

12 Given that in the past these policies were already the responsibility of the regions, what the new law did was to clarify the state's lack of concurrent powers – i.e. the ability to legislate without first consulting with the regions.

13 The 1996 law was officially motivated by the fact that the Single Market programme, guaranteeing the free circulation of people, goods and capital across national borders within the EU, came into effect on 1 January 1993, and so the national governments could not prevent regional presidents or other officials from travelling to Brussels to contact Commission officials. Another important motivating factor was the creation of the Committee of Regions in December 1993 that formalised the regional role in the EU process of decision-making and consultation.

14 Under art. 117 of the new title V of the Constitution: the Regions were given (exclusive) legislative power with respect to any matters not expressly under the preserve of State law (comma 4) and not included in concurrent legislation. The article listed a series of matters of concurrent legislation where the State would be allowed only to set the fundamental principles (comma 3) with regard to: regional international relations and relations with the EU; foreign trade; job protection and industrial safety; education; scientific research; protection of health; food safety; sport; civil protection; town planning; civil ports and airports; development of cultural and environmental resources; large-scale transport and navigation networks; energy; complementary social security, etc. The region could participate in decisions to establish Community instruments, and implementation of international agreements and EU instruments (comma 5).

15 Unfortunately, there is very little documentation available on the IMPs implementation and on the first cycle of SFs. The most reliable information is that found in the evaluation report carried out by external evaluators appointed by the region and the information acquired through my own interviews (cf. Chapter 5). What clearly emerges is that the regional government in Sicily did not have the means to manage the newly introduced programme, in contrast to the situation in Basilicata. In Sicily there was a blurring of responsibilities among

the administrative staff and the different assessorates, and the region was not familiar with any long-term planning or monitoring and evaluation processes (Arthur Andersen, 1995, 1997). Furthermore, the administrative bottlenecks were exacerbated by the constant interference of the political class and the continuous change of government and political leaders (interview with a member of the Regional European Community Group in charge of managing the IMP and SFs in Sicily, Palermo).

16 The author made a clear distinction between decentralised and centralised countries. In the latter the national authorities had much more power and dominated most of the process.

17 The Commission proposal for the 4 per cent reserve is contained in 'Implementation of the performance reserve for Objective 1, 2 and 3', Working Document 4, Directorate General, Programme Coordination and Evaluation of Operations.

18 A complete and detailed description of the Italian 6 per cent reserve criteria and mechanism design is contained in the 2000–2006 Objective 1 CSF (§6.5 and annex D) and in the document 'QCS Obiettivo 1, 2000–2006; Criteri e meccanismi di assegnazione della riserva di premialità del 6 per cento'.

Chapter 5

1 The Community Support Framework is defined by Art. 9 of Council Regulation 1260/99 (cf. section 2.1, n. 3)

2 The Management Authority tasks are defined by Art. 34 Reg. 1260/99.

3 In the 2000–2006 cycle, in addition to the ROP there were also the National Operative Programmes (NOP), managed by the central administrations: Scientific Research, Technological Development, Higher Education, the School for Development, Security for the Development of the South, Local Development, Transport, Fisheries and Technical Assistance.

4 According to Art. 9 of Council Regulation 1260/99 a measure is 'the means by which a priority is implemented over several years which enable operations to be financed'. The same article defines operations as 'any project or action carried out by the final beneficiaries of assistance'. Within the framework of European economic and social cohesion policy, a measure is the basic unit of programme management, consisting of a set of similar projects and disposing of a precisely defined budget. Each measure has a particular management apparatus. Measures generally consist of projects. Many measures are implemented through a process of Calls for Proposals and subsequent appraisal (Tavistock Institute, 2003: Glossary).

5 Investigations carried out in other countries have pointed to co-ordination as one of the main problems in the management of the programmes (ÖIR, 2003). Indeed, the Objective 1 Programme management structures in Burgenland (Austria) had a total of 17 departments from federal and land level involved in programme implementation, a number which is large in comparison with the

programme size. For the purpose of coordinating and guaranteeing integration of the measures undertaken by each department, fund-specific coordination meetings were instituted under the chairmanship of the MA. The coordinating meetings, which took place every six weeks, constituted the central decision-making body and played a major role in harmonising the varying interests of the federal level and the Länder.

6 This is the name of the programming documents in the first and second planning periods. In the third planning period the same document was called ROP.

7 Infrastructure and network; industry, craft and services; tourism; environmental protection; training; research and innovation; technical assistance, information and monitoring; agricultural infrastructure; environment protection; support to the enterprise income; human resources enhancement.

8 The evaluation reports for Sicily and Basilicata referred to in this chapter are listed in the primary sources section of the bibliography.

9 The general manager of the MA in Sicily, Gabriella Palocci, was the former Director of the Department of Development and Cohesion Policy at the Ministry of the Treasury, the Budget Ministry and the Ministry of Economic Programming.

10 The situation for the IMP appears to have been very similar: the programme was supposed to start in 1986 but was approved after significant delays in May 1988. During the IMP implementation phase the original programme was revised three times, in 1991, 1992 and 1993 respectively (Arthur Andersen, 1995: 7). This was due to a lack of correspondence between the initial strategy and the real needs of the region – i.e. the initial formulation of the programme was not well rooted in the reality of the socio-economic structure of the region.

11 Decision of the European Community Commission N.C (90) 2516/3, 14 December 1990

12 Decision of the European Community Commission N.C (90) 2989/2, 20 December 1990

13 Decision of the European Community Commission N.C (94) 3765, 16 December 1994

14 The general characteristics and purpose of the indicators are described by Art. 36: 'the indicators shall show the stage reached in terms of procedural, financial and physical implementation, results, and impacts'.

15 The Technical Assistance service was created at the national level to improve the institutional performance of public administration, and to enhance the implementation process of OPs and actions co-financed by SFs. Such a task implied technical assistance in helping regional and local governments to implement their programmes with the support of standard models and guidelines, analysis and surveys, shared indicators and databases, the exchange of best practices, and assistance to those in the network.

16 Together they create the defining characteristic of the implementation method in that they lie at the heart of an accountability loop involving all key players in

the EU decision-making process and which requires the EC to account for the expenditure of public money to Parliament and to the European Court of Auditors. From the point of view of the implementation method it has implications for all of the actors and involves the collection of data as a basis for arriving at an assessment of compliance with all of the rules, procedures and technical support measures provided for in the Regulations.

17   Regulation 1260/99, Art. 35 provides for the setting up of a Monitoring Committee which supervises the implementation of SFs. A representative of the Commission should participate in the work of the Monitoring Committee in an advisory capacity. The committee should discuss the implementation of the Funds every six months. Members of the Committee are the general managers of each department, representatives of the political class, socio-economic partners, non-governmental organisations, and representatives of the national government.

Chapter 6

1   The old system where pay and promotion were based on laws and procedures, paying little regard to quality and results was replaced by performance controls, and in particular financial incentives for managers based on position and performance. In addition, a fixed term of seven years was set for all the managers appointed, which could be terminated by poor performance. Lastly, 5 per cent of the state managers could now be selected from outside the civil service.

2   The cabinet implemented the law on 2 July 1997 with resolution 268.

3   The four steps are these: (1) the tender proposals are sent from the *assessorati* to the President of the Region, who forwards them to the Cabinet for the definition of the terms and conditions; (2) the Cabinet examines them and then passes them on to the Regional Assembly; (3) the various commissions which form the Regional Assembly, the Surveillance Committee and the Regional Cabinet separately examine the proposals and express their opinion; (4) the tender proposals are approved. Clearly, this process is extremely long and requires that the whole political system come to an agreement.

4   Annual official reports were prepared by Ecosfera *et al.* between 1999 and 2002: see the primary sources section for Basilicata in the Bibliography. They are cited in this chapter as Ecosfera *et al.* See also the primary sources section for Sicily.

5   The majority party (or majority coalition) in parliament selected the chief executive after a long negotiation process within parties and across the potential members of the governing coalition. The prime minister was elected by, and directly accountable to, the legislature, through the vote of confidence.

6   Since 1994 the prime minister designate has been more clearly defined during the electoral campaign, and the outcomes of the elections were in a position to clearly identify the person who would be designated as prime minister and the coalition that would rule the country.

7   The shortest government lasted nine days, under Andreotti in 1972, and the longest lasted three years, under Craxi in 1983. The Berlusconi government

began in 2001 and ran until the end of the 2006 legislature: it has been the longest serving government in Italian history.

8   Indeed, the Programming Complement was revised and amended 17 times in the last four years for which full data are available (2000–2004) in Sicily, compared with only seven times in Basilicata.

9   Indeed, political accountability has still not been institutionalised as a concept. The literature on accountability agrees that it has to be embedded in a mutually understood and pre-established set of rules (Persson *et al.*, 1997: 1164). Some of these may be formalised in constitutions, legal codes, or sworn oaths, but political accountability is not the same as legal, financial, or ethical accountability: 'More broadly, rulers can be investigated and held to account for actions that did not break the law or result in illicit personal enrichment or violate common mores. They may have simply made bad political choices that failed to produce their intended effect or cost vastly more than initially announced' (Schmitter, 2004: 48).

10   The logic is to allocate resources to local government in order to further local clientelistic boundaries, and ultimately to strengthen, at the local level, its own power. The internal antagonism at regional level leads the political class to reinforce the local request, and uses it to assert its power either within the belonging party or in front of other parties.

Chapter 7

1   The present paper is the result of independent research carried out by the authors. The research has benefited from a previous project in which both authors participated: the SOCCOH project, The Challenge of Socio-economic Cohesion in the Enlarged European Union, financed by the 6th EU Framework Programme for Research (Ref. 029003). We would like to thank Prof. Professor Jacint Jordana for his contribution during the SOCCOH project, Juan José Lirón for his help and support in Galicia and Antonio Valverde for his help in Andalusia. Special thanks also to José Antonio Zamora, Director of the General Department of Community Funds within the Ministry of Economy and Finance. Finally, any errors or omissions are the responsibility of the authors.

2   Indeed, since 1993 there have been only four years in which national political parties elected to government have had an absolute parliamentary majority; thoughout the remaining period they have needed to gain the support of regional nationalist parties, in particular from Catalonia and the Basque Country.

3   A region's developmental legislation can be more demanding than the national legislation – according to the preference of the territorial constituency – but it cannot run contrary to the basic state legislation.

4   Despite some peculiarities – Spain's 40-year dictatorship – the development of decentralisation in Spain during the 1970s and 1980s shares many features with comparable nations, such as Italy, France, Belgium, the United Kingdom and the Netherlands.

5 Ministry of Public Administration (2008)
6 For further details see, among others, Ramió and Salvador, 2000; Parrado, 2001; Cienfuegos, 2007.
7 In the 1960s and 1970s, the development plans and different laws that fostered regional incentives only represented a first and *shy* interest in regional issues.
8 Of the total amount of 97 billion euros (at 1999 prices) for the 1989–2006 period, 84 billion euro derived from SFs, whilst the remaining 13 billion euro are attributable to the Cohesion fund.
9 In the 2000–2006 CSF for Objective 1, the development strategy was defined through 23 OPs, 12 of which were regional (one for each Objective 1 region) and 11 multi-regional programmes. The latter were managed exclusively by the DGFC of the Ministry of Economy.
10 For instance, in 1989 the central government decided to submit three CSFs, one for each Community objective (1, 3 and 5a) instead of 17 separate ones covering each region. In doing so, the central government wanted to maintain control over the territorial redistribution of EU funds, limiting – *de facto* – the financial autonomy of regional governments (Closa and Heywood, 2004).
11 A common characteristic of the young democratic PAs was the 'sweeping capture of power centres and public positions by party activists and supporters' exactly at the most favourable historical moment for creating a democratic state administration and modern regional administrations 'which started from scratch or almost scratch' (Nieto, 1992).
12 For a very detailed investigation of the main characteristics of the Galician PA since the transition, see Bouzas' most recent works, which are very rich in data and valuable information.
13 In particular, Law 4/1991 on Reform of the Civil Service made it possible to rationalise the chaotic situation of the Galician public service until then. The target was to create a professionalised regional civil service able to efficiently and impartially serve general interests. By the beginning of the 1980s there were more than 1,700 temporary public workers in the regional administration's central services, many of them in the positions of assistant director or chief of service. In the following legislature the government found a public administration with more than 7,000 civil servants working with job stability. (Rodríguez, 2004: 240–5).
14 As the report of the Andalusian Ombudsman of 1995, on the selection and provision procedures for public servants, stated: 'Certainly, the Andalusian Civil Service is not an example for other public administrations: a radiography of its state allows us to describe it as inadequate, really deplorable, in a situation of temporality and improvisation whose final regulation is hard to conceive in the short-term. An administration can only work badly when its servants, its employees, are neither motivated nor confident with their jobs and, at the same time, an impression is given of favouritism for acceding to the civil service'. According to this report, in 1995, there were in Andalusian

PA more than 7,000 temporary public workers, many of which were politically designated on the basis of confidence (Informe del Defensor del Pueblo Andaluz, 1995).

15 The *Fundación*, which possesses two different locations – one in Brussels and the other in Santiago de Compostela – is charged with promoting the defence of Galician interests in the European arena, with diffusing all relevant information that can affect Galician society, and with promoting Galician culture (and language) abroad.

16 According to economists, however, SFs contributions can be evaluated positively in Galicia since they have meant 381+ euro per capita for Galician citizens with respect to an unfunded scenario (for the 1995–2006 period).

17 Some evidence from our interviews shows that in Galicia, for example, a bipartite coalition between PSOE and BNG brought about a more political redistribution of the Xunta's *Consellerias*, affecting, not always positively, the whole management of SFs in the region.

18 Or its previous definition as the Popular Alliance (Alianza Popular, AP)

19 According to Sartori, a predominant party system 'is such to the extent that, and as long as, its major party is consistently supported by a winning majority (the absolute majority of seats) of the voters. It follows that a predominant party can cease, at any moment, to be predominant' (Sartori 2005: 173–4).

20 The relationship between regional political stability in Spain and citizen support for regional government and the political system has been studied in depth by Mota (2008). The higher the regional political stability, the higher is the public opinion's support for the performance of regional government.

21 In fact, politicisation of the Spanish PA has continued and even increased over time, since both the socialist (1982–1996) and conservative (1996–2004) governments enlarged the political administrative sphere by increasing the number of politically appointed positions (Parrado, 2004).

22 In the end, as Porras concludes: 'All that, along with the likely misunderstanding of the political majority notion, contributed to the creation of a bureaucratic class closer to the old tradition of a spoiler system than to the modern requirements of a democratically flexible and efficient PA' (Porras, 1992: 504).

23 'Recommendations for improving the operative management' (recommendation A.6), in the *Midterm Updated Evaluation of the Integrated Operative Programme Andalusia 2000–2006*, vol. I (2005: 80). 'Implementation of the recommendations', in the *Midterm Updated Evaluation of the Integrated Operative Programme Galicia 2000–2006* (2005: 29).

24 Contrasting conclusions as regards to the political consequences of PER are stated in Corzo (2002).

Chapter 8

1 Only the tasks related to implementation were divided among other administrative units and governmental departments.

2   The CSF was adopted by Poland's Council of Ministers on 23 December 2003, based on the translation of the document accepted by the EC, which was confirmed by an official letter from the Commissioner for Regional Policy, Michel Barnier, on 18 December 2003 to the Deputy-Minister of Economy, Social Policy and Labour, Jerzy Hausner. The formal adoption of the CSF for Poland took place in May 2004 upon accession to the EU.

3   The budgetary appropriations for CEECs agreed during the 1999 Berlin European Council (and corrected by the Commission in 2002 to include all ten accession countries joining in 2004 rather than the 'Luxembourg group' only) anticipated the total allocation of 25.6 billion euro in 2004–2006 in the framework of the structural and cohesion Funds. Poland's share amounted to 12.8 billion euro, that is, around 50 per cent of this sum.

4   The regional contracts were signed by the management board of the voivodship and the minister in charge of regional development (Chapter V of the Act on the National Development Plan of 20 April 2004).

5   Law of 12 May 2000 on the principles of support for regional development.

6   Jerzy Regulski, a professor of the Łódź University, co-chaired the negotiations on local government reform during the Round Table talks. Government Plenipotentiary for Self-government Reform in 1989–1991. In 1998–1999 Chair of the Council for the Systemic Reform at the Prime Minister's Office.

7   Michał Kulesza, a professor at Warsaw University, in 1992–1994 Government Plenipotentiary for Public Administration Reform, from December 1997 until January 1999 Government Plenipotentiary for Systemic Reform, Under-Secretary of State in PM Chancellery until April 1999.

8   Although communist authorities banned the seminar after its first session, it continued to work as an informal gathering. After martial law was introduced in December 1981, research on self-governance in Poland was carried out by three major academic institutions: the Polish Academy of Science, Institute of Economic Science, the Łódź University, Institute of Cities' Development, and the team of Michał Kulesza at the University of Warsaw.

9   The question of self-governance and state decentralisation, however, appeared on the Round Table agenda. Jerzy Regulski, together with Kulesza and Jerzy Stępień, represented the 'Solidarity' side at the sub-table on pluralism of social organisations, later on replaced by the sub-table on self-governmental reform.

10 Interview with Michał Kulesza, Government Plenipotentiary for Territorial Reform in May 2003.

11 Liberty Union and small factions of the Election Action 'Solidarity' (AWS).

12 The major political players of the time were the post-communist Left Democratic Alliance (Sojusz Lewicy Demokratycznej, SLD), Polish Peasants Party (Polskie Stronnictwo Ludowe PSL), Democratic Union (Unia Demokratyczna, UD) Election Catholic Action (Wyborcza Akcja Katolicka, WAK), Confederation of Independent Poland (Konfederacja Polski Niepodległej,

KPN), Civic Agreement Centre (Porozumienie Obywatelskie Centrum, PC), Christian Democrats (Chrześcijańska Demokracja, ChD), and 'Solidarity' Trade Union.

13 Jerzy Buzek led the coalition between Election Action 'Solidarity' (AWS) and the Liberty Union (UW).

14 The AWS–UW government introduced major health, education and pension system reforms.

15 The reform was introduced in legal terms by the Act of 18 December 1998 on amendment of the Act on the governmental departments; Act of 5 June 1998 on voivodship self-government; Act of 26 November 1998 on income of territorial self-government units; Act of 26 November 1998 on public finance.

16 Substantiation of the resolution of the Council of Ministers in the matter of the principles of preparation and implementation of the public administration reform.

17 The authors' initial plans seemed more ambitious than the outcome, hammered out in the course of a series of political compromises.

18 As the interviewed official of the Commission Delegation in Warsaw stressed. Interview with PHARE Task Manager in the Commission Delegation in Poland in September 2003.

19 Ibid.

20 Interview with the Director of the Department of Support for the Committee of European Integration (in 2001–2004) in the Office of the Committee of European Integration in September 2008; interview with the Director of the Analytical Unit in the Department of Support for Accession Negotiations in March 2006.

21 Prior to the fifth enlargement.

22 Replaced by Council Regulation (EC) 1083/2006.

23 In parallel to these, large infrastructural and environmental investments are co-financed from the cohesion fund and smaller projects are realised within the framework of the Community Initiatives.

24 After the introduction of the Renovation Programme in November 2005, these roles were transferred to the newly established Ministry of Regional Development.

25 See http://isip.sejm.gov.pl/prawo/index.html, accessed February 2010.

26 See http://www.nik.gov.pl, accessed February 2010.

27 The OP Human Resources Development had the best rate in terms of agreements signed (reaching 28 per cent of available budget) while the worst results were observable in the OP Transport, with 0.1 per cent of funding assigned to the concrete projects (Ministry of Economy, 2005: 51).

28 The most problematic issue remained the low rate of absorption of the cohesion fund, which reached only around 50 per cent of the cohesion fund budget at the end of 2008. Thus, still considerable efforts are needed to successfully close the 2004–2006 budgetary perspective.

29 There were only eight applications for assistance in Priority II of the programme.

30 There were 16 million euros reallocated from Priority II of the programme (revival and modernisation of the fishing fleet), mostly to the measures financing the fish processing industry.

31 The Act was not created until the end of the first budgetary perspective. Interview with the President of the Fish Producers Organisation in Władysławowo in September 2008.

32 Interview with the Political Advisor to the Secretary of State in charge of Fisheries in the Ministry of Agriculture and Rural Development, from March 2006.

33 Leader of the Self-Defense party in governmental coalition with the Law and Order party, in power from October 2005 until November 2007. From May to September 2006 he was Minister of Agriculture in the government of Kazimierz Marcinkiewicz, and from October 2006 until July 2007 in the same post in the government of Jarosław Kaczyński.

34 Interview with the President of the Association of Maritime Fishermen in September 2008.

BIBLIOGRAPHY

Primary Sources

European

Commission of the European Communities (CEC)

'Report on the Regional Problems in the Enlarged Community', *Bulletin of the European Communities 6*, Supplement 8/73, 1973.

'Regional Development Programme Mezzogiorno, 1977–1980', Office for Official Publications of the European Communities, Luxembourg, 1979.

'Integrated Mediterranean Programmes 1988 Progress Report', *SEC(89)1665*, Brussels, 1989.

'Community SFs 1994–99: Revised Regulations and Comments', 1993.

'Fifth Annual Relation on SFs, 1993', Office for Official Publications of the European Communities, Luxembourg, 1994.

'Sixth Annual Relation on SFs, 1994', Office for Official Publications of the European Communities, Luxembourg, 1995.

'Seventh Annual Relation on SFs, 1995', Office for Official Publications of the European Communities, Luxembourg, 1996.

'Eight Annual Relation on SFs, 1996', Office for Official Publications of the European Communities, Luxembourg, 1997a.

'Agenda 2000 – Commission Opinion on Poland's Application for Membership of the EU', *DOC/97/16*, Brussels, 1997b.

'Agenda 2000: For a stronger and wider Union' *Bulletin of EU, Supplement 5/97*, 1997c.

'Ninth Annual Relation on SFs, 1997', Office for Official Publications of the European Communities, Luxembourg, 1998.

'Tenth Annual Relation on SFs, 1998', Office for Official Publications of the European Communities, Luxembourg, 1999a.

'Agenda 2000' 1999b http://europa.eu.int/comm/agenda2000/index_en.htm

'Evaluating Socio-economic Programmes', *MEANS Collection*, Office for Official Publications of the European Communities, Luxembourg, 1999c.

'Regular Report from the Commission on Poland's Progress towards Accession', Brussels 1999d.

'Poland, Accession Partnership 1999', *Enlargement DG*, Brussels, 1999e.

'Eleventh Annual Relation on SFs, 1999', Office for Official Publications of the European Communities, Luxembourg, 2000a.

'Implementation of the Performance Reserve for Objective 1, 2 and 3', *Working Document 4*, General Directorate for Regional and Cohesion Policies, 2000b.

'Second Report on Economic and Social Cohesion', Office for Official Publications of the European Communities, Luxembourg, 2001a.

'Twelfth Annual Relation on SFs, 2000', Office for Official Publications of the European Communities, Luxembourg, 2001b.

'EU Governance: A White Paper, 2001', *COM(2001) 428 final*, Brussels, 2001c.

'Regular Report from the Commission on Poland's Progress towards Accession', Brussels, 2001d.

'Thirteenth Annual Relation on SFs, 2001', Office for Official Publications of the European Communities, Luxembourg, 2002.

'Fourteenth Annual Relation on SFs, 2002', Office for Official Publications of the European Communities, Luxembourg, 2003a.

'Second Progress Report on Economic and Social Cohesion', Brussels, 2003b.

'Third Report on Economic and Social Cohesion', Office for Official Publications of the European Communities, Luxembourg, 2004a.

'Fifteenth Annual Relation on SFs, 2003', Office for Official Publications of the European Communities, Luxembourg, 2004b.

'A New Partnership for Cohesion. Convergence, Competitiveness, Cooperation. Third Report on Economic and Social Cohesion', Office for Official Publications of the European Communities Luxembourg, 2004c.

'Sixteenth Annual Relation on SFs, 2004', Office for Official Publications of the European Communities, Luxembourg, 2005a.

'Partnership in the 2000–2006 programming period', *Discussion paper of DG Regio (November)*, Brussels, 2005b.

'Third Progress Report on economic and Social Cohesion', Brussels, 2005c.

'Fourth Progress Report on Economic and Social Cohesion', Brussels, 2007.

Committee of the Regions

'White Paper on Multi-level Governance', *CdR 89/2009 fin FR/EXT/RS/GW/ym/ms*, Brussels, 2009.

Council of the European Communities

'Council Decision of 18 August 2006 on Community strategic guidelines on cohesion 2007/2013', Interinstitutional File: 2006/0131 (AVC).

'Council Decision of 6 October 2006 on Community strategic guidelines on cohesion 200//2013', (2006/702/EC), Official Journal L 291/11, 21/10/2006.

'Regulation (1985) No 2088/85 of 23 July 1985 concerning the Integrated Mediterranean Programmes', Official Journal L 197, 27/07/1985.

'Regulation (1988) No 2052/88 of 24 June 1988 on the tasks of the SFs and their effectiveness and on coordination of their activities between themselves and with the operations of the European Investment Bank and the other existing financial instruments', Official Journal L 185, 15/07/1988.

'Regulation (1988) No 4253/88 of 19 December 1988, laying down provisions for implementing Regulation (EEC) No 2052/88 as regards coordination of the activities of the different SFs between themselves and with the operations of the European Investment Bank and the other existing financial instruments', Official Journal L 374, 31/12/1988 P. 0001 – 0014 CONSLEG – 88R4253 – 24/12/1994 – 33 P.

'Regulation (1988) No 4254/88 of 19 December 1988, laying down provisions for implementing Regulation (EEC) No 2052/88 as regards the European Regional Development Fund', Official Journal L 374, 31/12/1988 p. 0015 – 0020 CONSLEG – 88R4254 – 31/07/1993 – 13 p.

'Regulation (1988) No 4255/88 of 19 December 1988, laying down provisions for implementing Regulation (EEC) No 2052/88 as regards the European Social Fund', Official Journal L 374, 31/12/1988 p. 0021–0024.

'Regulation (1988) No 4256/88 of 19 December 1988, laying down provisions for implementing Regulation (EEC) No 2052/88 as regards the EAGGF Guidance Section', Official Journal L 374, 31/12/1988, p. 0025–0028. Finnish special edition: Ch. 14, Vol. 2, p. 0003. Swedish special edition: Ch. 14, Vol. 2, p. 0003.

'Regulation (1993) No 2081/93 of 20 July 1993 amending Regulation (EEC) No 2052/88 on the tasks of the SFs and their effectiveness and on coordination of their activities between themselves and with the operations of the European Investment Bank and the other existing financial instruments', Official Journal L 193, 31/07/1993.

'Regulation (1993) No 2082/93 of 20 July 1993 amending Regulation (EEC) No 4253/88 laying down provisions for implementing Regulation (EEC) No 2052/88 as regards coordination of the activities of the different SFs between themselves and with the operations of the European Investment Bank and the other existing financial instruments', Official Journal L 193, 31/07/1993, p. 0020–0033.

'Regulation (1993) No 2083/93 of 20 July 1993 amending Regulation (EEC) No 4254/88 laying down provisions for implementing Regulation (EEC) No 2052/898 as regards the European Regional Development Fund', Official Journal L 193, 31/07/1993, p. 0034–0038.

'Regulation (1999) No1260/99 of 21 June 1999 laying down general provision on the SFs', Official Journal L 161/1, 26/06/1999.

'Regulation (1999) No 1447/1999 of 24 June 1999 establishing a list of types of behaviour which seriously infringe the rules of the common fisheries policy', Official Journal L 167, 02/07/1999, p. 0005–0006.

Italian Documents and Reports

Ministero del Tesoro

'Quadro Comunitario di Sostegno 1994/1999, Obiettivo 1, Italia', Dipartimento per le Politiche di Sviluppo, Roma, 1993.

'Quadro Comunitario di Sostegno 2000/2006, Obiettivo 1, Italia', Dipartimento per le Politiche di Sviluppo, Roma, 1999a.

'Documento di programmazione economico finanziaria 2000–2006', Dipartimento per le Politiche di Sviluppo, Roma, 1999b.

'Modernizzare e dare capacità alle amministrazioni Pubbliche', *Rapporto annuale 2000–2001*, Dipartimento per le Politiche di Sviluppo, Roma, 2002.

'Modernizzare e dare capacità alle amministrazioni Pubbliche', *Rapporto annuale 2002*, Dipartimento per le Politiche di Sviluppo, Roma, 2003.

'Modernizzare e dare capacità alle amministrazioni Pubbliche', *Rapporto annuale 2003*, Dipartimento per le Politiche di Sviluppo, Roma, 2004.

'Modernizzare e dare capacità alle amministrazioni Pubbliche', *Rapporto annuale 2004*, Dipartimento per le Politiche di Sviluppo, Roma, 2005.

'Modernizzare e dare capacità alle amministrazioni Pubbliche', *Rapporto annuale 2005*, Dipartimento per le Politiche di Sviluppo, Roma, 2006.

'Quadro strategico Nazionale 2007–2013', Dipartimento per le Politiche di Sviluppo, Roma, 2006a.

'Ex-post Evaluation of the Objective 1 1994–1999, National Report – ITALY', Ismeri Europa, 2002.

'Rapporto di Valutazione Intermedia QCS Obiettivo 1 2000/2006', LSE and Vision & Value, 2005.

'Domanda e Organizzazione della Valutazione Intermedia del QCS 2000–2006 Ob.1', *UVAL – Unità di valutazione degli investimenti pubblici,* Dipartimento per le Politiche di Sviluppo, Roma, 2002a.

'Relazione Finale sulla proposta di attribuzione della riserva del 6%', *UVAL – Unità di valutazione degli investimenti pubblici,* Dipartimento per le Politiche di Sviluppo, Roma, 2002b.

'Relazione Finale sulla proposta di attribuzione della riserva del 4%', *UVAL – Unità di valutazione degli investimenti pubblici,* Dipartimento per le Politiche di Sviluppo, Roma, 2003.

Sicily Documents and Reports

'Valutazione finale Progetti Integrati Mediterranei – Sicilia 1986–1992', Arthur Andersen, 1995.

'Valutazione finale Programma Operativo Plurifondo Sicilia 1989–1993', Arthur Andersen, 1996.

'Rapporto di Valutazione Intermedia POP Sicilia 1994/1999', CENSIS, Vision and Value, 2001.

'Rapporto Finale di Valutazione Intermedia POP Sicilia 1994/1999', CENSIS,

Vision and Value, 2002.

'Rapporto di Valutazione Intermedia POR Sicilia 2000–2006', Ernst & Young, Palermo: Regione Sicilia, 2003a.

Regione Sicilia (Document obtained by the Programming Department of the Region): 'Programma Integrato Mediterraneo', 1986.

'Programma Operativo Plurifondo – POP – 1989/1993', 1990.

'Programma Operativo Plurifondo – POP – 1994/1999', 1996.

'Programma Operativo Regionale – POR – 2000/2006', 2000a.

'Complemento di Programmazione –POR- 2000/2006', 2000b.

'Rapporto di Valutazione ex-ante – POR – 2000/2006', 2000c.

'Rapporto Annuale di Esecuzione 1997–1999', 2000d.

'Semaforo, n. 19 del 12 maggio', 1962.

Basilicata Documents and Reports

'Primo Rapporto di Valutazione Intermedia POP Basilicata 1994–1999', Ecosfera SPA, Reconta Ernst and Young SPA, Ernst and Young Corporate Finance Srl, 1999, available online at http://www.regione.basilicata.it/sportelloeuropa/default.cfm?dir=326&doc=&fuseaction=dir (accessed February 2010).

'Secondo Rapporto di Valutazione Intermedia POP Basilicata 1994–1999', 2000, available online at http://www.regione.basilicata.it/sportelloeuropa/default.cfm?dir=326&doc=&fuseaction=dir (accessed February 2010).

'Terzo Rapporto di Valutazione Intermedia POP Basilicata 1994–1999', 2001, available online at http://www.regione.basilicata.it/sportelloeuropa/default.cfm?dir=326&doc=&fuseaction=dir (accessed February 2010).

'Rapporto di Valutazione Finale POP Basilicata 1994–1999', 2002, available online at http://www.regione.basilicata.it/sportelloeuropa/default.cfm?dir=326&doc=&fuseaction=dir (accessed February 2010).

'Rapporto di Valutazione Intermedia POR Basilicata 2000–2006', Ernst & Young, Potenza: Regione Basilicata, 2003b.

Regione Basilicata (Document obtained by the Programming Department of the Region):

'Programma Integrato Mediterraneo – PIM – 1986/1992', 1986.

'Programma Operativo Plurifondo – POP – 1989/1993', 1989.

'Rapporto finale di esecuzione POP 1989/1993', 1995a.

'Programma Operativo Plurifondo – POP – 1994/199', 1995b.

'Rapporto di Esecuzione annuale 1994–1996', 1996a.

'Rapporto Finale di Valutazione PIM 1986/1992', 1996b.

'Rapporto finale di Esecuzione POP 1989/1993', 1997.

'Rapporto di Valutazione exante POR 2000/2006', 1999.

'Regional Operative Programme – POR – 2000/2006', 2000a.

'Complemento di Programmazione POR 2000/2006', 2000b.

'Rapporto di Esecuzione Annuale 2001', 2001a.

'Trent'anni di attività. Speciale n.100', 2001b.

Speech of Gaetano Michetti during the inauguration of the Cabinet, 19 June 1985.
Speech of Filippo Margiotta during the insediazione of the Cabinet, 19 June 1985.

Spanish Documents and Reports

'Mid-term Updated Evaluation of Andalucía POI 2000–2006', Consejería de Economía, Junta de Andalucía, 2005.
'Mid-term Updated Evaluation of Galicia POI 2000–2006', Consellería de Economía, Xunta de Galicia, 2005.
'Marco Comunitario de Apoyo (2000–2006 para la Regiones Españolas del Objetivo 1)', Ministerio de Hacienda y Economía, Ministerio de Economía-FEDER, Madrid, 2001.
'Las relaciones de colaboración Estado-Comunidades Autónomas'. *Informe Anual 2004*, Ministerio de Administraciones Publicas MAP, Madrid, 2005.
'La programación regional y sus instrumentos', *Informe Anual 2004*, Ministerio de Hacienda y Economía MHE, Madrid, 2005.
'Plan de Desenvolvementi Economico de Galicia 2000–2006', Xunta de Galicia, 2000, available online at http://www.xuntaeco.es/ga/pub/pedega/pedega.htm (accessed February 2010).

Polish Documents and Reports

'The Timetable of Preparation of the National Development Plan for 2004–2006', Ministry of Economy, Employment and Social Affairs, Warsaw, 2002.
'Act of 24 May 2004 on the National Development Plan', O.J. 2004.116.1206, 2004.
'The Report on the Implementation of the National Development Plan 2004–2006', Ministry of Economy, Employment and Social Affairs, Warsaw, 2005.
'Investments realized within the SOP "Fisheries and fish processing in 2004–2006" and the reasons behind varying interests of beneficiaries in particular types of projects', Ministry of Economy, Employment and Social Affairs, Warsaw, 2005a.
'Report on the course of the institutional adaptation processes in the public administration at central and regional level for absorption of the EU SFs and the Cohesion Fund', Ministry of Economy, Employment and Social Policy Department of the Structural Policy Coordination, Warsaw, 2003.
'The report on the implementation of the National Development Plan/Community Support Framework in 2004–2006', Ministry of Regional Development Department of Coordination of Implementation of the EU Funds, Warsaw, 2008.

Secondary Sources

Adserà, Alícia, Boix, Carles and Payne, Mark (2003) 'Are you being served? Political accountability and quality of government', *Journal of Law, Economics, & Organization,* 19/2, pp. 445–90.
Aja, Eliseo (2001) 'Spain: nations, nationalities and regions', in John Loughlin (ed.), *Subnational Democracy in the EU: Challenges and Opportunities,* Oxford: Oxford

University Press, pp. 229–53.

Alesina, Alberto, Ozler, Sule, Roubini, Nouriel and Swagel, Phillip (1996) 'Political instability and economic growth', *Journal of Economic Growth*, 1/2, pp. 189–211.

Allum, Felia and Cilento, Marco (2001) 'Parties and personalities: the case of Antonio Bassolino, former Mayor of Naples', *Regional and Federal Studies,* 11/1, pp. 1–26.

Anessi Pessina, Eugenio and Steccolini, Ileana (2005) 'Evolutions and limits of new public management-inspired budgeting practices in Italian local governments', *Public Budgeting & Finance*, 4/2, Summer 2005.

Anselmo, Iolanda and Raimondo, Laura (2000) 'The Objective 1 Italian performance reserve: a tool to enhance the effectiveness of programmes and the quality of evaluation', Unità di Valutazione degli Investimenti Pubblici – Ministero del Tesoro.

Armesto Piná, Jose Francisco (2008) 'El impacto de la política regional comunitaria en Galicia. Una Panorámica', *Revista Gallega de Economia*, vol. 17, número extraordinario.

Azfar, Omar, Kähkönen, Satu, Lanyi, Anthony, Meagher, Patrick and Rutherford, Diana (1999) *Decentralization, Governance and Public Services: The Impact of Institutional Arrangements*, IRIS Center, University of Maryland, College Park.

Bache, Ian (2008a) *Europeanization and Multi-level Governance: Cohesion Policy in the EU and Britain*, Lanham, MD: Rowman & Littlefield.

—— (2008b) 'Which challenges for multi-level governance?', in The Committee of the Regions, *The Contributions to the 2008 Ateliers*, Forward Studies/Cellule de Prospective, Brussels.

Bailey, David and De Propris, Lisa (2002) 'The 1988 reform of the European SFs: entitlement or empowerment?', *Journal of European Public Policy*, 9/3, pp. 408–28.

Barca, Fabrizio (2001a) 'Il ruolo del Dipartimento per le politiche di sviluppo e di coesione', *Le Istituzioni del federalismo*, 22/2, pp. 419–45

—— (2001b) 'New trends and the policy shift in the Italian *mezzogiorno*', *Daedalus*, 130/2, pp. 93–113.

—— (2009) *An Agenda for a Reformed Cohesion Policy: A Place-based Approach to Meeting EU Challenges and Expectations*, Independent Report prepared at the request of Danuta Hübner, Commissioner for Regional Policy, available online at http://territori.formez.it/files/report_barca_v2104.pdf (accessed November 2009).

Barro, Robert J. (1973) 'The control of politicians: an economic model', *Public Choice*, 14/1, pp.19–42.

—— (1991) 'Economic growth in a cross-section of countries', *Quarterly Journal of Economics*, 106/2, pp. 407–43.

—— (1996) 'Democracy and growth', *Journal of Economic Growth*, 1/1, pp. 1–27.

Basile, Roberto, de Nardis, Sergio and Girardi, Alessandro (2001) *Regional Inequalities and Cohesion Policies in the EU*, ISAE Working Papers 23 (Istituto di Studi e Analisi Economica), Roma.

Bassanini, Franco (2000a) 'La riforma della pubblica, amministrazione in Italia: un bilancio a fine 2000', *Le autonomie per lo sviluppo economico,* Congress of Unioncamere, Rome, 13 December 2000.

—— (2000b) 'Overview of administrative reform and implementation in Italy: organization, personnel, procedures and delivery of public services', *International Journal of Public Administration,* 23/2–3, pp. 229–52.

Begg, Iain (2008) 'Subsidiarity in regional policy' in George Gelauff, Isabel Grilo and Arjan Lejour (eds), *Subsidiarity and Economic Reform in Europe,* Berlin: Springer.

Bekemans, Leonce (2008) 'Multi-level governance and the EU in a global context: some introductory reflexions', in The Committee of the Regions, *The Contributions to the 2008 Ateliers,* Forward Studies/Cellule de prospective, Brussels.

Benz, Arthur and Eberlein, Burkard (1988) *Regions in European Governance: The Logic of Multi-Level Interaction,* European University Institute, Working Paper RSC No 98/31.

Berg, Elliot J. (1993) *Rethinking Technical Cooperation: Reforms for Capacity Building in Africa,* UNDP/DAI, Washington, DC.

Beutel, Jörg (2002) *The Economic Impact of Objective 1 Interventions for the Period 2000–2006,* Final report to the Regional Policy Directorate-General, European Commission. Konstanz, Germany, available online at http://europa.molisedati.it/molise/euromoli.nsf/910b783560442a51c12568400037dd56/f6009c828969dff3c1256bff0028f6fd/$FILE/final_report.pdf (accessed November 2009) .

Bianchi, Giuliano (1993) 'The IMPs: a missed opportunity?', in Leonardi, Robert (ed.), *The Regions and the European Community: The Regional Response to the Single Market in Underdeveloped Areas,* London: Frank Cass, pp. 47–70.

Bodo, Giorgio and Viesti, Gianfranco (1997) *La grande svolta,* Roma: Donzelli.

Boijmans, Pascal (2003) *Building Institutional Capacity,* paper presented to the Annual Meeting of ISPA Partners, Brussels, 9–10 April 2003.

Boissevain, Jeremy (1966) 'Patronage in Sicily', *Man,* New Series, 1/1, pp. 18–33.

Boland, Philip (1999) 'Contested multi-level governance: Merseyside and the European SFs', *European Planning Studies,* 7/5, pp. 647–64.

Bollen, Frank (2001) *Capacity Building for Integration: Managing EU SFs: Effective Capacity for Implementation as a Prerequisite,* Maastricht: Eipa.

Börzel, Tanja A. (2001) 'Non-compliance in the EU: pathology or statistical artefact?', *Journal of European Public Policy,* 8/5, (October 2001), pp. 803–24.

—— (2003) *Environmental Leaders and Laggards in Europe: Why There is (not) a 'Southern Problem',* Aldershot: Ashgate.

—— (2005) 'Europeanization: how the EU interacts with its Member States', in Simon Bulmer and Christian Lequesne (eds), *The Member States of the EU,* New York: Oxford University Press.

Börzel, Tanja A. and Panke, Diana (2005) *Policy Matters – But How? Explaining Success and Failure of Dispute Settlement in the EU,* Paper prepared for presentation at the annual convention of American Political Science Association (APSA), Washington, DC, September 2005, available online at http://userpage.fu-berlin.

de/~europe/forschung/docs/BoerzelPanke_APSA05finalversion.pdf (November 2009).

Borzel, Tanja A. and Risse, Thomas (2000) *When Europe Hits Home: Europeanization and Domestic Change*, European Integration online Papers (EIoP), 4/15, available online at http://eiop.or.at/eiop/texte/2000–015a.htm (November 2009).

Börzel, Tanja A., Dudziak, Meike, Hofmann, Tobias, Panke, Diana and Sprungk, Carina (2007) 'Recalcitrance, inefficiency, and support for European integration: why Member States do (not) comply with European law', Center for European Studies Working Paper Series #151, available online at http://www.people.fas.harvard.edu/~ces/publications/docs/pdfs/Borzel_CES_151.pdf (November 2009).

Bouzas, Ramon (1999) *Análisis Organizativo de la Administración de una Comunidad Autónoma: la Xunta de Galicia, 1982–1997*, Santiago de Compostela PhD thesis

—— (2004) *La organización administrativa de la Xunta de Galicia: 20 años de autonomía*, Institut de Ciencies Politiques i Socials, WP. Num. 235, Barcelona

Brown Weiss, Edith and Jacobson, Harold K. (1998) *Engaging Countries: Strengthening Compliance with International Environmental Accords*, Cambridge, MA: MIT Press.

Bull, Martin J. and Newell, James L. (1993) 'Italian politics and the 1992 elections: from "stable instability" to instability and change', *Parliamentary Affairs*, 46/2, pp. 203–27.

Bursens, Peter (2002) 'Why Denmark and Belgium have different implementation records: on transposition laggards and leaders in the EU', *Scandinavian Political Studies*, 25/2, pp. 173–95.

Buti, Marco (1995) 'Livello di governo e convergenza istituzionale. Verso una ridefinizione del triangolo di governo fra Unione europea, Stato e regioni' in Gianluigi Gorla e Orietta Vito-Colonna (a cura di), *Regione e sviluppo: modelli, politiche e riforme*, Milano: Franco Angeli, pp. 283–303.

Capano, Gilberto (2000) 'Le politiche amministrative: dall'improbabile riforma alla riforma permanente?', in Giuseppe Di Palma *et al.* (a cura di), *Condannata al successo*, Bologna: Il Mulino, pp. 153–98.

Cassese, Sabino (1984) 'The higher Civil Service in Italy', in Ezra N. Suleiman (ed.), *Bureaucrats and Policy Making*, New York, Holmes and Meier, pp. 35–71.

—— (2002) 'Come funziona lo "spoils system" all'italiana', *La voce*, 12/11/2002, available online at http://www.lavoce.info/articoli/pagina169–351.html (November 2009).

Cazorla, José (1994) *El clientelismo de partido en España ante la opinión pública. El medio rural, la Administración y las empresas.* Barcelona: ICPS Working Paper no. 86.

Ceccanti, Stefano and Vassallo, Salvatore (a cura di) (2004) *Come chiudere la transizione Cambiamento, apprendimento e adattamento nel sistema politico italiano*, Bologna: Il Mulino.

Cerbo, Pasquale (2002) 'Ragioni e problemi dello spoils system', *La voce*, 12/11/2002, available online at http://www.lavoce.info/articoli/pagina211–351.html (November 2009).

Checchi, Daniele and Garibaldi, Pietro (2002) 'Lo "spoils system" italiano è efficiente?', *Quotidiano La voce,* issue of 12/11/2002.

Checkel, Jeffrey T. (1999) 'Social construction and integration', *Journal of European Public Policy,* 6/4, pp. 545–60.

Chubb, Judith (1982) *Patronage, Power, and Poverty in Southern Italy: A Tale of Two Cities,* Cambridge: Cambridge University Press.

Cienfuegos, Manuel (2000) 'La coordinación de los asuntos europeos en las administraciones autonómicas', *Revista de Estudios Politicos,* 108, pp. 103–42.

—— (2007) *Las comunidades autónoma ante la integración europea,* Barcelona: UOC.

Closa, Carlos and Heywood, Paul M. (2004) *Spain and the EU,* London: Palgrave MacMillan.

Cohen, John M. (1993) *Building Sustainable Public Sector Managerial, Professional and Technical Capacity: A Framework for Analysis and Intervention,* Development Discussion Paper 473, Cambridge, MA: Harvard Institute for International Development.

Conzelmann, Thomas (2008) 'Towards a new concept of multi-level governance?', in The Committee of the Regions, *The Contributions to the 2008 Ateliers,* Forward Studies/Cellule de Prospective, Brussels.

Corzo, Susana (2002) *El clientelismo político. El plan de empleo rural en Andalucía. Un estudio de caso,* Granada: Universidad de Granada.

Cowles, Maria G., Caporaso, James A. and Risse, Thomas (eds) (2001) *Transforming Europe: Europeanization and Domestic Change,* Ithaca, NY: Cornell University Press.

D'Amico, Renato (a cura di) (1992) *Manuale di Scienza dell'amministrazione,* Roma: Edizioni Lavoro.

Desideri, Carlo and Santantonio, Vincenzo (1997) 'Building a third level in Europe: prospects and difficulties in Italy', in Charlie Jeffery (ed.), *The Regional Dimension of the EU: Towards a Third Level in Europe?,* London: Frank Cass.

Desveaux, James A. (1995) *Designing Bureaucracies: Institutional Capacity and Large-scale Problem Solving,* Stanford: Stanford University Press.

Diamanti, Ilvio (2001) *Politica all'Italiana. La parabola delle riforme incompiute,* Milano: Edizioni Il Sole 24 Ore.

DiMaggio, Paul J. and Powell, Walter W. (1991) 'The iron cage revisited: institutional isomorphism and collective rationality in organizational fields', in Paul J. Powell and Walter W. DiMaggio (eds), *The New Institutionalism in Organizational Analysis,* Chicago: University of Chicago Press.

Dimitrova, Antoaneta (2002) 'Enlargement, institution-building and the EU's administrative capacity requirement', *West European Politics,* 25/4, pp.171–90

Dipartimento della Funzione pubblica (2001) *Lo stato dell'amministrazione pubblica a 20 anni dal rapporto Giannini,* available online at http://www.funpub.it/home/fr_attivita.html.

Diz Otero, Isabel, Lagares Díez, Nieves, Rivera, José M. and Castro, Alfredo B. (1998) 'Sistema electoral y elecciones autonómicas en Galicia', in Juan Montabes (coord.), *El sistema electoral a debate: veinte años de rendimiento del sistema electoral español (1977–1997)*, Madrid: CIS (319–328)

Downs, George W., Rocke, David M. and Barsoom, Peter N. (1996) 'Is the good news about compliance good news about cooperation?', *International Organization*, 50/3, pp. 379–406.

Dudek, Carolyn M. (2005) *EU Accession and Spanish Regional Development: Winners and Losers.* Brussels: Peter Lang S.A.

Duina, Francesco (1997) 'Explaining legal implementation in the EU', *International Journal of the Sociology of Law*, 25/2, pp. 155–80.

Easterly, William and Levine, Ross (1997) 'Africa's growth tragedy: policies and ethnic divisions', *Quarterly Journal of Economics*, 112/4, pp. 1203–50.

Ederveen, Sjef, de Groot, Henri L.F. and Nahuis, Richard (2002) 'Fertile soil for SFs', Centraal Plan Bureau (CPB) (Netherlands Bureau for Economic Policy Analysis) Government of the Netherlands, *Discussion Paper n.10.*

Emilewicz, Jadwiga and Wołek, Artur (2002) *Reformers and Politicians: The Power Play for the 1998 Reform of Public Administration in Poland, as Seen by its Main Players*, Warsaw: Foundation in Support of Local Democracy.

Eurostat (2008) *Regional Statistics*, available online at http://epp.eurostat.ec.europa. eu (accessed June 2008).

Fabbrini, Sergio and Della Sala, Vincent (2004) *Italian Politics: Italy between Europeanization and Domestic Politics*, New York: Berghahan Books.

Falkner, Gerda, Treib, Oliver, Hartlapp, Miriam and Leiber, Simone (2005) *Complying with Europe: EU Harmonisation and Soft Law in the Member States*, Cambridge: Cambridge University Press.

Fanfani, Roberto (2001) 'La politica di sviluppo rurale e la sua attuazione in Italia', in *Le Istituzioni del Federalismo,* 2/1, pp. 507–39.

Fargion, Valeria, Morlino, Leonardo and Profeti, Stefania (eds) (2006) *Europeizzazione e rappresentanza territoriale: il caso italiano*, Bologna: Il Mulino.

Ferejohn, John (1986) 'Incumbent performance and electoral control', *Public Choice*, 50/1, pp. 5–26.

Ferrell, Odies C. and Hartline, Michael, D. (1998) *Marketing Strategy*, Orlando, FL: Dryden Press.

Ferrera, Maurizio (1984) *Il Welfare State in Italia*, Bologna: Il Mulino.

Finocchiaro Castro, Massimo and Rizzo, Ilde (2006) 'Performance measurement of heritage conservation activity in Sicily', *Working Paper Series del Dipartimento di Economia e Metodi Quantitativi (DEMQ)*, Università di Catania.

Forss, Kim, and Venson, Pelonomi (2002), 'An evaluation of the capacity building efforts of United Nations operational activities in Zimbabwe: 1980–1995', available online at http://www.un.org/esa/coordination/Chpt8.PDF (June 2005).

Fosu, Augustin Kwasi (1992) 'Political instability and economic growth: evidence from Sub-Saharan Africa', *Economic Development and Cultural Change*, 40/4, pp. 829–41.

Fukuda-Parr, Sakiko, Lopes, Carlos and Malik, Khalid (eds) (2002) 'Overview:

institutional innovations for capacity development', *Capacity for Development, New Solutions to Old Problems*, UNDP, Earthscan.

Gilowska, Zyta (2001) 'Possibilities and barriers in regional policy conduct', in Jan Szomburg (ed.), *State Regional Policy Amidst Institutional and Regulatory Entanglements*, Gdańsk: The Gdańsk Institute for Market Economics.

Gilowska, Zyta and Misiąg, Wojciech (2000) *Adaptation of the Income of Territorial Self-governments to the Constitutional Norms and European Standards*, Gdańsk: The Gdańsk Institute for Market Economics.

Gil-Ruiz, Carmen and Iglesias, Jaime (2007) 'El gasto público en España en un contexto descentralizado', in *Presupuesto y Gasto Público* 47/2007, pp. 185–206, IEF.

Giner, Salvador (1982) 'Political economy, legitimation and the state in Southern Europe', *British Journal of Sociology*, 33/2, pp. 172–99.

Giuliani, Marco (2003) 'Europeanization in perspective: institutional fit and adaptation', in Kevin Featherstone and Claudio Radaelli (eds.), *The Politics of Europeanization*, Oxford: Oxford University Press.

Glusman, Justyna (2008) *When is EU Conditionality Effective? The Terms of Poland's Accession* (Unpublished), London School of Economics and Political Science.

Goetz, Klaus H. and Hix, Simon (2000) *Europeanised Politics? European Integration and National Political Systems*, Portland, OR: Frank Cass.

Gow, James I. and Dufour, Caroline (2000) 'Is the new public management a paradigm? Does it matter?', *International Review of Administrative Sciences*, 66/4, pp. 573–97.

Grabbe, H. (2002) 'EU conditionality and the *acquis communautaire*', *International Political Science Review*, 23/3, pp. 249–68.

Grosse, Tomasz Grzegorz (2003b) *The Twilight of Decentralization in Poland? Development Policy in the Voivodships in the Context of European Integration*, Warszawa, The Institute of Public Affairs.

—— (2003a) *The Preparations for Absorption of the SFs: Assessment of the Undertaken Actions and Recommendations*, The Institute of Public Affairs, Analysis and Opinions 7.

—— (2004) *State of Preparation of the Regional Administration to Absorb the EU Structural Assistance*, The Institute of Public Affairs, Analysis and Opinions 18.

Grote, Jürgen R. (1996) *Regioni e sviluppo: modelli, politiche, riforme*, Rome: Edizioni Franco Angeli.

Gualini, Enrico (2004) *Multi-level Governance and Institutional Change: The Europeanization of Regional Policy in Italy*, Aldershot: Ashgate.

Gzel, M. (2002) *Preparation of Poland's Central and Territorial Administration to Realisation of the Common Fisheries Policy*, available online at www.cie.gov.pl/fundusze/kondanreg/gdansk_mat/adm_wpr.pdf.

Hanf, Kenneth and Scharpf, Fritz W. (eds) (1978) *Interorganizational Policy Making*, London: Sage Publications.

Hausner, Jerzy (2001) 'Regional policy mechanisms', in Jan Szomburg (ed), *State Regional Policy Amidst Institutional and Regulatory Entanglements*, Gdańsk: The Gdańsk Institute for Market Economics.

Hausner, Jerzy and Marody, Miroslawa (2000) *The Quality of Governance: Poland Closer to the EU?*, Cracow, Małopolska School of Public Administration, Cracow University of Economics, Friedrich-Ebert Stiftung.

Haverland, Markus and Romeijn, Marleen (2007) 'Do Member States make European policies work? Analysing the EU transposition deficit', *Public Administration*, 85/3, pp. 757–78.

Héritier, Adrienne (2001) 'Differential Europe: national administrative responses to community policy', in Maria G. Cowles, James A. Caporaso and Thomas Risse (eds) (2001) *Transforming Europe: Europeanization and Domestic Change*, Ithaca, NY: Cornell University Press.

Hilderbrand, Mary E. and Grindle, Merilee S. (1994) *Building Sustainable Capacity: Challenges for the Public Sector*, Harvard Institute for International Development, Boston, MA.

Hine, David (1993) *Governing Italy: The Politics of Bargained Pluralism*, Oxford: Clarendon Press.

Honadle, Beth Walter (1981) 'A capacity-building framework: a search for concept and purpose', *Public Administration Review,* 41/5, pp. 575–80.

Hooghe, Liesbet (1996) *Cohesion Policy and European Integration: Building Multi-level Governance*, Oxford: Oxford University Press.

—— (1998) 'EU cohesion policy and competing models of European capitalism', *Journal of Common Market Studies,* 36/4, pp. 457–77.

Hooghe, Liesbet and Marks, Gary (2001) 'Types of multi-level governance', *European Integration online Papers (EIoP)*, 5/11, October 12, 2001, available online at http://papers.ssrn.com/sol3/papers.cfm?abstract_id=302786 (November 2009).

—— (2003) 'Unraveling the central state, but how? Types of multi-level governance', *American Political Science Review*, 97/2, pp. 233–43.

Hughes, James, Sasse, Gwendolyn and Gordon, Claire E. (2001) 'The regional deficit in Eastward enlargement of the EU: top down policies and bottom up reactions', *ESRC One Europe or Several?,* Programme Working Paper 29/01.

—— (2003) 'EU enlargement and power asymmetries: conditionality and the Commission's role in regionalisation in Central and Eastern Europe', ESRC, *One Europe or Several?*, Programme Working Paper 49/03.

—— (2004a) 'Conditionality and compliance in the EU's Eastward enlargement: regional policy and the reform of sub-national government', *Journal of Common Market Studies*, 42/3, pp. 523–51.

—— (2004b) *Europeanization and Regionalization in the EU's Enlargement to Central and Eastern Europe: The Myth of Conditionality*, London: Palgrave.

Hurd, Ian (1999) 'Legitimacy and authority in international politics', *International Organization*, 53/2, pp. 379–408.

Informe del defensor del pueblo andaluz (1995), *Procedimientos de selección y provisión en la administración de la Junta de Andalucía*, available online at http://www.defensor-and.es/informes_y_publicaciones/informes_estudios_y_resoluciones/informes_especiales/informe_0000/descargas/txt_procedimientos.doc.

Jeffery, Charlie (1996) 'Towards a "third level" in Europe? The German *Länder* in the EU', *Political Studies*, 44/2, pp. 253–66.

Jimenez Blanco, José (1977) *La conciencia regional en España*, Madrid: CIS.

John, Peter (2000) 'The Europeanization of sub-national governance', *Urban Studies*, 37/5–6, pp. 877–94.

Johnson, Janet (2005) *Political Science Research Methods*, Washington, DC: CQ Press.

Jönsson, Christer and Tallberg, Jonas (1998) 'Compliance and post-agreement bargaining', *European Journal of International Relations*, 4/4, pp. 371–408.

Jordan, Andrew (1999) 'The implementation of EU environmental policy; a policy problem without a political solution?', *CSERGE, Environment and Planning C: Government and Policy 1999*, 17/1, pp. 69–90.

Katz, Richard S. and Ignazi, Piero (1996) *Italian Politics: The Year of the Tycoon*, Boulder, CO: Westview Press.

Keating, Michael (1995a) 'A comment on Robert Leonardi, *Cohesion in the European Community: Illusion or Reality?*', *West European Politics*, 18/2, pp. 408–12.

—— (1995b) 'Europeanism and regionalism', in B. Jones and M. Keating (eds.), *The EU and the Regions*, Clarendon Press, Oxford.

—— (1998) *The New Regionalism in Western Europe: Territorial Restructuring and Political Change*, Cheltenham: Edward Elgar Ltd.

—— (2008) 'A quarter century of the Europe of the regions', *Regional and Federal Studies*, 18/5, pp. 629–35.

Keohane, Robert O. (1988) 'International institutions: two approaches', *International Studies Quarterly*, 32/4, pp. 379–96.

Klasik, Andrzej (2001) 'Institutional contingencies of the state regional policy and voivodship development policy', in Jan Szomburg (ed), *State Regional Policy Amidst Institutional and Regulatory Entanglements*, Gdańsk: The Gdańsk Institute for Market Economics.

Knack, Stephen and Keefer, Philip (1995) 'Institutions and economic performance: cross-country tests using alternative institutional measures', *Economic and Politics*, vol. 7, pp. 207–27.

Knight, Jack (1992) *Institutions and Social Conflict*, Cambridge: Cambridge University Press.

Knill, Christoph (2006) 'Implementation', in Jeremy Richardson (ed.), *EU: Power And Policy-making*, 3rd edn, London: Routledge.

Kohler-Koch, Beate and Rittberger, Berthold (2006) 'The governance turn in EU studies', *Journal of Common Market Studies*, Sep. 2006 Supplement, 44/1, pp. 27–49.

Kulesza, Michal (2002) 'Methods and techniques of managing decentralization reforms in CEE countries: the Polish experience', in Gábor Péteri (ed.), *Mastering Decentralization and Public Administration Reforms in Central and Eastern Europe*, Budapest: Open Society Institute, Budapest.

Kun-Buczko, Magdalena (2004) *The Capacity Building of the Institutional System as one of the Elements Necessary to the Effective SFs Absorption*, The 12th NISPAcee

Annual Conference. Central and Eastern European Countries Inside and Outside the EU: Avoiding a New Divide, Vilnius, Lithuania, 13–15 May.

Kuznets, S. S. (1966) *Modern Economic Growth: Rate, Structure, and Spread*. New Haven, CT: Yale University Press

La Spina, Antonio and Sciortino, Giuseppe (1993) 'Common agenda, Southern rules: European integration and environmental change in the Mediterranean states', in J. Duncan Liefferink *et al.* (eds.), *European Integration and Environmental Policy*, London: Belhaven Press.

Laakso, Markku and Taagepera, Rein (1979) 'Effective number of parties: a measure with application to West Europe', *Comparative Political Studies*, 12/1, pp. 13–27.

Lampinen, Risto and Uusikylä, Petri (1998) 'Implementation deficit: why Member States do not comply with EU directives', *Scandinavian Political Studies*, 21/3, pp. 231–51.

Leonardi, Robert (1993) *The Regions and the European Community: The Regional Response to the Single Market in the Underdeveloped Areas*, London: Frank Cass.

—— (1995) *Convergence, Cohesion and Integration in the European Union*, London: Macmillan.

—— (2005) *Cohesion Policy in the EU: The Building of Europe*, New York: Palgrave.

Leonardi, Robert and Nanetti, Raffaella Y. (1991) *The Regions and European Integration: The Case of Emilia-Romagna*, London: Pinter.

—— (eds.) (1998) *Regional Development in a Modern European Economy: The Case of Tuscany*, 2nd edn, London and Washington, DC: Pinter.

Leonardi, Robert, Putnam, R. and Nanetti, R. (1987) *Il Caso Basilicata*, Ricerche e studi dell'Istituto Cattaneo. Bologna: Il Mulino.

Leopoldo, Franchetti (2000) *Condizioni politiche e amministrative della Sicilia*, Roma: Donzelli Editore.

Londregan, John B. and Poole, Keith T. (1990) 'Poverty, the coup trap, and the seizure of executive power', *World Politics*, 62/2, pp.151–83.

Loubser, Jan J. (1993) 'Capacity development – a conceptual overview', paper presented at a Workshop on Capacity Development at the Institute on Governance, Ottawa, Canada.

Mairate, Andrea (2006) 'The added value of EU cohesion policy', *Regional Studies*, 40/2, pp. 167–77.

Mancinelli, Emma (2001) 'Istituzioni e sviluppo economico', in Sergio Vellante (a cura di), *Mezzogiorno Rurale Risorse Endogene e Sviluppo: il caso Basilicata*, Roma: Donzelli Editore.

March, James G. and Olsen, Johan P. (1998) 'The institutional dynamics of international political orders', *International Organization*, 52/4, pp. 943–69.

Marks, Gary and Hooghe, Liesbet (2004) 'Contrasting visions of multi-level governance' in Ian Bache and Matthew Flinders (eds), *Multi-level Governance*, Oxford: Oxford University Press.

Marks, Gary, Hooghe, Liesbet and Blank, Kermit (1995) *European Integration and the State*, EUI Working Paper RSC n. 95/7, Badia Fiesolana, San Domenico (FI).

Marks, Gary, Hooghe, Liesbet and Blank, Kermit (1996b) 'European integration from the 1980s: state-centric v. multi-level governance', *Journal of Common Market Studies,* 34/3, pp. 341–78.

Marks, Gary, Nielsen, Francois, Ray, Leonard and Salk, Jane (1996a) 'Competencies, cracks and conflicts: regional mobilization in the EU', in Gary Marks, Fritz W. Scharpf, Philippe Schmitter and Wolfgang Streeck (eds), *Governance in the EU,* London: Sage Publications.

Martin, Lisa L. (1993) 'The rational state choice of multilateralism', in John G. Ruggie (ed.), *Multilateralism Matters: The Theory and Practice of an International Form,* New York: Columbia University Press.

Mastenbroeck, Ellen (2005) 'EU compliance: still a "black hole"?', *Journal of European Public Policy,* 12/6, pp. 1103–20.

Mauro, Paolo (1995) 'Corruption and growth', *Quarterly Journal of Economics,* 110/3, pp. 681–712.

—— (1998) 'Corruption and the composition of government expenditure', *Journal of Public Economics,* 69/2, pp. 263–79.

Mayntze, Renate (1999) 'Multilevel governance, German federalism and the EU', in Carl Lankowski (ed.), *Governing Beyond the Nation State: Global Public Policy, Regionalism or Going Local?,* The American Institute for Contemporary German Studies, The Johns Hopkins University, AICGS Research Report No. 11.

Melis, Guido (1996) *Storia dell'amministrazione italiana. 1861–1993,* Bologna: Il Mulino.

Mentz, J.C.N. (1997) *Personal and Institutional Factors in Capacity Building and Institutional Development,* ECDPM Working Paper No. 14. Maastricht.

Milen, Anneli (2001) *What Do We Know About Capacity Building?,* Geneva: World Health Organization, available online at http://afronets.org/files/capacity.pdf (November 2009).

Milio, Simona (2007) 'Can administrative capacity explain differences in regional performances? Evidence from SFs implementation in Southern Italy', *Regional Studies,* 41/4, pp. 429–42.

—— (2008) 'How political stability shapes administrative performance: the Italian case', *West European Politics,* 31/5, pp. 915–36.

Montabes, Juan and Torres, Javier (1998) 'Elecciones, partidos y proceso político en Andalucía (1977–1996)', in Manuel Alcántara and Antonia Martínez (eds.), *Las elecciones autonómicas en España, 1980–1997,* Madrid: CIS (9–50).

Moravcsik, Andrew (1993) 'Preferences and power in the European Community: a liberal intergovernmentalist approach', *Journal of Common Market Studies,* 31/4, pp. 473–524.

—— (1995) 'Liberal intergovernmentalism and integration: a rejoinder', *Journal of Common Market Studies,* 33/4, pp. 611–28.

Morisi, Massimo (1993) *Far politica in Sicilia: deferenza, consenso e protesta,* Milano: Feltrinelli.

Mota, Fabiola (2008) *Capital social y gobernabilidad en el rendimiento político autonómico*. Madrid: Centro de Estudios Políticos y Constitucionales.

Nanetti, Raffaella Y. (1996) 'EU cohesion and territorial restructuring in the Member States', in Liesbet Hooghe (ed.), *European Integration, Cohesion Policy and Subnational Mobilization*, Oxford: Oxford University Press.

—— (2007) 'The Context of Italian Politics', in M. Donald Hancock, *Politics in Europe,* 4th edn, Washington, DC: CQ Press.

Newell, James L. (2000) *Parties and Democracy in Italy,* Aldershot: Ashgate.

Nieto, Alejandro (1992) 'La reforma del administración pública en España', *Revista Vasca de Administración pública*, 34/2.

North, W. Haven (1992) *Capacity Building and Technical Cooperation: Managing the Connection,* New York: UNDP.

ÖIR (2003) *A Study on the Efficiency of the Implementation Methods for SFs: Final Report*, ÖIR in association with LRDP and IDOM, commissioned by the EU DG Regional Policy.

Olsen, Johan P. (1996) 'Europeanization and nation-state dynamics', in Sverker Gustavsson and Leif Lewin (eds.), *The Future of the Nation-state*, London: Routledge.

Olvera, Fermín (2003) *La emergencia de la administración pública andaluza (1978–1985)*, Granada: Universidad de Granada.

Page, Edward C. (2003) 'Europeanization and the persistence of administrative systems', in Jack Hayward and Anand Menon (eds.), *Governing Europe*, Oxford: Oxford University Press, Ch.10, pp.162–76.

Papantoniadou, Sofia (2004) 'The pre-accession programmes of EU and the development possibilities they provide to the candidate and acceding countries', 17.05.2004 Blagoevgrad, available online at thttp://www.elieff.bg/cep/cbcbook/Phare,%20ISPA,%20SAPARD/phare-ispa-sapard.doc (November 2009).

Parrado, Salvador (2001) 'The development and current features of the Spanish Civil Service system', in Hans Bekke and Frits van der Meer (eds.), *Civil Service Systems in Comparative Perspectives*, Cheltenham: Edward Elgar.

—— (2004) 'Politicisation of the Spanish civil service: continuity in 1982 and 1996', in B. Guy Peters and Jon Pierre (eds), *Politicization of the Civil Service in Comparative Perspective*, London: Routledge, pp. 227–56.

Perez Tremps, Pablo, Espierrez, Cabellos, Ángel, Miguel and Roig Moles, Eduard (1998) *La participación europea y la acción exterior de las Comunidades Autónomas*, Madrid/Barcelona: Generalitat de Catalunya/Marcial Pons.

Persson, Torsten, Roland, Gerard and Tabellini, Guido (1997) 'Separation of powers and political accountability', *Quarterly Journal of Economics*, 112/4, pp.1163–1202.

Peters, Guy B. (1997) 'Policy transfers between governments: the case of administrative reforms', *West European Politics*, 20/4, pp. 71–88.

—— (2001) *The Politics of Bureaucracy*, 5th edn, London: Routledge.

Piattoni, Simona (1997) 'Local political class and economic development: the cases of Abruzzo and Puglia in the 1970s and 1980s' in Michael Keating and John Loughlin (eds), *The Political Economy of Regionalism*, London: Frank Cass.

Piattoni, Simona (1998a) 'Virtuous clientelism: the Southern question resolved?', in Jane Schneider (ed.), *Italy's Southern Question: Orientalism in One Country?*, Oxford: Berg, pp. 225–43.

—— (1998b) 'Clientelism revisited: clientelist politics and economic development in postwar Italy', *Italian Politics and Society*, 49, pp. 44–62.

—— (2008) 'Subnational governments and non-governmental organizations: a difficult coexistence within multi-level governance?' in Committee of the Regions, *The Contributions to the 2008 Ateliers*, Forward Studies/Cellule de prospective, Brussels.

Piattoni, Simona and Smyrl, Marc (2002) 'Building effective institutions: Italian regions and the EU SFs', in Jeanie Bukowski *et al.* (eds.), *Between Europeanization and Local Societies: The Space for Territorial Governance in Europe*, Lanham, MD: Rowman & Littlefield Publishers, pp. 133–56.

PM Chancellery (2000) 'Regional policy and co-ordination of structural instruments', *Reply to EU Common Position*, Plenipotentiary of the Government for the Accession Negotiations about Poland's Membership in the EU, CONF-PL 43/00: 6 July 2000.

Pollack, Mark A. (1995) 'Regional actors in an intergovernmental play: the making and implementation of EC structural policy', in Carolyn Rhodes and Sonia Mazey (eds.), *The State of the EU*, Boulder, CO: Lynne Rienner Publishers.

Porras Nadales, Antonio J. (1992) 'Representación política y clientelismo: El caso de Andalucía', in *Revista de Fomento Social*, 47/188, pp. 495–510.

—— (2005) 'La reforma de la administración Andaluza y los desafíos de la segunda modernización', *Revista de Fomento Social*, 60/239, pp. 463–90.

Pressman, Jeffrey L. and Wildavsky, Aaron, B. (1973) *Implementation: How Great Expectations in Washington are Dashed in Oakland: or, why it's amazing that federal programs work at all, this being the saga of the Economic Development Administration as told by two sympathetic observers who seek to build morals on foundation of ruined hopes*, Berkeley: University of California Press.

Putnam, Robert D., Leonardi, Robert and Nanetti, Raffaella Y. (1985) *La Pianta e le Radici*, Ricerche e studi dell'Istituto Cattaneo, Bologna: Il Mulino.

—— (1993) *Making Democracy Work: Civic Traditions in Modern Italy*, Princeton, NJ: Princeton University Press.

Pyszkowski, Andrzej and Szlachta J. (2000) *Institutional model of the Regional Development Policy in Poland*, Gdańsk: The Gdańsk Institute for Market Economics.

Ramió, Carles and Salvador, Miquel (2002) 'La configuración de las administraciones de las comunidades autónomas; entre la inercia y la innovación institucional', in Joan Subirats and Raquel Gallego (eds.), *Veinte años de autonomías en España*, Madrid: CIS.

Rebora, Gianfranco (1999) *Un decennio di riforme*, Milano: Guerini.

Risse, Thomas (2002) 'Constructivism and the study of international institutions: towards conversations across paradigms', in Helen V. Milner and Ira Katznelson (eds), *Political Science as Discipline? Reconsidering Power, Choice and the State at the Century's End,* New York: W. W. Norton.

Rivera, José Manuel et al. (1998) 'Las elecciones autonómicas en Galicia', in Manuel Alcántara and Antonia Martínez (eds), *Las elecciones autonómicas en España, 1980–1997,* Madrid: CIS (285–308).

Rhodes, Martin (ed.) (1995) *The Regions and the New Europe: Patterns in Core and Periphery Development,* Manchester: Manchester University Press.

Roberts, Peter (2003) 'Partnerships, programmes and the promotion of regional development: an evaluation of the operation of the SFs regional programmes', *Progress in Planning,* 59/1, pp. 1–69.

Rodriguez-Arana, Jaime (2004) 'El Estatuto de 1981 y la administración pública gallega', in Martin Bassols (ed.), *Las administraciones públicas de las comunidades autònomas,* Madrid: INAP, pp. 227–59.

Rodríguez-Pose, Andrés (1998) *Dynamics of Regional Growth in Europe: Social and Political Factors,* New York: Clarendon Press.

Sapienza, Rosario (1993) 'Considerazione sull'attuazione dei PIM: il caso italiano', *Rivista Giuridica del Mezzogiorno,* 7/2, pp. 315–19.

Sartori, Giovanni (2005) *Parties and Party Systems: A Framework for Analy*sis, Essex: ECPR.

Scharpf, Fritz W. (1988) 'The joint decision trap: lessons from German federalism and European integration', *Public Administration,* 66/3, pp. 239–78.

Schmitter, Philippe C. (2004) 'The ambiguous virtues of accountability', *Journal of Democracy* 15/4, pp. 47–60.

Schofield, Jill (2001) 'Time for revival? Public policy implementation: a review of the literature and an agenda for future research', *International Journal of Management Reviews,* 3/3, pp. 245–63.

Segnestam, Lisa, Persson, Asa, Nilsson, Mans and Arvidsson, Anders (2002) *Country Environment Analysis: A Review of International Experience,* Stockholm Environment Institute, Draft, 2002.

Shoylekova, Mina (2004) 'Building capacity for policy making: experience from the Bulgarian administrative reforms', The 12th NISPAcee Annual Conference. Central and Eastern European Countries Inside and Outside the EU: Avoiding a New Divide, Vilnius, Lithuania, 13–15 May.

Smyrl, Marc E. (1997) 'Does European Community regional policy empower the regions?', *Governance,* 10/3, pp. 287–309.

Stone, Clarence N. (1985) 'Efficiency versus social learning: a reconsideration of the implementation process', *Policy Studies Review,* 4/3, pp. 484–96.

Sverdrup, Ulf (2007) 'Implementation', in Paolo Graziano and Maarten P. Vink (eds), *Europeanization: New Research Agendas,* Basingstoke: Palgrave Macmillan.

Szomburg, Jan (2001) *State Regional Policy Amidst Institutional and Regulatory Entanglement*s, Gdańsk: The Gdańsk Institute for Market Economics.

Talani, Leila S. (2004) *European Political Economy: Political Science Perspectives*, Aldershot: Ashgate.

Tallberg, Jonas (2002) "Paths to compliance: enforcement, management, and the EU', *International Organization, 56/3*, pp. 609–43.

Taylor, Sandra, Rooney, Mary L and Bachtler, John (1999) *Outsourcing Programme Management: A Comparative Assessment*, Final Report to the Ministry of Economics and SMEs, Technology and Transport of the Land of Nordrhein-Westfalen.

Taylor, Sandra, Bachtler, John and Polverari, Laura (2001) *Information into Intelligence: Monitoring for Effective Structural Fund Programming* (with executive summary). IQ-Net Thematic Paper. European Policies Research Centre, University of Strathclyde, Glasgow.

Tavistock Institute (2003) *The Evaluation of Socio-economic Development – The Guide,* (in association with GHK and IRIS) Brussels: European Commission.

Tömmel, Ingeborg (1987) 'Regional policy in the European Community: its impact on regional policies and public administration in the Member States', *Environment and Planning C: Government and Policy,* 5/3, pp. 369–81.

Torreblanca, José I. (2005) *¿Adiós a los fondos? Las claves para entender la posición de España a la hora de negociar el presupuesto del UE para 2007–2013*, Real Instituto Elcano, Documento de Trabajo, 21/2005.

Trigilia, Carlo (1992) *Sviluppo senza autonomia: effetti perversi delle politiche nel Mezzogiorno,* Bologna: il Mulino.

Tsebelis, George (2002) *Veto Players: How Political Institutions Work*, Princeton, NJ: Princeton University Press.

USAID Center for Development Information and Evaluation (2000) 'Measuring Institutional Capacity', *Recent Practices in Monitoring and Evaluation TIPS*, number 15.

Verheijen, A. J. G. (2000) *Administrative Capacity Development: A Race Against Time?*, WRR, Scientific Council for Government Policy Working Documents, W 107.

Viesti, Gianfranco (2003) *Abolire il Mezzogiorno*, Bari-Roma: Laterza.

White, Joseph (2003) 'Three meanings of capacity: or, why the federal government is most likely to lead on insurance access issues', *Journal of Health Politics, Policy and Law,* 28/2–3, pp. 217–44.

Willems, Stephane and Baumert, Kevin (2003) 'Institutional capacity and climate actions', OECD Environment Directorate International Energy Agency.

Wojtuch, Magdalena (2006) 'How do we monitor EU money?', *Gazeta Prawna*, Warsaw, 68.

Żuber, P. (2002) 'Poland's management system of the financial resources from the EU', available online at http://www.ukie.gov.pl/kurs/pszf/pszf.pdf.

INDEX